The Middle English Stanzaic Versions
of the
Life of Saint Anne

Early English Text Society.

Original Series, No. 174.

1928 (for 1927).

COPY OF PAGE FROM 'LIFE OF ST. ANNE'
University of Minnesota, U.S.A., MSS.

The Middle English Stanzaic Versions
of the
Life of Saint Anne

EDITED BY
ROSCOE E. PARKER

LONDON:
PUBLISHED FOR THE EARLY ENGLISH TEXT SOCIETY
BY HUMPHREY MILFORD, OXFORD UNIVERSITY PRESS,
AMEN HOUSE, E.C. 4,
1928.

KRAUS REPRINT
Millwood, N.Y.
1987

OXFORD

UNIVERSITY PRESS

Great Clarendon Street, Oxford OX2 6DP
United Kingdom

Oxford University Press is a department of the University of Oxford.
It furthers the University's objective of excellence in research, scholarship,
and education by publishing worldwide. Oxford is a registered trade mark of
Oxford University Press in the UK and in certain other countries

© The Early English Text Society 1928

The moral rights of the authors have been asserted

Database right Oxford University Press (maker)

First Edition published in 1928

All rights reserved. No part of this publication may be reproduced,
stored in a retrieval system, or transmitted, in any form or by any means,
without the prior permission in writing of Oxford University Press,
or as expressly permitted by law, or under terms agreed with the appropriate
reprographics rights organization. Enquiries concerning reproduction
outside the scope of the above should be sent to the Rights Department,
Oxford University Press, at the address above

You must not circulate this book in any other form
and you must impose this same condition on any acquirer

Published in the United States of America by Oxford University Press
198 Madison Avenue, New York, NY 10016, United States of America

British Library Cataloguing in Publication Data
Data available

Library of Congress Cataloging in Publication Data
Data available

Original Series, 174

ISBN 978-0-85-991683-7

PREFACE

THIS edition of the Middle English stanzaic versions of the life of St. Anne was undertaken several years ago at the suggestion of Professor Carleton Brown, to whom I am under the greatest obligations for counsel and assistance at almost every step of its preparation. Although the pressure of other duties has perhaps unduly delayed the completion of the task, he has never lost interest in its progress nor failed to lend of his store of knowledge and wisdom.

In the preparation of this edition, I have constantly endeavoured to keep in mind Ritson's dictum: "To correct the obvious errors of an illiterate transcribeer, to supply irremediable defects, and to make sense of nonsense, are certainly dutys of an editour of ancient poetry." Fortunately, there have been few "obvious errors" to correct or "irremediable defects" to supply. I have contented myself, therefore, with trying to present an accurate text accompanied by such information in the introduction and notes as would "make sense" of what might otherwise be "nonsense" to those not familiar with the peculiarities and associations of "ancient poetry." All textual expansions have accordingly been italicized, and all orthographic and linguistic peculiarities have been dealt with in the notes to the text. In order to prevent undue expansion of the introduction, the lists of words used to illustrate phonological changes have been made typical rather than complete for each poem.

It is a pleasure to acknowledge my indebtedness to Professor Arthur G. Brodeur, of the University of California, for his generous assistance, especially in the philological study of these poems. I have constantly drawn on his thorough knowledge of early English dialects in my phonological investigations and have always profited from his criticisms. My thanks are also due to Professor George R. Noyes, of the same University, for his kindly assistance in the final revision of my copy. My greatest debt of gratitude, however, is due my wife, who has shared the labour of collating the entire text with the MSS. and has contributed largely to whatever of accuracy and value this edition may possess.

ROSCOE E. PARKER.

University of Tennessee.

CONTENTS

	PAGE
INTRODUCTION:	
I. BACKGROUND	ix
II. MANUSCRIPTS AND DIALECTS	xi
III. AUTHORSHIP AND SOURCES	xxvi
IV. INFLUENCES	xxxiv
V. CONCLUSIONS	liii
TEXT FROM MS. UNIVERSITY OF MINNESOTA, Z. 822, N. 81	1
TEXT FROM MS. TRINITY COLLEGE, CAMBRIDGE, 601	90
TEXT FROM MS. BODLEIAN, 10234	110
NOTES TO MINNESOTA MS. VERSION	127
NOTES TO TRINITY COLLEGE, CAMBRIDGE, MS. VERSION	134
NOTES TO BODLEIAN, 10234, MS. VERSION	136
BIBLIOGRAPHY	138

INTRODUCTION

I. BACKGROUND.

WITH the single exception of the version contained in Osbern Bokenham's *Lyuys of Seyntys*, the Middle English stanzaic versions of the life of St. Anne have not been printed heretofore nor made the object of special study. This is somewhat surprising, since the life of St. Anne is almost inseparably connected with the life and miracles of the Blessed Virgin and with the stories of the childhood of Jesus, both of which contributed much to English life, literature, and thought during the thirteenth, fourteenth, and fifteenth centuries. We have, it is true, the Joachim and Anna story in the *Legenda Aurea* and the *Cursor Mundi*; but these are parts of larger cycles and neither is stanzaic in form. Of these stanzaic versions we have heard little, although modern scholarship has devoted considerable attention to the closely related legends of Mary. Although the body of extant literature in honour of St. Anne is smaller than that in honour of the Virgin Mary, the popularity of St. Anne was persistent in both France and England until the end of the fifteenth century; and the extant Middle English stanzaic versions of the life of St. Anne are here presented for the first time in the belief that they afford significant contributions to our knowledge of Middle English life and literature.

The medieval popularity of St. Anne as a patron saint, the widespread observance of St. Anne's Day, and the considerable body of literature celebrating the life of St. Anne bear witness to her influence in both France and England. The evidence of this influence is to be found in guild records, religious festivals, and literary productions. A brief summary of this evidence reveals the following facts: St. Anne was the patron saint of the first strictly religious guild recorded in the city of London. This was the St. Anne's Guild in the Church of St. Owen, Newgate, established during the reign of King John.[1] Before the end of the fourteenth century similar guilds were flourishing in Lincoln, Lynn,

[1] Westlake, H. F., *The Parish Gilds of Mediaeval England*, London, 1909, p. 16.

Bury St. Edmunds, and other places.[1] By this time the number of St. Anne's Guilds in the city of London had increased to four.[2] The St. Anne's Guild at Lincoln was active in dramatic productions throughout the fifteenth century and was still in existence at the middle of the sixteenth century.[3] Doubtless there were many similar guilds throughout England whose records are no longer extant.

St. Anne's popularity as a patron saint was greatly enhanced by the ecclesiastical sanction of the Feast of St. Anne. This festival, which originated in the Oriental Church during the fourth century, was celebrated by the Church at Constantinople, during the first half of the eighth century, on July 25. It eventually received recognition throughout the province of the Western Church, and July 26 was set apart as St. Anne's Day. On this day the Feast of St. Anne was celebrated at Doune in 1291. Pope Urban VI introduced the festival into England by an edict dated November 21, 1378.[4] Thereafter St. Anne's Day was celebrated in play, poetry, and festival.[5] The relation of the popular festivals to the poems published herewith will be discussed hereafter.

As has been stated already, the poems in celebration of St. Anne were numerous both in France and in England. The French poems are, on the whole, earlier and perhaps more numerous than the English. M. Chabaneau has published the most important of the French versions, *Le Romanz de Saint Fanuel et de Sainte Anne et de Nostre Dame et de Nostre Segnor et de Ses Apostres*, a long poem of the thirteenth or fourteenth century, from MS. Montpelier 350.[6] Another poem containing practically the same material is to be found in MS. Grenoble 1137, which belongs to the fourteenth century.[7] In addition to these long poems, M. P. Meyer has pointed out a number of shorter poems on the same subject.[8] Likewise many English poems in celebration of or supplication

---

[1] Westlake, H. F., *The Parish Gilds of Mediaeval England*, London, 1909, pp. 168, 196, and 226.

[2] Unwin, George, *The Guilds and Companies of London*, London and New York, 1909, pp. 367-369.

[3] Leach, Arthur F., "Some English Plays and Players" in *An Old English Miscellany Presented to Dr. F. J. Furnivall*, Oxford, 1901, pp. 233 ff. See also *14th Report of the British Historical MSS. Commission*, Appendix 8, pp. 32-40.

[4] For a summary of the history of St. Anne's Day, see *The Catholic Encyclopedia*, New York, 1907, I, 538-539; Baring-Gould, S., *Lives of the Saints*, London and New York, 1898, VIII, 564 ff.; and Budge, Sir E. A. Wallis, *Legends of Our Lady Mary the Perpetual Virgin and Her Mother Hanna*, London, 1922, xxv-l.

[5] Chambers, E. K., *The Mediaeval Stage*, Oxford, 1903, II, 118, and Leach, *op. cit.*

[6] *Revue des langues romanes*, XXVII, 157-258. I am indebted to Professor George L. Hamilton of Cornell for directing my attention to this poem.

[7] Bonnard, Jean, *Les Traductions de la Bible en Vers Français au Moyen Age*, Paris, 1884, pp. 181-193.

[8] *Romania*, XV, 271 and 334 ff.; XVI, 44 ff.; XXV, 542 ff.

Introduction

to St. Anne were written between the end of the thirteenth and the beginning of the sixteenth centuries. In addition to those of unknown authorship, poems in honour of St. Anne were written by John Audelay, John Lydgate, and Osbern Bokenham.[1] All these things—guild records, festivals, and literary productions—are evidences of the medieval popularity of St. Anne and indicate, to some extent, the position which she occupies in the annals of hagiography.

The foregoing summary of the history and popularity of the cult of St. Anne furnishes the necessary background for the study of her life as it is presented herewith. Such study as seems necessary will now be made of the date, content, and language of these poems. This will be followed by a study of their sources and an attempt to estimate their influence on Middle English drama.

II. Manuscripts and Dialects.

Three Middle English stanzaic versions of the life of St. Anne, none of which has been printed heretofore, are known to be in existence; and two of these versions have survived in two MSS. each. These versions are contained in the University of Minnesota MS. Z. 822, N. 81 (formerly Phillips 8122), Trinity College Cambridge 601 (English Poets R. 3. 21), Chetham Library 8009, Bodleian 10234 (Tanner 407), and Harley 4012. The first of these versions is in twelve-line stanzas, the two copies of the second are in rime royal, and the two copies of the third are in four-line stanzas. In both form and content they constitute three different types, or groups; and all of them, in their present form, probably belong to the fifteenth century.

The oldest, longest, and most significant of these poems appears as an insertion at f. 185*b* of the Minnesota MS., which is a North English Homily Collection, and continues through f. 215*a*.[2] That this is not the original version of the poem is indicated by certain scribal errors, omissions, and dialectal inconsistencies which will be discussed hereafter. This poem is written, nevertheless, by the same hand as the body of the MS.—a hand of the end of the fourteenth or beginning of the fifteenth

---

[1] Brown, Carleton, *A Register of Middle English Religious and Didactic Verse*, Oxford, 1920, II, 407.
[2] This is not the last poem in the MS., as was erroneously stated by Professor G. H. Gerould in his dissertation, *The North English Homily Collection*, p. 7. It is followed by a fragment of the life of St. George. This was printed in *Modern Language Notes*, XXXVIII, 97 ff.

century.[1] The writing of the MS. is clear and offers little, if any, variation from the usual hand of the beginning of the fifteenth century. The scribe generally uses γ (þ) for an initial *th*- and sometimes for a final -*th*. He also uses the stroked *ll* and *h*, though apparently without significance, and employs the usual stroke over a final vowel to indicate the addition of an *m* or *n*. The same stroke is sometimes used over *m* or *n* to indicate the insertion of a preceding *u*. The curved stroke is so indiscriminately employed after a final consonant that it apparently has little significance. It occasionally seems to suggest the addition of a final -*e*, but it is just as frequently used where such an addition would be preposterous. The long stroked *s*, however, is consistently used for *ser*, and the stroked *p* for *per* and for *pre* or *pro* is distinguished by a straight and a curved stroke respectively. Medial vowels in þ*at* and *with* are generally omitted, and the *t* in these words is written above the initial consonant. The ʒ is frequently used for *y*, especially in pronouns; and it is sometimes used for *z* and for final -*gh*. Expansion of these contractions is indicated throughout the text by the use of italics. The stroked *h* and *ll*, on the other hand, have been disregarded except in cases where they clearly indicate contractions.

This poem is written in twelve-line stanzas riming aabccbddbeeb. The riming couplets are four-stressed lines and the tail rime lines are three-stressed lines. The long lines are written down the left side of the MS. pages and the b-rime lines are written down the margins at the right of the pages. These b-rime lines do not, however, constitute a refrain so far as the thought of the stanza is concerned. On the contrary, they carry forward the thought of the stanza just as the other lines do. This method is consistently maintained throughout the 3456 lines of the poem, which relates the whole life of St. Anne after her marriage to Joachim and includes the life of the Virgin and of Jesus to the time of the calling of the first six disciples.

The dialect of the poem is generally Northern, but it contains many Midland and a few Southern forms, as the following summary will show.[2]

---

[1] The writing is apparently that of the early fifteenth century. Wells, J. E., says, however, in his *Manual of the Writings in Middle English*, p. 290, "not before 1375-1400." Gerould, G. H., *op. cit.*, says, "not earlier than the last quarter of the fourteenth century." The same authority, in his *Saints' Legends*, p. 171, thinks it safe to regard the original *North English Homily Collection* "as a pioduct of the earlier fourteenth century."

[2] See the bibliography for a complete list of the works consulted in the preparation of this section.

Words in the phonological tables are starred if they occur in rime in one of the places listed, except in cases where the occurrence of the word in rime is of no significance.

Introduction xiii

1. O.E. *ā* appears in two forms :
   a. Nth. *ā* 305 times : ane 422, 641, 937 ; bane(s) 564, 2433 ; hame* 98, 161, 169 ; swa* 15.
   b. Mid. or Sth. *ǭ* 233 times : one* 545, 986, 1450 ; bone* 117, 197, 690 ; home 725, 1725, 1837.
2. O.E. *a* is lengthened in open syllables to *ā* : name* 17, 2065 ; shame* 97 ; tale 2605.
3. Merc. *a*, W.S. *ea + ld* appears in two forms :
   a. Nth. *ā* 133 times : ald(e) 493, 497, 712 ; bald* 2150, 2457, 2491 ; hald(e)* 139, 680, 1029.
   b. Mid. *ǭ* 31 times : old(e) 409, 568, 871 ; hold* 2924.
4. O.E. *aē + r* in adverbs and verbs appears in three forms :
   a. Nth. *ā* 54 times : whare 1076, 1508, 1833 ; þar(e)* 227, 420.
   Note : war(e)* (O.N. **vāru**) occurs 54 times : 221, 295, 320.
   b. Mid. *ē* 162 times ; wer(e) 472, 475, 476 ; þer* 536, 637, 1076.
   c. Sth. *ǭ* three times : thore 1485, 2080 ; whore 2160.
   Note : wore* (O.N. **vǭru**) occurs twice in 362, 1376.
5. O.E. *y, ȳ* appears as Nth. *i, ī*, written '*y* : ffyrste 968 ; fyre 226 ; hyll* 159, 1062, 2374 ; syn* 676, 848, 991.
6. O.E. *c* appears in two forms :
   a. *k* in guttural positions and before palatal vowels arising from umlaut : knaw* 1773, 1895 ; ylkane* 1921, 2356, 2543 ; kepe 432, 605 ; kyng* 893, 1246 ; mykyll 2617, 2654, 2933.
   b. *ch* in palatal positions : chese 423 and child, childer regularly.
   Note : O.N. *k* appears as Nth. M.E. *k* in kyrke 1054. (Possibly <O.E. **cyrice**.)
7. O.E. initial palatal *g* is written ȝ or *yh-* :
   a. ȝ : ȝere(s) 164, 2083, etc.
   b. *yh* : yhong(e) 158, 182, etc.
8. The O.E. guttural stop *g* remained : god 20, 42, 66 ; gude 57, etc.
9. O.E. *h* in the combination *h + t* appears as follows :
   a. *gh* : bryght* 2002 ; broght* 172, 2062.
   b. *tgh* : rytght 19.
   c. ȝ : noȝt* 89, 124, 153.
   d. ȝ*th* : noȝth 98, 165, etc.

10. O.E. *sc* appears in several forms:
   a. Nth. *s* 210 times initially in unstressed words: sall, suld.
   b. Normal *s(s)h*: bys(s)hop(e) 310, 339, 344; fisshers 3200; shame 97, 168, 170; shent 577; worships 2746.
   c. The alternative spelling *sch* appears in the following words, each occurring once: bischope, schere, schrayfe, schryfe, schype.
   d. O.N. *sk*, which is a Nth. characteristic, appears in **skarthes** 2270; and the spelling **skole** 2087 may be an indication of the derivation of the word through O.N. **skoli**.
11. O.E. *hw* appears in three forms:
   a. Nth. (or E. Mid.) *qw* 41 times: qwen 140, 284, 391; qwhen 24, 649, 2159; qwhat 726, 927, 1600.
   b. Mid. *wh* 167 times: what 7, 312, 563; when 508, 524, 724; whare 1076, 1263, 1303.
   c. Sth. *w* five times: war(e) 2880, 2886; wilk 3167; wils 1719; wylke 2323.
12. The personal pronouns are Nth. in form:
   a. Feminine singular, third person: scho 145 times; sho 13 times.
   b. Nominative of the third person plural: þai 396 times; þay twice; and þi once.
   c. Possessive of the third person plural: þer 86 times and occasionally þere and þar(e).
   d. Objective of the third person plural: þam 174 times and occasionally þaim and þaym.
13. Plural substantives have the following endings:
   a. *-es* 244 times: bestes 254, 1063, 1101; clothes 296; frendes 424, 1162, 1174.
   b. *-s* 114 times: damsels 293, 627; danteʒs (= danteys) 3262; maydens 262, 469, 607; tempils 2831; 2876.
   c. *-ys* 41 times: bestys 2500, 2515; frendys 1661, 1835.
   d. *-n* regularly in children and once in eyn (O.E. **ēagan**) 2002.
   e. *-us* in the following Latin words: *pharaseus* 2173 and *tribus* 485.
   f. The following words of O.F. origin write the pl. *-ts* as *-tʒ*: presantʒ 2609; rentʒ 2599; spirytʒ 3007.
   g. The plural *seruauntes* is sometimes two syllables and sometimes three. It occurs in the following forms:

Introduction

seruaunde3s 3314; seruuand3es 3281; seruandt3es 3304; seruaunte3s 3266, 3289.

14. Verbs regularly end in -*es* in the present indicative, second person singular: begynnes 934; haves 152, 674; knawes 127, 866; and as follows in the present indicative, third person singular.
   a. -*es* regularly: comes 92, 441; spekes 2142, 2153; standes 1318.
   b. -*s* in *says* regularly, three times in *bers*, and once in each of the following verbs: begyns, bids, ligs, lys.
   c. -*se* occurs three times: lyse 1805, 2429, 3154.
   d. -*ys* occurs: rynnys 3170; standys 3079; suffys 3173.
15. Verbs regularly have the characteristic Nth. ending -*es* in the pres. ind. pl. The pres. ind. pl. of the anomalous verb **ben** is always the Nth. **er** except for **bes** 2256, and the Nth. contracted forms **has** 1085 and **seys** 2012 occur. **Comys** 1249 is a variant spelling of Nth. **comes**.
16. Present participles of strong verbs have the following endings:
   a. Nth. -*and(e)* 49 times: brynnand 226; walkand 999.
   b. -*yng* four times: plesyng* 1532, shynyng* 1247, spekyng 2587, standyng 1101.
17. Preterit participles of strong verbs regularly end in -*en* and are without prefix: comen 56, 185, 1030; funden 1078; benomen 1031, 1749.
18. Preterit participles of weak verbs end in -*ed* or -*id*: betrayde 415; cursyd 448; sayde 201; wayfed 415; weddid 408.
19. Special forms peculiar to the North: among, emang 368, 479, 485; at (= that) 42, 45, 246, 432, 747, 974, 2358, 3380; bus 810, 1174, 1176; childer 59; gas 161; gudnes 403; helles 99; hende 177, 1031, 1387, 2180; herkens 3, 71; lufed 868; luke 577; tane 929, 1803, 2828; þas 607, 610, 985; thusgate 148, 499, 736, 2461; tyll (= to) 104, 323, 585.
20. The first two hundred lines of the poem contain the following Scandinavian loan-words: at (= that) 42, 45; ay 138, 175; bath 22; bayth 62; boyth 61; bo3th 23; er 72, 84; fell 36, 101; fra 105, 130; fro 120, 152, 172, 185; fyrth 36; gar 176; hende 177; husband 120, 122, 153; yll 154, 168; neke 22; ryn 81; sam 59, 164; sere 93;

xvi   *Introduction*

skyll 162; slyke 28; thusgate 148; til 110; toke 32; tyll 103; þai 35, 50, 57, 59, 62, 67, 76, 84; þaim 76; þer 68, 72, 178, 180,; þithen 103; were (n.) 96, 157.[1] These two hundred lines contain, therefore, twenty-four separate words of Scandinavian origin occurring fifty-three times in an approximate total of 1190 words, or a percentage of 4.7, leaving out of consideration words which may have been influenced by Scandinavian phonology.

This study has shown the following facts concerning the life of St. Anne as it is contained in the Minnesota MS.: the language is predominantly Northern, but contains a considerable Midland element; the poem contains a considerable number of words which are peculiar to the Northern dialect, and must have been in the original version; the Scandinavian element in the language is larger than would be expected in a Midland text, but is not so large as would be expected in a pure Northern text. (No exact statistics are available, and this statement of the case is based on impressions gained from reading in various M.E. dialects.) It will be shown later (p. xxvii) that this version of the poem is a copy of an older original. We may conclude, therefore, that the original version of this poem was a Northern text and that the extant copy was made by a Midland scribe either in the southern part of the Northern territory or in the northern or north-eastern part of the Midland territory.

A shorter version of the life of St. Anne is that in MS. Trinity College, Cambridge, 601. It begins at f. 221a and extends through f. 232b; it contains ninety-four rime royal stanzas. The MS., which contains poems chiefly by Lydgate, belongs to the time of Edward IV.[2] The writing is clear and contains a surprisingly small number of contractions and peculiarities of orthography. Almost the only contractions used are those for -er, which is indicated by a curl above and to the right of the preceding letter, and for *with* which is written w^t. Aside from the usual prologue of deprecation and supplication, the poem is an exposition of the facts concerning the lives of St. Anne and the Virgin up to and including the birth of Christ. It ends with a prayer to St. Anne.

The following analysis will show that the dialect of this poem is approximately the same as that of Lydgate, whose name has been added at the top of f. 221a and at the bottom of f. 222a by a hand different

[1] This study is based primarily on the authority of Erik Björkman's *Scandinavian Loan-words in Middle English*, in *Studien zur Englischen Philologie*, VII, 1–191, and XI, 19–360.

[2] See Brown, *op. cit.*, I, 242, and the *Catalogue of Western MSS. in Trinity College, Cambridge*, II, 83, for the date and more detailed description of this MS.

Introduction xvii

from and later than that in which the MS. is written. (Lydgate's name was probably added by Stowe, to whom the MS. once belonged.)

1. O.E. *ā* regularly appears as *ǭ*, which is the characteristic form for the Midland and Southern dialects : holy 37, 127, 128, 172; more 54, 196, 274, 283; sory* 27, 73; stone 31, 225, 236.
   Exceptions : In the following unaccented positions it appears as *a* : nat 52, 347, 518; notwithstanding, 28, 522.
2. O.E. *a* is lengthened in open syllables to *ā* : make 13, 244; name 211; shame* 59.
3. Merc. *a*, W.S. *ea + ld* appears as *ǭ* : manyfolde* 119, 472; old* 29, 118, 177.
4. O.E. *āe + r* in adverbs and verbs regularly appears as Midland *ē* : there 233, 329; were 15, 18, 258, 271.
5. O.E. *y*, *ȳ*, appears in two forms :
   a. Nth. or E. Mid. *i*, *ī* (written *y*) : fyrst 97; synners 46, 206, 469, 640.
   b. Sth. *u* : furst 381; suche (<O.E. swylc by absorption of *w* and loss of *l*. N.E.D.) 197, 203, 404, 528.
6. O.E. *c* appears as follows :
   a. *k* (sometimes written *c*) generally in guttural positions and before palatal vowels arising from umlaut : come* 171, 251; derk 267; eke 9, 96, 97, 184; kynrede* 242, 293.
   b. *ch* in palatal positions : chose 100, 369; chyrche* 127, 461; chyld 172, 359.
   Exceptions : mykell* 281; moche 289, 399; suche 10, 197, 203; whyche 23, 81, 85, 110, 135.
7. O.E. palatal *g* appears regularly as *y* : yaue 31; yef 35; yefte 338; yeres 327; yeuyng* 131, 226, 266.
8. O.E. guttural stop *g* remained : god 31; good 21.
   Exception : owne (O.E. **āgen**) 45, 198, 246 by diphthongization of *ā* (N.E.D.).
9. O.E. *h* in the combination *ht* appears as *gh* : brought 139, 164; doughter 334; lyght(e)* 3, 266; myghty 243, 271, 274.
10. O.E. *hw* appears as Mid *wh* : what 337; where 18, 40; whom 120.
11. O.E. *sc* regularly appears as *sh* : shall 56, 68, 69; shuld 122, 198, 337; flessh(e) 258, 333; shynyng 294.
12. The third person of the feminine singular pronoun appears only as *she*.

13. The third person of the plural pronoun appears as :
    a. Nom. they 221, 271, 274.
    b. Poss. theyr(e) 204, 205, 226.
    c. Obj. theym 40, 41, 300; hem 236, 285, 503, 510.
14. The regular endings of plural substantives are :
    a. -es, sometimes written -ys : beames 226 ; goodes 321 ; goodys 270 ; storyes 36, 262 ; thornes 299.
    b. -s : herts 65 ; moders 195 ; pylgryms 320 ; vergyns 148.
    c. -n in brethern 106 and regularly.
15. The present indicative, third person singular, of verbs ends in -eth : apereth 107 ; causeth 38 ; ffedeth 167 ; hath 34, 54, 228.
16. The present indicative, third person plural, of verbs appears in two forms :
    a. -n ending : byn 88 ; 224, 251 ; shewyn 262.
    b. Without ending : halow 108 ; worshyp 108 ; support 219.
17. Present participles end in -yng : bryngyng* 122 ; encresyng 277 ; preysyng 132 ; yeuyng* 131, 266.
18. Past participles of strong verbs end in -en or -yn and are without prefix : holdyn 129 ; forsaken 111 ; knowyn 360.

This analysis points unmistakably to the S.E. Midlands as the home of this poem. The language is so similar to that of Lydgate that it is a practical certainty that the MS. belongs to the neighbourhood of Suffolk.[1]

Chetham Library MS. 8009 contains, beginning at f. 19a, another copy of the same version of the life of St. Anne as that in Trinity College, Cambridge, 601, although there are slight variations between the two copies. The Chetham Library MS. belongs to the latter half of the fifteenth century.[2] It contains a few more of the usual contractions than Trinity College, Cambridge, 601, and is written with more flourish. The variant readings of this MS. are given with the text from Trinity College, Cambridge, 601. An analysis of the language of the Chetham version follows.

1. O.E. $\bar{a}$ regularly appears as $\bar{o}$: holy(e) 37, 83, 127 ; stone 31, 237 ; sore 42, 68, 154 ; two 237 ; wo* 91, 203, 339.

---

[1] For a discussion of the language of Lydgate see E.E.T.S. 80, 89, 97, and 103.
[2] Cf. Brown, op. cit., I, 454.

Introduction xix

2. O.E. *a* appears in two forms:
   a. *ā* in open syllables: lak(e) 9, 17; name 211; scham* 59.
   b. *ō* before a nasal + a voiced consonant: honde* 10; lond* 108; stonde* 214.
3. Merc. *a*, W.S. *ea* + *-ld* regularly appears as *ǭ* : manyfolde* 119, 472; olde* 29, 118, 177.
4. O.E. *aē* + *r* regularly becomes *ē* in adverbs and verbs: therfor(e) 62, 77, 127, 200; wer(e) 15, 18, 33; wherfor 30, 48, 131, 190.
5. O.E. *y*, *ȳ* generally appears as *i*, *ī* (*y*): fyrst 97, 381; sinnarys 46; synnarys 469; synnerys 206.
   Exceptions: letyll (Kentish) 278, 399 and such 197, 203 (O.E. swylc by absorption of *w* and loss of *l* (N.E.D.). It may be Sth.
6. O.E. *c* appears in two forms:
   a. *k* in guttural positions and before palatal vowels arising from umlaut: derk 161; eke 9, 96; kepe 53; kynred 242, 394; mekyll 281, 368.
   b. *ch* in palatal positions: besechyng 7; cherche 127, 461; werche 462; which 32, 85, 110.
7. O.E. *g* appears in three forms:
   a. Guttural *g* remained: god, good, gaff 31.
   b. Palatal *g* became *y*: yeff 35; yeuyng 226; yefte 338; yerys 327.
   c. Medial *g* became *w* in *owne* (O.E. āgen) 45, 58 by diphthongization of *ā*.
8. O.E. spirant *h* + *t* appears with three spellings:
   a. *gh*: brought(e) 173, 186; nought 60; ryght 8.
   b. ȝ: brouȝte 164, 342; hyȝe 79, 163, 182.
   c. ȝ*th*: myȝthi 271, 274; myȝthly 233.
9. O.E. *hw-* regularly appears as Mid. *wh-*: wherfor 13, 30, 48; whom(e) 120, 159, 204; whose 145, 165, 172.
   Exceptions: Nth. *wase* (= whose) 40 and Mid. or Sth. *woso* (= whoso) 449.
10. O.E. *sc-* appears regularly as *sch-*: schall 56, 68, 69; schene 232, 367; schulde 122, 188, 337; worschipe 108, 192.
    Exceptions: fleche 258, 333; flesshly 121.
11. The third person singular of the feminine pronoun appears only as *sche*.

12. The third person plural of the personal pronoun appears as follows:
   a. Nom. they 221, 271, 274, 278.
   b. Poss. ther (þer) 204, 205, 226, 280.
   c. Obj. hem. regularly; them 285, 306.
13. Plural substantives regularly end as follows:
   a. -*es* or -*ys*: angellys 116, 167; branches 158; costes 146; flowrys 142, 143, 150; wallys 237.
   b. -*s*: prophetts 118, sayntts 115; wytts 34.
   c. -*n*: brethern 106, 212.
14. The present indicative, third person singular, of verbs ends in -*eth*: causeth 38; cometh 29; ffedeth 167.
15. The present indicative, third person plural, of verbs ends in -*e*: beleve 252; bene 150, 224; supporte 219; worschipe 108; but shewith 262.
16. Present participles end in -*yng*: abydyng 104, 209; puttyng 42; submittyng 94; unconnyng 95.
17. Past participles of strong verbs end in -*yn*: forsakyn 111; holdyn 129.

The foregoing analysis shows the language of this poem to be closely related to that of the Trinity College, Cambridge, 601 version, but it also shows certain important variations. The regular occurrence of *sch* instead of *sh* from O.E. *sc*, the use of *sche* instead of *she* for the third person feminine of the personal pronoun, and the -*e* instead of the -*n* ending of the present indicative, third person plural, of verbs indicate that this is a more northern text than the Trinity College, Cambridge. It is not, however, a Northern text, for the O.E. $\bar{a}$ always appears as $\bar{\rho}$, O.E. *y* appears as *e* in *letyll* (278, 1399), *hem* is the more common objective form of the third person pl. of the pronoun, and the present participle ends in -*yng*. This text, therefore, must belong to that part of the E. Midlands where certain Northern forms occur regularly. It is probably an E. Midland copy of a S.E. Midland original. The distinctive variations recorded in the collations with the text from Trinity College, Camb., 601, indicate, however, that this is not a direct copy of the Trinity College, Cambridge, version, but that both are copies from an unknown original written in the S.E. Midlands.

The best version of the third stanzaic form of the life of St. Anne is ound in MS. Bodl. 10234 (Tanner 407), which also belongs to the fifteenth century.[1] The poem begins at f. 21*a* and contains 115 stanzas of four

---

[1] Cf. Brown, *op. cit.*, I, 96.

Introduction xxi

long lines each riming abab. The scribe's use of contractions is confined largely to the omission of the vowel in *with*, the use of a back stroke over a final consonant to indicate the addition of a final *-e*, and the writing of a curled stroke above and to the right of a consonant for the addition of *-er*. A distinct peculiarity of this MS. appears in a series of dots similar to periods in modern punctuation. Sometimes they appear in the middle of a line, sometimes at the end of a line, and sometimes at the end of a stanza. For the sake of reproducing this interesting peculiarity, I have transcribed the poem without adding further punctuation. I have also retained the capitalization of the MS.

The following analysis of the language of this version shows several inconsistencies in dialect.

1. O.E. $\bar{a}$ regularly appears as $\bar{\rho}$: hom(e) 181, 183, 200; ston(e)* 225, 293; tokene 185, 339.
   Exception in unaccented word: na 270.
2. O.E. *a* appears in two forms:
   a. $\bar{a}$ in open syllables: name* 9, 11, 22; same 211; schame 114, 388.
   b. $\bar{\rho}$ before a nasal + voiced consonant: hond(e)* 212, 317, 318; lombe* 108; lond* 301, 395.
3. Merc. *a*, W.S. *ea* + *-ld* appears as $\bar{\rho}$: bold* 256; holde 358; olde 149, 219; told 191, 192.
4. O.E. $a\bar{e}$ + *r* in adverbs and verbs regularly appears as $\bar{e}$: ther(e) 194, 201, 224; wer(e) 78, 96, 110; wher 191.
5. O.E. *y*, $\bar{y}$ appears in two forms:
   a. *i*, $\bar{i}$ (written *y*): fyrst 10, 27; kynde* 150; lytel 139, 311; mankynde 128; swyche 230, 370; synne 272.
   b. *e*: mankende 131; meche 201, 369; merthe 201; sweche 230; weche 120, etc.
6. O.E. *c* appears in two forms:
   a. *k* in guttural positions and before palatal vowels arising from umlaut generally: boke 34, 70, 80; derk 248; kome 213 (come also appears); kynred 74; mekyl 91.
   b. *ch* in palatal positions generally: chyld* 15, 17, 22; chyrche 84; swych(e) 348, 370.
      Note: O.E. *c* is not palatalized to *ch* in *mekyl* 91 but is in *mechyl* 356 and *meche* 201, 369. O.N. *k* remains in *kyrk* 244.

7. O.E. palatal *g* appears in two forms:
    a. ȝ regularly: aȝen 65, 143, 247; ȝe(e)r(e)* 56, 93, 217; ȝyf 1, 95, 133; ȝong 228, 230, 371.
    b. *g*: gate* 186, 193.
       Note: the *g* appears as *w* in *morwen* 244 by labialization and in *owyn* 89, 133, 176 by diphthongization of *ā*.
8. O.E. spirant *h* + *t* appears with two spellings:
    a. *-gh*: hyght 49, 61; myght* 17, 18, 95; nyght* 20; ryght 13, 159, 249; thurgh 177.
    b. *-th*: bryth* 231; brouth 53, 147, 250; nouth 105, 114, 125.
       Note: the spirant *h* disappears in *dowter(ys)* 8, 33, 54, 439, leaving a trace of its influence in the diphthong *ow*.
9. O.E. *hw-* appears in three forms:
    a. *wh-* regularly: whan 103, 117, 213; what 65, 68, 110; who 57, 59, 68; whom 66, 452.
    b. *qw-*: qwan 243; qwat 263, 265, 312, 407, 418; qwom 324; qwose 320; qwy 285, 342.
    c. *w-*: weche 120, 236, 346.
10. O.E. *sc* regularly appears as *sch*: byschopis 257; schall 119, 139, 163; schame 114, 388; schuld 20, 91, 95.
    Exceptions: bysshopys 254, 279, 281, 293, 299; fleysshlly 129; flexly 138; freyssh 215, 443; worchepe 56, 212; wurchepe 35; wurchepful 72.
11. The third person singular of the feminine pronoun appears regularly as *sche*; but *she* appears in 34, 50, 196, 237.
12. The third person plural of the personal pronoun appears as follows:
    a. Nom. they, þei, þey indiscriminately, though the spelling they is slightly predominant.
    b. Poss. her(e) regularly except there 199.
    c. Obj. hem always.
13. Plural substantives have four endings:
    a. *-ys* is the prevailing form: bokys 156, 207; dowterys 8, 54; frendys 102, 182, 214; pasys 224, 228.
    b. *-es* occurs frequently: almes 85; dayes 36, 78, 126; ryches 81, 82.
    c. *-s* occurs frequently: days 87; housbonds 28, 50; tonggs 3; tydynggs 122.
    d. *-yn*: chylderyn 8, 38, 58; drynkyn 259.

Introduction xxiii

14. The present indicative, third person singular, of verbs regularly ends in *-yth*: beryth 70; byddyth 314; chargyth 314; makyth 184.
    Exceptions: sayes 34, 80, 168; tellys 67, 261.
15. The present indicative, third person plural, of verbs regularly ends in *-n*: answeryn 377; ben 86, 161, 320; han 88, 129, 141, 144; mowen 63, 162, 318; seyn 42, 164, 223.
    Exceptions: be 224; beryth 127; come 146; tel 156, 202, 436; wene 130.
16. Present participles of verbs end in *-yng*: levyng 36; weuyng 246; passyng 428.
17. Preterit participles of strong verbs end in *-yn*: getyn 33, 105, 402; helpyn 304; knowyn 367; wretyn 38, 70, 167.

The foregoing analysis shows that this text is predominantly Midland in dialect; and the occurrence of O.E. *sc-* as *sch-* and as *x*, of the personal pronouns *sche* and *þei*, and of O.E. *hw-* as *qw-* indicates that it belongs to the N.E. Midlands. There are, however, certain forms which must be of Northern origin: O.E. *c* (k) occurs as *k* in *kome, kyrk*, etc.; and O.E. *hw-* survives as *qw-*. On the other hand, there are certain Southern or S. Midland characteristics: O.E. *y, ȳ* becomes *e, ē* in several instances; and *hem* occurs regularly; the present indicative, third person singular, of verbs regularly ends in *-yth* and the corresponding plural in *-n*. But the *e, ē* from O.E. *y, ȳ* is distinctly Kentish. We must conclude, therefore, that the original of this version is of Northern provenience, that this original was copied in the dialect of London, and that the present text was made in the N.E. Midlands from the London copy.

Another copy of this four-line stanzaic version of the life of St. Anne is contained in MS. Harley 4012 at f. 130b. It also is a product of the fifteenth century.[1] It is written with considerable flourish and decoration, but contains no significant peculiarities of composition or orthography. Wherever the reading of this MS. varies from that of Bodl. 10234 the variant readings are given with the Bodl. text.

The following analysis of the dialect of the Harley MS. version will show that the language is slightly different from that of the Bodl. MS. version.

[1] Brown, *op. cit.*, I, 339.

Introduction

1. O.E. ā appears as ǭ: home 181, 336; holigost* 177, 320; one 50, 51, 52; token 185, 307, 339; too* (numeral) 47, 172, 432.
2. O.E. a occurs in two forms:
   a. ā in open syllables: name* 9, 22, 42; same 211, 445; shame 114, 388.
   b. ǭ before a nasal + voiced consonant: honde* 212, 329 (hande 318), londe* 301, 395; sonde* 210.
3. Merc. a, W.S. ea + -ld appears as ō: bolde* 256; holde 358; tolde 191, 206; wolde (N.E. old) 149, 151, 219.
4. O.E. āe + r in adverbs and verbs regularly becomes ē: þer 15, 115, 194; wer(e) 13, 19, 52; wher 68, 103, 191.
5. O.E. y, ȳ regularly appears as i, ī: first 10, 27; liste* 46; mankinde 76; synne 240, 272.
   Exceptions: moche 12, 91, etc.; suche 230, 348, 370.
6. O.E. c appears as follows:
   a. k generally in guttural positions and before palatal vowels arising from umlaut: derke 248; kallid 34, 44, 74; kam(me) 103, 199, 213; kowde 12, 110.
   b. ch generally in palatal positions: children 38, 112; chulde 51; suche 230, 348, 370.
   Exceptions: k remains in O.N. kirk* 242 but is palatalized to ch in cherch(e) 84, 98. O.E. c appears as k in wirk 242 but is palatalized to ch in eche 51, 244 and in moche 12, 91, 142, 369.
7. O.E. palatal g regularly appears as y(ȝ): yeate 193; ȝeate 186; ȝeris 78, 126; yode 101; yofen 33; younge 228, 315, 326, 371.
   Exceptions: awne 133, 160 by diphthongization of ā.
8. O.E. spirant h + t appears as gh: broght 53, 250; doghter 33, 439; myght* 18, 95; right* 136, 240.
9. O.E. hw- regularly appears as wh-: what 110, 302, 390; when 103, 117; which(e) 75, 120; but hoo (N.E. who) 57, 59, 153.
10. O.E. sc- appears as sh-: bisshoppis 254, 257, 293; flesh 443; shall 5, 26, 119; shame 114; short. 21.
11. The third person singular of the feminine pronoun is always she.

Introduction

12. The third person plural of the personal pronoun appears as follows:
    a. Nom. þei (occasionally þey, they) 13, 14, 17, 19.
    b. Poss. þer 14, 82, 83, 89.
    c. Obj. þem 33, 43, 99.
13. Plural substantives have five different endings:
    a. *-es* most frequently: daes 36, 78; frendes 1; husbondes 50; trifelles 3.
    b. *-is* almost as frequently as *-es*: husbondis 7, 28; frendis 102; seruauntis 90.
    c. *-s* occurs occasionally: doghters 8, 54.
    d. *-n*: childern(e) 8, 47, 54.
    e. *-us*: almus 85.
14. The present indicative, third person singular, of verbs regularly ends in *-ith*: berith 70; biddith 314; knawith 407; makith 184.
    Exceptions: sa(i)es 34, 80, 168; tellis 67, 261.
15. The present indicative, third person plural, of verbs regularly ends in *-ith*: berith 127; makith 55; saith 223; tellipe 378.
    Exceptions: haue 141, 162; sayne 225; telle 202, 436; wene 130.
16. Present participles of strong verbs end in *-yng*: ffulfillyng 86; leuyng 36; walkyng 195; sitting 123.
17. Preterit participles of strong verbs end in *en*: knawen 367; writen 38; yofen 33; gotyn 106, 402.

Since this text retains certain of the Northern and Kentish characteristics of the Bodl. text; has þei, þer, þem regularly for the third person of the plural pronoun; has the *-ith* ending for both the singular and the plural of verbs in the third person, present indicative; and has the present participle in *-yng*, we may safely conclude that it is an E. Midland version of the same provenience as the N.E. Midland version contained in the Bodl. MS.

That the Harley 4012 copy is a variant version rather than a copy of the Bodl. version is indicated by the great variation in the use of pronouns, by the difference in form of the plural indicative of verbs, by the fact that the two MSS. have only this poem in common, and by the further fact that the Bodl. copy was definitely made for the purpose of celebrating St. Anne's Day while the Harleian copy as definitely was not. A copyist would undoubtedly make certain changes in the form of words in order to bring these words into accord with the usage of his own dialect, but it is highly improbable that he would make changes as radical and consistent as those which appear in the Harleian copy. The evidence, therefore, indicates that the two copies are from a common original.

On a basis of the preceding studies, the versions of the life of St. Anne which are under consideration may be classified as follows:

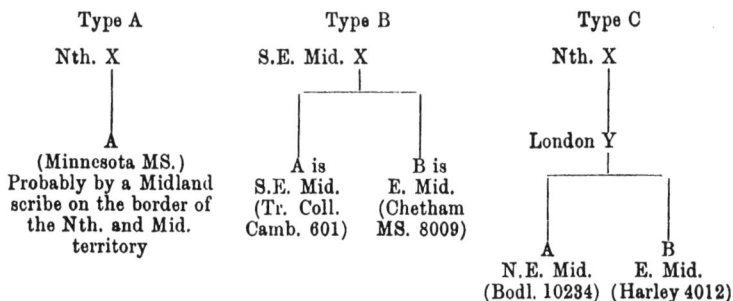

III. AUTHORSHIP AND SOURCES.

While it is in every case impossible to determine the authorship of these stanzaic versions of the life of St. Anne, there are certain facts concerning the occasion and relationships of these poems which can be stated with a fair degree of certainty. The sources of the poems also, whenever they are at all definite, can be determined with comparative certainty. It is to these problems that this section is devoted.

The version of the life of St. Anne contained in the Minnesota MS. is written by the same scribe who wrote the remainder of the MS. The identity of this scribe, however, has not been determined. The only clue to his identity—if such it is—is to be found at the bottom of f. 185*a*. Here is written, in the same hand that wrote the entire MS., Nome*n* scri*p*toris R.G. plenus amoris. Ecce quam bonu*m* et quam Iocu*n*dum h*a*bitare frat*r*es i*n* unu*m*.[1] The R.G. may be the initials of the scribe. If they are, the quotation would imply that he belonged to a monastery. They may, on the other hand, be the initials of the author, as Professor Gerould surmises, or even of Robert de Gretham, whose *Miroir* (*Les Euangiles des*

---

[1] The quotation is from *Liber Psalmorum* 132:1. I read R.G. and not R.S. as does Professor Gerould, who thinks that these may be the initials of the R. Stoundone of Cambridge University MS. Dd. I. 1. (Cf Gerould. G. H., *Saints' Legends*, p. 169.) I should hesitate to disagree with so distinguished a scholar as Professor Gerould had not my reading been concurred in by experienced scholars to whom I have shown these initials.

Domees) may have been the model for the *North English Homily Collection*.¹ However that may be, the scribe was hardly the author, for this is not the original version of the poem. This fact is evidenced by such scribal errors as the writing of *Joseph* for *Jesus* at l. 2671 and the omission of three verses from each of six different stanzas of the poem. The problem of the authorship of this poem, therefore, must for the present remain unsettled.

The source of the poem is not difficult to determine. In the first stanza the author says that his "lytill tretice" follows the story

>Of anna & hyr doghter dere,
>Mary þat maydyn fre,
>How scho was born & in what land,
>Als seynt mathew yt wretyn fand
>In grew & þerfor he
>Made it in latyn out of grewe
>Als seynt Ierom þe doctour trew
>Witnes it suld be.

This corresponds closely with the heading of the apocryphal Gospel of Pseudo-Matthew in codex A (Vaticani Codicis), which reads as follows: *Incipit Liber de ortu Beatae Mariae et Infantia Salvatoris a Beato Matthaeo Evangelista Hebraice in Latinum translatus*.² Then, near the end of the poem (ll. 3413 ff.), the author declares that he has recorded the story

>Als saynt Iohn euangelyst it wrate,
>For next hym best he couth.
>. . . . .
>Bot saynt mathew eftyrward wele & fyn
>Out of grew turnyd yt in latyn
>& had þus in doyng,
>At þe prayer of byshoppes two,
>Cromassij and Elydon called þai so,
>Twa gude men of lyfyng.
>& for all þis ȝyt es þer some
>Þat says it es apocrysome
>& none autentyk thyng.

This in turn corresponds with the same Pseudo-Matthew in codex B (Codicis Laurentiani), which states that *Sanctus apostolus et evangelista Iohannes manu sua scripsit hunc libellum hebraicis litteris consignatum, quem Ieronimus doctor ille perspicuus de hebraico in latinum deduxit*.³ The source of the poem, therefore, is the Gospel of Pseudo-Matthew.

---
¹ Cf. Gerould, *op. cit.*, p. 168.
² Tischendorf, C., *Evangelia Apocrypha*, p. 51.
³ *Ibid.*, p. 112.

An examination of the text shows, however, that the author did not follow the apocryphal codex A, but codex B, which contains a larger proportion of miraculous material. But even this version he did not follow " fro sentence to sentence " beyond a certain point, if we assume that the author was using one of the extant versions of the Pseudo-Matthew—an assumption which is unwarranted in view of our present knowledge of the large fund of biblical and hagiographical lore available in the ancient seats of learning.[1] In ll. 1837-2076 are recorded events which do not occur in any of the various extant versions of the Pseudo-Matthew printed by Tischendorf. The same thing is true of ll. 2377-2940, where the author inserts legends from Jacobus de Voragine's *Legenda Aurea*, Peter Comestor's *Historia Scholastica*, and others for which I have found no source. Again, in ll. 2989-3408, he recounts certain miracles from the canonical Gospels of Matthew and Luke.[2]

[1] See, for example, the *Catalogi Veteres Librorum Ecclesiae Cathedralis Dunelmensis* in the *Publications of the Surtees Society*, VII, 54-58.

[2] For convenience, I give below a tabular view of the more important differences between the A and B versions of the Gospel of Pseudo-Matthew as printed by Tischendorf in his *Evangelia Apocrypha*. The life of St. Anne follows the B version in these cases. Detailed differences will be given in the notes to the text of the poem.

Chap.	A Version.	B Version.
II.	Joachim's offering is refused by Reubin.	Refused by Ysachar.
IV.	The birth of Mary and her consecration in the temple.	Gives the additional incident of Mary ascending the fifteen steps of the temple unaided.
VII.	Mary refuses to marry when she is 14 years old.	Mary is 12 years old.
VIII.	A dove ascends from Joseph's rod as a sign that he is to marry Mary.	Joseph's rod flowers and bears nuts.
IX.	The Annunciation " iuxta fontem."	The Annunciation in the " habitationem " of Mary.
XVI.	The coming of the Magi. No names are given.	The names of the Magi are Guaspar, Melchior, and Balthasar.
XXII.	Joseph and Mary, upon their arrival in Egypt, lodge in the temple at Sotinen.	They lodge in the house of a widow at Sotrina, where Jesus restores a dead child to life.
XXVI.	The miracle of the lake and the restoration of the dead boy.	Only the first part of the miracle is given.
XXX.	Zachyas advises that Jesus be sent to school.	Combines A version XXX, XXXI, and XXXVIII.
XXXI.	Zachyas becomes the teacher of Jesus and is put to shame by the wisdom of the Child.	A friend of Joseph becomes the teacher of Jesus and is surprised at the wisdom of the Child.
XXXIII.	Mary sends Jesus to the well. He performs the miracle of the broken pitcher.	Mary sends a maid for the water. Jesus performs the miracle of the broken pitcher.

Introduction xxix

Although the author of this version of the life of St. Anne, like Osbern Bokenham in his life of Anna,[1] may have been following a compilation unknown to us, it is evident that he was no slavish copyist. It is also evident that the principal source of his poem is the B version of the Gospel of Pseudo-Matthew and that this is one of the many poems produced for the purpose of furnishing entertaining religious instruction.

There is nothing to suggest the identity of the author of the rime royal version of the life of St. Anne contained in MS. Trinity College, Cambridge, 601. Lydgate's name, it is true, appears at f. 221*a* and again at f. 222*a*; but this name is written in a later hand than that in which the poem is written. Moreover, Professor MacCracken excludes this poem from the Lydgate canon because it breaks "all Lydgate's rhyming habits, while closely imitating his general style" and because, he thinks, "it is of a later date than Lydgate."[2] While the ascription of the poem to Lydgate might not be denied conclusively on account of date, Professor MacCracken's rime tests seem definitely to exclude it from the Lydgate canon and to leave the problem of its authorship unsettled.

Although the authorship of this poem remains a mystery, the occasion for which it was written is certain. In ll. 247 ff. the author says:

> Thys day, dere brethern, most specyally
> In honou*r* of thys matrone ferre and nere,
> Most worshipfull and blessyd entyerly,
> As we haue seyde before, now v*er*yly
> And in thys day togyder we byn come.

XXXIV.	The miracle of the wheat.	The miracle of the wheat and of the healing of James Alpheus, who was bitten by a serpent.
XXXV.	The miracle of Jesus and the lioness.	Not in the B version.
XXXVI.	Jesus parts the waters and crosses the Jordan.	Not in the B version.
XXXVII.	Jesus lengthens the beam for Joseph.	Jesus lengthens the beam for "quidam architector lignifaber." Jesus surprises his playmates by leaping on a sunbeam.
XXXVIII.	Jesus is sent to school a second time.	Given under XXX in the B version.
XXXIX.	Jesus teaches his schoolmaster.	Given under XXXI in the B version.
XLII.	The banquet of Joseph and his sons.	The death of Joseph and the account of Anne's three husbands and her children.

[1] *Englische Studien*, XII, 34.
[2] MacCracken, H. N., *The Minor Poems of John Lydgate*, London, 1911, I, xxxix and xl.

And in ll. 642 ff. he says :

> And to vs all worshippyng in what place.
> Of thys same day and the gret solempnyte
> She bryngeth grace of hyr benygnyte.

Since the title of the poem reads "Incipit Vita Sancte Anne matris Sancte Marie Virginis," there is only one day to which the poem would be appropriate. "Thys day" must be St. Anne's Day (July 26), and the poem must have been written for the celebration of the Feast of St. Anne. In view of the fact that this poem shows a marked similarity to the works of Lydgate, to whose locality the MS. certainly belongs, it appears more than probable that the poem was written, or at least copied, for the celebration of the annual festival of the St. Anne's Guild of Bury St. Edmunds, where such a guild flourished after about 1309.[1]

The source of this poem is not so definite as of that contained in the Minnesota MS. The prologue contains the typical apology of the medieval clerk for his lack of ability; it also contains something more. The author apologizes not only for his lack of ability but also for the offence which he may give. He addresses himself to "ye cruell herts mercyless" and admonishes them that "man witout mercy mercy shall mys." The burden of this prologue is a plea for pity and mercy. Whether such a plea has any reference to contemporary events I am unable to say, for it contains no specific references. It is possible, however, that the author had in mind such events as those following Jack Cade's Rebellion and the slaughter of citizens, both innocent and guilty, attending the accession of Edward IV to the throne.[2] There is no reference to these affairs beyond the prologue, although the author dwells upon the mercy and pity of God and of St. Anne. In doing this he seems to have followed the general outline of the Gospel of the Nativity of Mary, which was attributed to St. Matthew. There are also evidences that the poet was familiar with the *Legenda Aurea*, Gospel of Pseudo-Matthew, and the canonical scriptures.[3] The items taken from these sources are interspersed with the author's comments and explanations, thereby giving an appearance of originality to the poem which renders the location of the definite source more difficult than would otherwise be the case.

---

[1] Cf. Westlake, *op. cit.*, p. 226.
[2] Cf. Gardner, S. R., *A Student's History of England*, London, 1911, I, 322–337.
[3] The sources of the various parts of the poem, in so far as I have been able to determine them, are indicated in the notes to the text. The problem of originality will be discussed in connection with the Chetham MS.

Introduction xxxi

A variant of this version of the life of St. Anne is to be found in Chetham Library MS. 8009 at f. 19*a*. There is, however, considerable variation between the two poems, both in phraseology and in dialect. In general, wherever differences in phraseology occur, the reading of the Trinity College MS. is preferable. This fact may be illustrated by the following passages :

Trinity College MS.	Chetham Society MS.
1. To let I wyll nat whatsoeue*r* befall ; I wyll kepe forth my p*ur*pose as I ment.	To let I wyll not what so be falle ; I wyll kepe forth myne entent.
2. O p*er*fyte charyte whyche art w*i*touten pere.	A parfet man which whith ou3te arte pere.
3. Ffor all ve*r*tues byn groundyd apon the.	For all rownd are gronddyd on the.
4. Of bethlem, forsoth, that nobyll cyte Of Dauid, Anne ys gone out sycurly.	Off bethlem, forsoth, þ*a*t noble cyte Off Anne, dauyth ys gonne ou3te sekyrly.

The reading of the Chetham MS. version in the last instance cited is probably a case of accidental transposition by a careless scribe, for it does not accord with the reading of any possible source material that I have been able to find. The reading of the Trinity College MS. is preferable moreover, on account of both sense and meter, as the lines just quoted and the variants recorded in the collations will illustrate. That the two versions are as different in dialect as in phraseology has been shown already.

If either of these versions had been copied from the other, it is quite likely that the two poems would show a greater similarity in both phraseology and dialect, for the differences between the two do not appear to be the result of careless copying. Additional evidence against the one having been copied from the other appears in the fact that this is the only piece which the two MSS. have in common.[1] This evidence points to a common original for these two poems and supports the dialectal evidence already deduced. The home of this original has already been shown to have been the S.E. Midlands, but its authorship and definite location remain undetermined.

[1] Cf. Brown, *op. cit.*, I, 96 and 454.

xxxii *Introduction*

The third type of the stanzaic life of St. Anne is contained in MS. Bodl. 10234 (Tanner 407) at f. 21a. This MS. is a Commonplace Book compiled by Robert Reynys, a churchwarden of Accle, toward the end of the fifteenth century.[1] Accle, or Acle, is situated in East Norfolk, a fact of importance in locating the home of the poem. While it is extremely improbable that Reynys, who was probably a carpenter, wrote the poem, it is certain that the dialect of the poem is N.E. Midland. It is also certain that this poem was produced for the celebration of the Feast of St. Anne. Evidence for this statement is to be found in ll. 53 ff., which read as follows :

> Now blyssyd be sent anne þat brouth forth þis berth
> and blyssyd be these dowterys and her chylderyn infere ;
> and blyssyd be all tho þat make onest merth
> in the worchepe of sent anne in thys tyme of ȝeere.

The occasion for which the poem was produced is even more definitely set forth in the two final stanzas, save one :

> Now blyssyd be þis barne þat born was of a mayde
> and blyssyd be this maydyn þat brouth forth þis berth
> and blyssyd be sent anne her moder as men saye
> in the worchep of whom we make alle oure merth
>
> And mary and her moder maynteth this gylde
> to þe worchep of god and of his plesaunce
> and all þat it mayntene it be it man or chylde
> god of his hey grace ȝeue hem good chaunce.

These stanzas indicate that the poem was written for the annual festival of a St. Anne's Guild and that it was read on St. Anne's Day. Whether the parish church at Accle had such a guild I have been unable to discover. The nearest one recorded by Westlake (*op. cit.*, p. 197) was at Lynn. He has recorded only those guilds, however, which afford the best types of parochial guilds or are some variation from the type ; consequently his failure to record such a guild in the Hundred of South Walsham, in which Accle is situated, is no evidence that such a guild did not exist there.[2]

[1] Calderhead, Iris G., "Morality Fragments from Norfolk," *Modern Philology*, XIV, 1-9.
[2] Cf. Westlake, *op. cit.*, p. vi. I have not been able to examine Blomefield's *History of the County of Norfolk*. Miss Julia M. Maynard, who has examined the index of the copy of Blomefield in the Harvard Library writes me as follows : "Casual inspection of the index reveals no mention of Robert Reynys, nor do I find

The source of this poem seems to be the *Legenda Aurea*, Chap. CXXXI: "De Nativitate beatae Mariae Virginis," which it follows closely throughout.[1]

MS. Harley 4012, f. 130*b*, contains a poor copy, as has been indicated on p. xxv, from the same original from which the Bodleian version of the life of St. Anne was made. That the Harleian version is a copy is indicated by the dialect and by the omission of verses at ll. 23, 207, 412, 424, and 454; by such scribal errors as the writing of *boye or knaue* for *mayde or knaue* at l. 19; and by the many variant readings which are listed in the collations of this study. A rather interesting example of the carelessness, or ignorance, of the scribe who made this copy is shown in his rendering of ll. 221-22. In the Bodleian version these lines stand as follows:

> On to þe grete temple of jerusalem
> þat semely is set on hey as j wene.

Harley MS. has

> Vnto þe tempell of Iersalem
> þat semely is set on his ass as I wene.

Furthermore, the fact that this is a version which was not intended for a guild celebration of the Feast of St. Anne is shown by the rather hopeless attempt of the scribe to recast ll. 453-457 so as to omit the reference to the guild—an attempt which he abandoned after writing two verses of the stanza.

There are, then, three types of the stanzaic versions of the life of St. Anne which are different in origin, in structure, in dialect, and in authorship. The long version, following the apocryphal Gospel of Pseudo-Matthew, is written in twelve-line stanzas and was probably intended for religious instruction—possibly it was read as a homily on St. Anne's Day. The rime royal version, which seems to follow the apocryphal Gospel of the Nativity, was certainly written for the celebration of the Feast of St. Anne, probably for the St. Anne's Guild at Bury St. Edmunds and for a similar guild in the E. Midlands. And the four-line stanzaic version, based on the *Legenda Aurea*, was written also for the celebration of the Feast of St. Anne by a St. Anne's

---

any Saint Anne's Guild whatever—though there are numerous other saints." But she notes the following comment of the librarian under date of 1854: "The Indexes not to be depended on either as to accuracy of reference or completeness." Miss Calderhead's discoveries verify this comment.

[1] Tho. Graesse, 3rd Ed., 1890, pp. 585-590.

xxxiv *Introduction*

Guild. In all, five MSS., none of which is the original version, are extant; but the authorship of all three poems, contained in five MSS., remains undetermined.

IV. INFLUENCES.

We may now ask whether any significance can be attached to the stanzaic versions of the life of St. Anne beyond the interest inherent in the poems and in their exemplification of the continued interest in the theme with which they deal. This inquiry leads naturally to a study of the relation of these poems to other Middle English literary productions which can be dated subsequent to the beginning of the fifteenth century. In such a study of relationships, one inevitably comes to the dramatic cycles, that considerable body of fifteenth-century literature which was compiled for popular consumption and edification. Such a study, however, reveals no relation between these poems and the *York*, *Chester*, or *Towneley* cycles of plays; but it does reveal what is apparently an important influence of one of these poems on the *Ludus Coventriae*, or *Hegge Plays*.

A comparative study of the Minnesota MS. version of the life of St. Anne and the *Ludus Coventriae* almost forces one to the conclusion that the life of St. Anne is the source of that group of plays in the *Ludus Coventriae* cycle which deals with the life of the Virgin from her conception to the birth of Christ, with the exception of the *Visit to Elizabeth*. This conclusion is induced by the relative dates of the two compositions, by the probability of the origin of the *Ludus Coventriae* in the N.E. Midlands, by dialectal similarities, by the peculiar history of the Virgin plays, and by convincing resemblances in content, phraseology, and rime words.

It has been shown already that the extant copy of the life of St. Anne, as it is found in the Minnesota MS., is not later than the first quarter of the fifteenth century and that it may belong to the last quarter of the fourteenth. Since the *Ludus Coventriae* belongs to the third quarter of the fifteenth century, there remains no question of the possibility of the use of the St. Anne material as a source by the author of the plays. Even if the Virgin plays constitute an older cycle which was incorporated into the *Ludus Coventriae*, as they probably do,[1] the life of St. Anne was composed early enough to permit of its use

---

[1] Block, K. S., *Ludus Coventriae or The Plaie Called Corpus Christi*, London, 1922 (E.E.T.S., Extra Series, cxx), p. xx.

Introduction

half a century before the compilation of the *Ludus Coventriae* cycle as we now have it.

The relative dates of these two compositions would have no significance, however, so far as the possible relationship between the two is concerned, were it not for the fact that the *Ludus Coventriae* devotes so many scenes to St. Anne, the Virgin, and the childhood of Christ. But the cycle is peculiar in this respect; and this peculiarity has led Chambers to suggest that the cycle was performed on St. Anne's Day rather than at Corpus Christi.[1] Professor Hardin Craig has championed this suggestion and has urged Lincoln as the home of the cycle. "I wish," he says, "to make the last [Chambers'] suggestion much more definitely, having arrived at considerable certainty with regard to it from other points of view. There are, I think, good reasons for fixing upon Lincoln as the home of these plays. The somewhat scanty records of the Lincoln plays seem to point to a Corpus Christi play which was transferred to St. Anne's day, and acted regularly as a St. Anne's play until near the middle of the sixteenth century. It was apparently an ordinary cyclic play with certain features appropriate to St. Anne's day. The so-called Coventry cycle, or to use the name of a former owner of the manuscript, the Hegge cycle, is unique in the possession of a group of plays dealing with the nativity and childhood of the Virgin Mary, a subject of unmistakable connection with St. Anne's day. The Corporation records show that each Lincoln alderman was required to furnish a silk gown for one of the 'kings' in the procession of St. Anne. . . .

"The suggestion that the plays belonged to Lincoln has been made before, and there are apparent agreements in the matter of dialect and content with what we should expect to find there. The hypothesis explains at a glance many of the perplexities and problems which have involved the cycle. In fact it would be so rare to find in any other place such a set of conditions as those of Lincoln that the identification must gain in credibility the more it is considered. Lincoln was a great ecclesiastical centre, and at that place we have a close and intimate connection between the cathedral clergy and the town plays, a set of circumstances which exactly accounts for the remarkable homiletic and apocryphal interest of the Hegge cycle."[2]

This theory is supported, in part, by scholars who assign the dialect

---

[1] Chambers, E. K., *The Mediaeval Stage*, Oxford, 1903, ii, 126-127, 421.
[2] *University of Minnesota Studies in Language and Literature*, I, 75, 76, 81.

of the *Ludus Coventriae* to the N.E. Midlands.[1] And if the N.E. Midlands was the home of the cycle, a knowledge of the life of St. Anne by the author of the plays is brought within the realm of possibility, for it has already been shown that the Minnesota version of the life of St. Anne, in its extant form, was made from a Northern original by a Midland scribe, either in the southern part of the Northern territory or in the N.E. part of the Midland territory. This possibility becomes more convincing as one repeatedly finds in the cycle such Northern forms as *lare, same, gan, knawe, thare*, and present participles in *-ande*. A study of these forms has led Professor Greg to conclude: "If we eliminate the Visit to Elizabeth and the Assumption the proportion of northern to southern forms actually established by rime is three to four."[2] Furthermore, Miss Block, the latest editor of the cycle, finds evidence that the manuscript has been worked over "for the purpose of removing archaic or dialectal (Northern) forms: *selkowth⟩, mervelus, shene⟩ bright, carpynge⟩ spekyng, barne⟩ child, bale⟩, sorow, buske⟩ go, tholyn⟩ suffer, . . . beth⟩ be, euy⟩ heuy, dede⟩ dyde, fende⟩ fynde, glathe⟩ gladd, thei⟩ they, perysche⟩ pers, blysse⟩ comfort*," etc. The most important changes, moreover, have been made in the plays of *Cain and Abel, Mary in the Temple, Trial of Joseph and Mary, Birth of Christ, Purification, Shepherds, Visit of the Magi, Harrowing of Hell*, and *Three Maries*, several of which fall within the group apparently showing the influence of the life of St. Anne.[3] It is a significant fact that many of these words which have been changed occur several times in the Minnesota MS. version of the life of St. Anne, and all of the changes are exactly those which a Midland scribe using Northern material would be expected to make. The language of the *Ludus Coventriae*, therefore, is not far removed from the language of the Minnesota MS. version of the life of St. Anne. In fact, all the linguistic evidence points toward the probable use of the life of St. Anne as the source of the Virgin group of the *Ludus Coventriae*.

The conclusion drawn from the linguistic evidence is supported by the two most recent studies of the composition of the cycle—that of Miss Esther L. Swenson[4] and that of Miss K. S. Block. Although these

---

[1] Ten Brink, *English Literature*, II, 283; M. Kramer, *Sprache und Heimat des sogen. L.C.*; A. W. Pollard, *English Miracle Plays*, p. xxxvii; W. W. Greg, *The Assumption of the Virgin. A Miracle Play from the N-Town Cycle*, Oxford, 1915, pp. 9–21.
[2] Greg, *op. cit.*, pp. 18–19.
[3] Cf. Block, *op. cit.*, pp. xvii–xviii.
[4] *An inquiry into the Composition and Structure of the Ludus Coventriae*, in the *University of Minnesota Studies in Language and Literature*, No. 1.

Introduction

investigators have reached different conclusions concerning the origin of the Virgin group (plays VIII to XV, exclusive of XIII, the *Visit to Elizabeth*), their studies of its composition lend weight to the theory that the group is based on the life of St. Anne. It seems worth while, therefore, to review their conclusions in some detail.

"The evidence," says Miss Block, "as to the composition of the series to be drawn from the characteristics of the MS. is complicated and often ambiguous, but the following points emerge:

"1. MS. Vesp. D. VIII is the compiler's book, not a transcript from another MS.

"2. It contains a collection of plays made according to a plan which was subject to alteration as it proceeded.

"3. Some of the plays and groups of plays had had a separate existence, having been acted as separate plays or groups.

"One portion of the MS. certainly, and probably two, quires N, P, Q, R, and quires S, T, have also had a separate existence."[1] Now, one of these groups which has had a separate existence is that dealing with the life of the Virgin Mary. Miss Block says that the "compiler is here grafting the plays of the *Contemplacio* series—*The Conception of Mary, Mary in the Temple*, and *The Visit to Elizabeth* with a *Dissponsacion* or *Betrothal* and a *Salutation and Conception* play not used, plays of an ecclesiastical character based in part on *Legenda aurea*,—on to another series of Mary plays described in the Proclamation—*The Betrothal, Return of Joseph, Trial of Joseph and Mary, Birth of Christ*, with a *Salutation and Conception* play not used, plays of a simpler and more popular character based directly . . . on the Pseudo gospel of Matthew; and that a later revision or alteration of purpose led to the substitution of a more elaborate *Salutation and Conception* and to some additions, based on Bonaventura's *Meditationes Vitae Christi*."[2]

Miss Swenson's conclusions are slightly different. "It will be noted," she says, "that the prologue states that the prophets shall prophesy, not of Christ, but of a 'qwene the whiche xal staunche our stryff and moote'; and an examination of the prophecies will show that the emphasis lies upon the birth of the Virgin, and not of Christ. . . . The fact that the prologue specifically provides for the prophecies of this nature indicates that the unusual interest in the Virgin Mary was a peculiarity of the cycle originally and not to be ascribed to the period of revision . . .

---

[1] Block *op. cit.*, pp. xxxiii.
[2] Block, *op. cit.*, pp. xxiv–xxv.

"After these two plays [VI, *Moses and the Laws*, and VII, *The Prophets*], which are comparatively simple, we have the introduction of an Expositor who is called Contemplacio. He recites, before the play proper of Anna and Joachim begins, a general prologue promising to present to the people (1) the story of Anna and Joachim, (2) Mary's presentation in the Temple, (3) her Betrothal, (4) the story of the Salutation, and finally, (5) Mary's visit to Elizabeth. . . . Then follow these five plays dealing with the life of the Virgin which in general tone and style are very different from the plays we have examined so far. The ecclesiastical element is very prominent in these plays, and there can be little doubt that they were introduced into the cycle at some time later than the writing of the Prologue. I do not think, however, that an entirely new group of plays was simply incorporated as a whole into the cycle without any modification. Some of the plays indicate clearly that old material has been combined with new. The Prologue provides for plays on two of these subjects, Mary's Betrothal and the Salutation. The other three plays promised by Contemplacio are not provided for in the Prologue, and in the case of the first two, the Barrenness of Anna and Mary's Presentation, there can be little doubt that they are entirely new. The Visit of Elizabeth, however, bears internal evidence of the combination of two versions."[1]

Now, whether we agree with Miss Block that the Virgin group of plays in the *Ludus Coventriae* is a composite of two older cycles or with Miss Swenson that it consists of an interpolation of new plays into an old group which has been modified for the purpose, there can be little doubt that the group, with the exception of the *Visit to Elizabeth* (*L.C.* XIII), is a separate entity. As such, it constituted a cycle of plays suitable for performance on St. Anne's day; and it probably was so performed by some St. Anne's guild.[2] It seems more probable, therefore, that the original version of this series of plays was based on the life of St. Anne than on the several sources to which it is attributed by Miss Block, Halliwell, and others: *Legenda Aurea*, Gospel of Pseudo-Matthew, and Bonaventura's *Meditationes*, translated by Nicholas Love as *The Mirrour of the Blessed Lyf of Jesu Christ*. The fact that no one of these possible sources contains all the material of the plays, as well as the fact that the plays deal with the lives of St. Anne and the Virgin Mary, militates against this attribution. On the other hand, practically all the

---

[1] Swenson, *op. cit.*, pp. 17, 26.
[2] Cf. Dodds, M.H., *The Problem of the Ludus Coventriae*, in *Modern Language Review*, IX. 79 ff.

Introduction

material contained in the plays of *Joachim and Anna* (VIII), *Mary in the Temple* (IX), *The Betrothal of Mary* (X), *The Salutation and Conception* (XI), *The Return of Joseph* (XII), *The Trial of Joseph and Mary* (XIV), and *The Birth of Christ* (XV), with the exception of the Parliament in Heaven—an allegory familiar to all medieval minds—is to be found in the life of St. Anne. Furthermore, the order of arrangement of the material is precisely the same in both the poem and the plays, as the following tabular view will show:

St. Anne. Subject.	Ludus Coventriae.
ll. 1–288, *Joachim and Anna—Conception of Mary*,	VIII, ll. 1–226.
ll. 289–408, *Mary in the Temple*,	IX, ll. 84–143, Exposition of fifteen graces. 152–175, Commandments of the high priests. 212–227, Mary's seven petitions.
ll. 409–600, *Betrothal of Mary*,	ll. 1–486.
ll. 601–708, *Salutation and Conception*,	ll. 1–216, Parliament in Heaven. 217–340, Salutation and Conception.
ll. 709–795, *Return of Joseph*,	ll. 1–224.
ll. 799–876, *Trial of Joseph and Mary*,	ll. 1–100, The Detractors. 101–372, The Trial.
ll. 877–1059, *Birth of Christ*,	ll. 1–320.

If it be argued that this arrangement is due to source material common to all the Middle English cycles of plays, my answer is that no other cycle contains *The Conception of Mary* (*Joachim and Anna*), *Mary in the Temple*, *The Betrothal*, or *The Trial of Joseph and Mary*, and that no other cycle follows this arrangement in the same order of detail. A comparative study will incontestably establish these facts. Moreover, the poem on the life of St. Anne contains much material of a dramatic nature. There is an abundance of dialogue in it, and the incidents are narrated with considerable feeling for their dramatic significance; hence it would lend itself easily to dramatization of the sort found in the cycle plays.

Finally, both the poem and the Virgin Mary plays contain an unusual amount of legendary and apocryphal material. The *Ludus Coventriae* is the most legendary of the Middle English cycles of plays; but all the legendary material of the Virgin group, with the exception of the cherry-tree episode, is to be found in the life of St. Anne. These facts, supported by the peculiar history of the composition of this group of plays, indicate something more than mere coincidence and point to the use of the life of St. Anne as the source of the Virgin group of the *Ludus Coventriae*.

Still more convincing evidence in support of this theory is to be found in the close verbal similarities of the two compositions, similarities which occasionally extend to the use of identical rimes. It now remains to tabulate these similarities. Since, however, Miss Block, in her recent edition of the *Ludus Coventriae*, has carefully listed the sources of this group of plays, so far as these sources were known to her, it seems better to discuss each play separately before tabulating corresponding passages, in order that the relative merits of all possible sources may be examined.[1]

The first of the Virgin group of the cycle is the *Joachim and Anna-Conception of Mary* play (*L.C.* VIII). According to Miss Block, "It can . . . be shown that the *Legenda aurea* was the actual authority used for the *Conception of Mary* at least. The marginal genealogies on folios preceding the *Conception of Mary* are taken from Chapter 130 of the *Legenda aurea*; the phrase *regale sacerdocium* (cf. *Conception of Mary*, l. 15) occurs in it and not in the gospel *De Nativitate*; and the words used of the rejection of Joachim's offering in *Legenda aurea*, *cum indignatione nimi repulsit*, seem rather to be echoed in '*with grett indygnacion þin offeryng I refuse*' than the words in the gospel: *despexit eum et munera eius sprevit*."[2] Convincing as this argument may seem, it is not conclusive. The genealogies preceding this play in the manuscript are also to be found in the life of St. Anne, ll. 3049-3084; *Legenda Aurea* gives no name to the priest who refuses Joachim's offering, whereas the life of St. Anne gives his name as *Isakar* and the play as *Ysakar*; and the verbal resemblances of the play and the poem, as will appear from the following comparison, are even more striking in many points than those cited by Miss Block. It appears more probable, therefore, that such variations from the poem as occur in the play are the result of the revision which this play obviously underwent at the time of its incorporation into the cycle than that they are the result of the influence of the *Legenda Aurea*. This view is supported by the following list of parallels:

---

[1] I have used Miss K. S. Block's edition of the *Ludus Coventriae*, and references are given by play and line to this edition.
[2] Block, *op. cit.*, p. xiv.

Life of St. Anne.

& of þe frute þat god hym sent
He parted it wit gud entent
In iij partes als I say :
A party to gyf wald he noȝt spare
To þam þat in þe tempyll ware
At serued god nyght & day.
Þe secunde part gayf he neuerþe-
  lesse
To widows & childer fadyrlesse
& other pouer at lay.
Þe thryd parte alway ordand he
To susten hym & hys meynhe ;
Þis was all hys aray.
  (ll. 37–48)

Boyth day & nyght bisili þai prayed
& wit a voyce bayth þai sayde
To gret god on þis wyse :
If he walde of hys curtasy
Sende þam sum frute of hyr body
To offer yt to god seruysse.
  (ll. 61–66)

Of his comyng was Ioachim
  agrysed,
For he hym & hys offryng dispysed
  & sayd on þis maner.
Oute of þis tempyll fast þu wende ;
Among gude men sall þu noȝt lende
To make non offryng here,
Ffor gode has vised þam ylkane ;
& frute of þe comes per ryght nane,
  Male ne famal sere :
& god cursse þam þat no fruyte
  beres.
Ioachym þan wit wepyng teres
  Away went in were.
    (ll. 85–96)

Ludus Coventriae.

I am clepyd Ryghtful why wole ȝe
  se
Ffor my godys in to thre partys I
  devyde
On to þe temple. *and* hom þat þer
  servynge be
A nodyr to þe pylgrimys *and* pore
  men.
Þe iijde ffor hem with me abyde
So xulde euery curat in þis werde
  wyde
ȝeve a part to his chauncel i-wys
A part to his parochonerys þat to
  povert slyde
the thryd part to kepe for hym *and*
  his
  (VIII, ll. 25–32)

but this I Avow to God with all
  the mekenes I can
ȝyff of his mercy he wole a childe
  us devyse
We xal offre it up in the temple to
  be goddys man
  (ll. 38–40)

But blyssyd wyff Anne sore I
  drede
In þe temple þis time to make
  sacryfice
Be cawse þat no frute of us doth
  procede
I fere me greatly þe prest wole me
  dysspice
  (ll. 33–36)
Þou *and* þi Wyff arn barrany *and*
  bare
neyther of ȝow. ffruteful nevyr ȝett
  ware
Whow durste þou a-monge fruteful
  presume *and* Abuse
It is a tokyn þou art cursyd þare.
  (ll. 76–80)
Þou joachym I charge the fast
  out þe temple þou go
    (l. 83)

Life of St. Anne.	*Ludus Coventriae.*
& for neghburs herd hys shame Þerfore durst he noȝth wend hame. (ll. 97-98)	Ffor hevynes I dare not go hom to my wyff And amonge my neyborys. I dare not abyde ffor shame. (ll. 96-97)
So for þu me no childer sent My husband now away es went, Ded trow I best he be; & whore to fynd hym wate I noȝt Þat he to beryng myght be broght; Forþi full wo es me. (ll. 121-126)	Alas ffor myn husbond. me is full wo I xal go seke him. what so evyr be falle I wote not in erth which wey is he go ffadyr of hefne ffor mercy. to ȝour ffete I falle (ll. 187-190)
Anna, drede þow þe no dele, For god has herd þi prayer wele & sothely I þe say Þi brith in gods awn counsel is. (ll. 133-136)	and as I seyd to hym so to þe sey I xal god hath herd þi prayour. and þi wepynge (ll. 193-194)

Attention is called to two corresponding rimes in these passages: *seruyse* (l. 66): *devyse* (l. 39) and *shame* (l. 97): *shame* (l. 97).

For the *Mary in the Temple* play (*L.C.* IX) there are several possible sources: Lydgate's *Lyf of Our Lady*, Love's *Mirrour* (translated from Bonaventura's *Meditationes*), *Legenda Aurea*, the apocryphal *De Nativitate* and *Pseudo-Matthew*, and the *Life of St. Anne*. Miss Block considers the first four of these possible sources and decides in favour of the *Meditationes* because in it "the three precepts observed by Mary are distinct from the seven petitions, though they correspond to the first three. Lydgate gives only the seven petitions."[1] But it is to be noted that the *Meditationes* does not mention the fifteen steps of the temple which Mary ascends alone, the steps which represent the fifteen graces and correspond to the fifteen Gradual Psalms, and the exposition of which occupies a fourth of the entire play. The three precepts, on the other hand, are simply a statement of the two Great Commandments combined with the ecclesiastical injunction to hate the devil; and the seven petitions are prayers for the well known seven virtues.[2] The heart of the play is the exposition of the fifteen graces and of the manner of life which the Virgin Mary led during her years in the temple; these

---

[1] Block, *op. cit.*, pp. xlvi-xlvii.
[2] Cf. Mark's Gospel 12: 29-31; E.E.T.S. 26, 1; Wells, *A Manual of the Writings in Middle English*, pp. 348, 484.

Introduction xliii

are likewise the things emphasized in the life of St. Anne, ll. 289-408. Hence the assumption that these central themes, taken from the poem, constituted the source of the original play and that the precepts and petitions are the additions of the reviser would appear to be a safe one. This assumption is supported by the following tabulation of resemblances :

Life of St. Anne.	*Ludus Coventriae*, IX.
Wit other damsels þaym was dere To þe temple þai hyr led. (ll. 293-294)	late us take mary our dowtere us be-twen and to þe temple with here procede (ll. 10-11)
Þer xv greces so lang and brade In þe honor of þe xv psalmes was made Þat þis childe wente up by. (ll. 313-315)	If þe fyftene grees. þou may Ascende It is meracle if þou do. now god þe dyffende Ffrom babylony to hevynly jherusalem þis is þe way Every man þat thynk his lyff to Amende þe fiftene psalmys in memorye of þis mayde say (ll. 79-84)
We offer up here to goddes servyse Oure child our god to knawe & to serue als we haue hith. (ll. 341-343)	Sere prince of prestes and it plese ȝow We þat were barreyn god hath sent us a childe to offre here to goddys service we mad oure avow here is þe same mayde. mary moste mylde. (ll. 33-36)
Þe bisshops wer glad of þat syght. Þer þai stod all on rawe & merualyd þat so ȝohng a thyng All hyr werkys to goddes plesyng So sone couth dresse & drawe. (ll. 344-348)	A gracyous lord þis is A mervelyous thynge þat we se here all in syght A babe of thre ȝer age so ȝynge to come up þese greces. so upryght It is An hey meracle and by goddys myght no dowth of she xal be gracyous. (ll. 144-149)

In these parallel passages the following corresponding rimes appear : *syght* (l. 344) : *syght* (l. 145), *thyng* (l. 346) : *thynge* (l. 144), *plesyng* (l. 347) : *ȝynge* (l. 146).

The dependence of the *Betrothal of Mary* (*L.C.* X) on the life of St.

Anne is even more obvious. Of the possible sources usually considered, the *Meditationes* is silent; in Lydgate and Pseudo-Matthew only the dove appears on Joseph's rod; neither *Legenda Aurea* nor the apocryphal *De Nativitate* gives the names of the maidens who attend the Virgin, their names being found only in Pseudo-Matthew and Lydgate's *Lyf of Oure Lady*; and *Legenda Aurea* and *De Nativitate* represent the priest as neglecting Joseph's rod, whereas in the play Joseph himself is at fault. The life of St. Anne, on the other hand, contains the flowering rod which " doth blome and bere," gives the names of two of the maidens as they appear in the play (with three additional names not given in the play), and portrays Joseph as the delinquent in the presentation of his rod.[1] This is the only possible source known which contains all these elements approximately as they appear in the play; hence it would seem to be the source of the play. This claim is substantiated by the following resemblances in phraseology:

Life of St. Anne.

Late be, syrys, it may no3t be done
  þat I suld wax so wyld
To knawe a husbande no3 3yt he me;
  I haue gyfne myn vyrgynyte
    To god at kep unfylde.
      (ll. 428–432.)

þe prest þan of þe trybe als faste
  Befor hym ded he call
All men þat war unweddid þan
  & oppenly byfor ylke man
    Charged both gret & small

On þe morne þat þai suld ald & yhyng
Euer ylkon to þe tempyll bryng
  þe yherd of a vyne tre
. . . . .
Als þare offrand yow lay þam þare
  & byd þe folke þat þai noght spare
þat day & nyght to pray.
On þe morne put þe yherdes in þe handes,
& in qwhilke yherde þis selkouth standes
  Gyf hym mary alway.
    (ll. 488–495, 511–516)

Ludus Coventriae, X.

A3ens þe lawe wyl I nevyr be
  but mannys ffelachep xal nevyr folwe me
I wyl levyn evyr in chastyte
  be þe grace of goddys wylle
    (ll. 36–39)

This is goddys owyn byddyng
þat all kynsmen of dauyd þe kyng
to þe temple xul brynge here offryng
with whyte 3ardys in þer honde

loke wele what tyme þei offere there
all here 3ardys in þin hand þou take
take heed whose 3erde doth blome and bere
and he xal be þe maydenys make
    (ll. 125–132)

---
[1] Cf. Block, *op. cit.*, pp. xlvii-xlviii.

Life of St. Anne.	*Ludus Coventriae,* X.
He saw þat Iosep yherd hade none,	Episcopus
& to þe tempell hade he broght one ;	Whath joseph why stande ȝe there
Fforþi to hym he ȝhede.	by-hynde
. . . . .	I-wys sere ȝe be to blame
Bot Iosep ȝyt had moste drede.	Joseph
	sere I kan nat my rodde ffynde
Ffor ferde þe byshop suld hym blame	to come þer in trowth me thynkyht shame
Iosep couth speke no wrode for shame	sere he may Euyl go þat is ner lame
Bot stode & lokyd myldly.	in soth I cam as fast as I may
(ll. 544–546, 552–555)	
	Episcopus
	offyr up ȝour rodde sere in goddys name
	why do ȝe not as men ȝow pray.
	(ll. 233–241)
Þe bysshop & all þat hym behelde	
Sayd : man, þou erte blist in þine elde,	
Fful wele es þe forthy ;	Episcopus
Of god allone þu es chosen here	Þou mayst be blyth with game and gle
To haue þis damysell þat us es dere	A mayd to wedde þou must gone
Att wede hyr oppynly.	be þis meracle I do wel se
He sayde to þam : for shame, lat be !	Mary is here name
What suld a yhong wench do wit me ?	Joseph
My banes er old & dry.	What xulde I wedde god for-bede
	I am an old man so god me spede
& god haues sent me childre also ;	and with a wyff now. to levyn in drede
Þerfore wyfys will I haue no mo.	It wore nyther sport nere game
Lat sum ȝong man hyr take.	(ll. 264–271)
(ll. 557–567)	
Iosep answerd þan on þis wyse :	*Joseph*
Godes byddyng wil I noȝt dispise,	A-ȝens my God not do I may
For I am lowed & still	here wardeyn and kepere wyl I evyr be
Redy at do þat ȝe commande.	(ll. 289–290)
(ll. 580–583)	
& for hyr solace & hyr game	Þer fore Euyl langage for to swage
Ffyue virgnis sal be wit ȝou same,	þat ȝour good fame may leste longe
Þe best in al þis place.	iij damysellys xul dwelle with ȝow in stage
. . . . .	With þi wyff to be evyr more a-monge
Þe name of þas v I vnderstande	I xal these iij here take
Als we in þe boke þam wreten fande	Susanne þe fyrst xal be
Herkens wit gude intent :	

Life of St. Anne.

Gentea & sophora hyght þe twa,
Sussanna and albigia,
Þe fyfte hyght agabell.
(ll. 589–591, 608–615)

Ludus Coventriae, X.

Rebecca þe secunde xal go with the
Sephore þe thrydde. loke þat ȝe thre
þis maydon nevyr ȝe for-sake.
(ll. 348–356)

The following corresponding rimes appear in the above passages: *me* (l. 430): *me* (l. 37), *vyrgynyte* (l. 431): *chastyte* (l. 38), *yhyng* (l. 493): *kyng* (l. 126), *bryng* (l. 494): *offryng* (l. 127), *blame* (l. 553): *blame* (l. 235), *shame* (l. 554): *shame* (l. 237).

The *Salutation and Conception* play (*L.C.* XI) has long been a puzzle to commentators, largely on account of the discrepancy between the character of the play announced in the Prologue and that of the play which appears in the cycle. Professor Greg states the problem of this play as follows: "It begins with what Contemplatio . . . calls the 'parlement of hefne,' the well-known contention of the four daughters of God, and then proceeds to a Salutation simple in design, but elaborate and distinctly ecclesiastical in composition. Now the stanza in the Prologue describes a quite simple Annunciation play of the usual type, and cannot by any possibility have been written for the play we have in the text. Observe in particular that Mary's three maidens hear the Angel's voice but see no one, while the text makes no mention of them whatever."[1] Miss Swenson similarly states the problem and adds: "This ecclesiastical tone so pervades the whole play that it would almost seem as if none of the original cycle play had been preserved, and that this play, like the Barrenness of Anna (*L.C.* VIII) and Mary's Presentation (*L.C.* IX), had been substituted entirely from the Virgin play."[2] And Miss Block believes "that a later [than the date of the composition of the Prologue] revision or alteration of purpose led to the substitution of a more elaborate *Salutation and Conception* and to some additions, based on Bonaventura's *Meditationes Vitae Christi*."[3] She bases her belief, so far as it concerns the *Meditationes* of Bonaventura, on certain verbal resemblances to Love's *Mirrour*, p. 29; but there are even closer resemblances, as the following tabulation will show, to the life of St. Anne. This poem, however, does not contain the Parliament in Heaven, which occupies 216 of the 340 lines of the play as we have it now. In the poem, on the other hand, the Virgin's attending maidens

---

[1] W. W. Greg, *Bibliographical and Textual Problems of the English Miracle Cycles*, London, 1914, p. 128.
[2] Swenson, *op. cit.*, p. 30.
[3] Block, *op. cit.*, pp. xxiv–xxv, xlv, xlviii.

do overhear the first salutation of the Angel Gabriel, who appears at the moment when they are blaming the Virgin for attempting to become their "qwhene." The facts, then, seem to be these: the Prologue was written for a simple *Salutation and Conception* play of an ecclesiastical nature, based on the life of St. Anne, which was later revised by prefixing the familiar and popular Parliament in Heaven and reworking the salutation scene so as to bring it into accord with the additional scene. This view is supported by the fact that the life of St. Anne devotes 103 lines to the subject and the play, exclusive of the Parliament in Heaven, 123 lines. It is also supported by the following verbal resemblances:

Life of St. Anne.	*Ludus Coventriae,* XI.
mary, full of grace, God is wit þe þis day; Of all women blyssede by yhow. (ll. 665-667)	Heyl fful of grace god is with the Amonge All women blyssyd art thu (ll. 217-218)
Þe angell sayd: mary, dred þe no3th; Þe grace þat þu so lange haues soght In god has fon it clere. Be you sall consaue witouten syn & bere a child þu clen virgyn, Ihesus is name is here. He sall be gret & goddes son calde; Hys fader sall gyf hym þe see to hald Of dauid þat is hym dere. In þe huse of Iacob þan sall he lende & regne in heuen witouten ende & in erth fer & nere. (ll. 673-684)	Mary in þis take 3e no drede Ffor At God. grace ffownde haue 3e 3e xal conceyve in 3our wombe in dede A childe þe sone of þe trynyte His name of 3ow jhesu clepyd xal be He xal be grett. þe son of þe hyest. clepyd of kende and of his ffadyr davyd. þe lord xal 3eve hym þe se Reynyng in þe hous of jacob. of which regne xal be no ende. (ll. 237-244)
How suld þis thyng on me be layde & man knew I neuer none? (ll. 686-687)	In what manere of wyse xal þis be Ffor knowyng of man I haue non now. (ll. 246-247)
To þis þe anngell þan answerd he & sayd: þe halygost sall light in þe, Umlap þe blod & bone. On þe sall born be goddes awn child;	The holy gost xal come fro Above to the and þe vertu of hym hyest xal schadu þe so. Ther fore þat holy gost of þe xal be bore.

Life of St. Anne.	*Ludus Coventriae*, XI.
& se eliȝabeth, þi cosyne so mylde, Sex monethes ys yt now gone. Þai called hyr baran in toun & felde; Now haues scho consaued in hyr elde Of goddes gret grace allone; Nothyng impossible may be forthy To god; þerfore dred þe noȝth, mary. (ll. 688–698)	he xal be clepyd þe son of god sage And se Elyȝabeth ȝour cosyn thore She hath conseyvid A son in hyre Age This is þe sexte monyth of here passage. Of here þat clepyd was bareyn no thynge is impossyble to goddys vsage. (ll. 251–259)
Goddes awn handmaydyn es me here; Als he wyll be yt don. (ll. 701–702)	Se here þe hand-mayden of oure lorde Aftyr þi worde. be it don to me. (ll. 287–288)

The following rimes occur in the passages above in corresponding context: *yhow* (l. 667) : *thu* (l. 218), *lende* (l. 682) : *kende* (l. 243), *ende* (l. 683) : *ende* (l. 244), *þe* (l. 689) : *the* (l. 251).

The *Return of Joseph* (*L.C.* XII) is accepted by critics as belonging to the original cycle, and Miss Block assigns the Pseudo-Matthew as its source. The verbal evidence, however, indicates that it is not based directly on the Pseudo-Matthew but on the life of St. Anne, ll. 709–795, which, as has been shown already, is a paraphrase of Pseudo-Matthew. Additional evidence of this fact is to be found in the prevailing verse form of the play, which is a ten-line stanza riming aabaabbcbc. This seems to show the influence of the aabccbddbeeb stanzaic structure of the poem. The following passages show similarities in phraseology:

Life of St. Anne.	*Ludus Coventriae*, XII.
Scho rase up myldly hym agayne & of hyr wambe was he noȝt fayne, Bot it myght noȝt be hid. For qwen he saw þat it was so grete All þe fyue vergnis fast gon he threte & lowd began to cry. He fell done & thus gate he sayde: What happ, lord, has þu for me layde? So ald a man als I	That semyth evyl I am afrayd þi wombe to hyȝe doth stonde I drede me sore I am be-trayd Sum other man þe had in honde Hens sythe þat I went Thy Wombe is gret it gynnyth to reyse than hast þou be-gownne a synfull gyse telle me now in what wyse thy self þow Ast þus schent (ll. 25–33)

Introduction

Life of St. Anne.	*Ludus Coventriae,* XII.

Sall now haue more shame & more anger.
Lord, lat me are lyfe no longere
  Bot dight me here to dy;
And damoyselles, he sayd, wo yow be;
Ffalsly have ȝe desseuede me,
  So haue ȝe don mary.
    (ll. 730–744)	

ȝe say þan þe angell made hir wit child:
Nay, sum lyke an angell has hyr begiled,
  A ȝong man wit sum gyn.
    (ll. 766–768)
	It was sum boy be-gan þis game
	þat clothyd was clene *and* gay
	and ȝe ȝeve hym now an anngel name.
	    (ll. 57–77)

What me ys best wate I noght now;
I wax als heuy as led.
& I dare loke no man in þe face
In þe tempyll no in na place
  For shame. Why ne were I ded?
    (ll. 770–774)
	Now alas whedyr xal I gone
	I wot nevyr whedyr nor to what place
	ffor oftyn tyme sorwe comyth sone
	and longe it is or it pace
	no comforte may I haue here
	    (ll. 118–122)

Þe angell appered to hym þat nyght,
  Bad: Iosep, turn þi red
& dred ye noȝthyng of þis lyf
For to take mary to þi wyf,
  Ne thynke wit hyr no shame.
Þe child þat scho sall bere in hast
Scho has consayued thurgh þe halygast,
  & jhesus sall be hys name;
Gret gods awn power sall haue
All hys folke fra syn to saue
  Þat adam broght in blame.
Iosep at morne he went belyue
To mary & to þis vergnis fyue
  & told þam all þis same.
He thankyd god & was full glad,
Bot of þe suspecion he to þam had
  He asked mary forgayfnes.
    (ll. 779–795)
	I know wel I haue myswrought
	I walk to my pore place
	and Aske ffor-gyfnes I haue mys-thought
	
	Now is þe tyme sen At eye
	þat þe childe is now to veryfye
	  which xal saue mankende
	As it was spoke be prophesye
	I thank þe god þat syttys on hye
	  with hert wyl *and* mende
	þat evyr þou woldyst me bynde
	to wedde mary to my wyff
	þi blysful sone. se nere to fynde
	In his presens. to lede my lyff.
	    (ll. 167–179)

These passages have the following corresponding rimes: *place* (l.

l Introduction

773) : *place* (l. 119), *face* (l. 772) : *pace* (l. 121), *lyf* (l. 781) : *lyff* (l. 179), *wyf* (l. 782) : *wyff* (l. 172).

The life of St. Anne does not mention the *Visit to Elizabeth* (*L.C.* XIII); neither does the Pseudo-Matthew nor *De Nativitate* mention it. It is not provided for in the Prologue and may, therefore, be considered as a later addition to the cycle; hence it could not have belonged in the original Virgin group of plays.

The *Trial of Joseph and Mary* (*L.C.* XIV) is a combination of coarse humour (contained in the speeches of the slanderers) with the simple and reverent dignity of the purgation ceremony. "The Prologue to this play," says Miss Swenson, ". . . is a simple quatrain. It does not adequately represent the play, but simply speaks of the fact that Joseph and Mary were slandered and went to their purgation. The purgation scene itself is simple and reverent enough and may possibly have been a part of the original cycle.

"The introductory speech of Den, with its long list of alliterative and allegorical names, is written into the manuscript in a different hand before the figure 14 occurs and belongs probably to a later period." She also notes the return of the name "Abiyachar" for the bishop rather than "Ysakar."[1] Miss Block does not think that the speech of Den is written by a different hand, but agrees that this play is one of those which was subjected to the process of "dovetailing and revision." She thinks it is probably based on Pseudo-Matthew, which it does not follow closely.[2] But it is to be noted that the life of St. Anne, ll. 799 ff., exactly follows the scheme of the play given in the Prologue. Joseph and Mary are "wreghed" by all the people, "for þam yll thoght," are brought to trial before "abythar . . . byshop of þe lawe," and are acquitted of all blame by the purgation ceremony. Now the name "Abyathar" might easily be confused with "Abiyachar" by a scribe; and this is probably what happened in this case as in many others of which we know. The history of the play, then, would seem to be this: the original Virgin group of plays contained a simple *Trial of Joseph and Mary* which was ecclesiastical in tone and based on the life of St. Anne; but this play was revised by the compiler of the *Ludus Coventriae* cycle, who added the horse-play of the detractors and the bit of poetic justice by which one of the chief detractors was forced to drink of the purgation water. This conclusion is attested by the following verbal resemblances:

[1] Swenson, *op. cit.*, pp. 32–33.
[2] Block, *op. cit.*, pp. xxiv, xlviii.

Introduction

Life of St. Anne.	*Ludus Coventriae*, XIV.
Iosep swore fast & mad hym clene To god gon witnesse drawe Þat he neuer wit wyll hyr knew ne wyst So mekyll þat scho a man aues kyst.	Sche is for me a trewe clene mayde And I for hire am clene Also of ffleschly synne I nevyr a-sayde sythyn þat sche was weddyd me to (ll. 193–196)
. . . .	
Iosep sayd : ȝe sall all wele wytt Þat scho ys clene vergyn ȝytt Boyth in thoght & dede. (ll. 812–815, 820–822)	
& many other prestes þat þare wasse Sayd : so lyghtly sall þu noȝt passe, Wit swilke lyrtes us lede. A maner of watyr þai had perfore In þe tempyll was kepyd in store For thyng þat was in drede	Thus xalt not schape from vs ȝitt so Fyrst þou xalte tellyn us a-nother lay Streyt to þe Awtere þou xalt go Þe drynge of vengeawns per to a-say. (ll. 197–200)
Þat whoso ware of a thyng gilty & drank perof suld haue oppenly A gret spot in hys face. Þai gar hym drynke þar he stode. (ll. 823–832)	
To drynk þarof had scho na drede, & boute þe auter sithen scho ȝede Seuen sythes witouten more. (ll. 856–858)	Here xal I drynke. be-fore ȝour face A-bowth þis Awtere than xal I fonde vij tymes to go by godys grace. (ll. 262–264)

"The use of the *Pseudo-Matthew* Gospel is clearest in the *Birth* play," says Miss Block, " where the incident of the midwives follows the original very closely. . . . The suggestion of the cherry-tree incident comes also from this gospel where a similar story is told of a palm-tree passed on the journey into Egypt."[1] But again the verbal similarities point to the use of the life of St. Anne, which follows the Pseudo-Matthew Gospel very closely at this point. Both differ from the play (*L.C.* XV) in that in them Christ is born in a cave instead of in " an hous of haras . . . amonge bestys," and in that they have Mary's vision of the two peoples, Jews and pagans, instead of the cherry-tree episode. The life of St. Anne, following the B-version of Pseudo-Matthew, gives the names of the two midwives as Ȝebell and Salome instead of Ȝelomy

[1] Block, *op. cit.*, p. xlviii.

and Salome. But both pairs of names were common (*Legenda Aurea*, p. 42, Graesse Ed., has Zebel and Salome), and the confusion is easily accounted for either by scribal error or by metrical demands. As for the cherry-tree episode, it must have been substituted for the vision of the Jews and pagans or for the similar date-tree incident (St. Anne, ll. 1500 ff.) under the influence of a popular poem such as that printed by Hone.[1] The essential elements of the play, however, are contained in the life of St. Anne; and the following resemblances in phraseology are convincing proof of its use by the author of the *Birth of Christ* play :

Life of St. Anne.	*Ludus Coventriae*, XV.
He spake þan unto mylde mary & saide: leve doghter myne, Me bus wende now bedlam unto At pay þer als our neghboures do ; Þerfore heygh we us heyne. (ll. 908–912)	Now my wyff mary. what sey ȝe to this For sekyr nedys I must fforth wende On to þe cyte of bedleem ffer hens i-wys Þus to labore I must my body bende. (ll. 9–12)
Iosep ȝohod to mary þan, Sayd: here er two mydwyfs þat can Of women preuetes knaw ; & mary smyled. Laghes þu ? sayd he. He saw a knaue child on hyr kne ; Þan sayde he : I was ouer slaw. (ll. 1003–1008)	the for to comforte in gesyne þis day tweyn gode mydwyuis I haue brought here . . . . Why do ȝe lawgh wyff ȝe be to blame I pray ȝow spowse do no more so (ll. 171–172, 181–182)
Lord god, scho sayde, mercy. Þe syght þat I se here ! Here hys a meruayll was neuer none swylke: I felt hyr two pappes full of milke & a childe frely borne, & wymbe of birth es here non sene ; Scho moder es als a mayden clene. Þis was neuer sene beforne. (ll. 1019–1026)	O myghtfull god have mercy on me A merveyle þat nevyr was herd be-forn Here opynly I fele *and* se A fayr child of a maydon is born And nedyth no waschynge as other don Fful clene *and* pure for soth is he with-outyn spot or ony polucyon his modyr nott hurte of virgynite. (ll. 225–232)

[1] William Hone, *Ancient Mysteries Described*, pp. 90–93.

Introduction

Life of St. Anne.	Ludus Coventriae, XV.
Allas, scho sayd, I am lorne. Ffull wele I wote I haue done mys; For my mystrowyng all haf I þis þat I lyfed in a drede; & god þu wote I lufed nyght & day Women & chylder to help þam ay. Holpe now me in þis nede. (ll. 1032–1038)	O lord of myght þou knowyst þe trowth þat I have evyr had dred of þe on every power whyght evyr I have rowthe and 3ove hem almes for loue of þe Bothe wyff and wedowe þat Askyght for the And frendles chyledryn þat haddyn grett nede I dude them cure and all for the and toke no rewarde of them nor mede. (ll. 265–272)
Gabrell bad hyr aske mary forgyfnes And sayde: touche þe childe þat borne es Þu sall be hale gude spede. (ll. 1039–1041)	Woman þi sorwe to haue de-layde wurchep þat childe þat þer is born towch þe clothis þer he is layde ffor he xal saue all þat is lorn (ll. 277–280)

In these parallel passages are found the following corresponding rimes: *drede* (l. 1035): *nede* (l. 270), *nede* (l. 1038): *mede* (l. 272).

Although the life of St. Anne contains the stories found in the *Adoration of the Shephards, Purification, Magi, Massacre of the Innocents and Death of Herod*, and the *Dispute between Christ and the Doctors*, the verbal similarities to the *Ludus Coventriae* cease with the *Birth of Christ*, except in three or four short passages common to all accounts of the events in which they occur. We must conclude, therefore, either that the series of striking similarities of the Virgin group of plays in the *Ludus Coventriae* cycle to the corresponding parts of the life of St. Anne constitutes a rare coincidence or that the life of St. Anne is the source of the original Virgin group of the cycle. Since all the evidence indicates that this series of similarities is not a coincidence, we may assert with a considerable degree of confidence that the Minnesota MS. version of the life of St. Anne is the source of that group of plays in the *Ludus Coventriae* which portrays the life of St. Anne, the life of the Virgin Mary, and the birth of Christ.

V. CONCLUSIONS.

These hitherto inaccessible poems are of considerable interest to the student of Middle English literature, for they deal with a subject intimately connected with the life of the period. Saints' lives were inextricably interwoven with the religious, social, and commercial life of Medieval England; and St. Anne, around whose cult the legends of the Virgin and the Christ centred, was an important figure in all these phases of life. This fact is emphasized by the stanzaic versions of her life, for the five poems belong to three different types in origin, structure, and content. With the originals from which they are descended, they cover a period of considerably more than a century; and they illustrate how throughout this long period the two great storehouses of medieval religious lore, the apocryphal gospels and the *Legenda Aurea*, were drawn upon by both church and guild. These poems show that the patron saint of church or guild was frequently also the patron saint of didactic poetry written for popular consumption.

The linguistic significance of these poems must also be taken into account. Since the poems cover almost half of England, they illustrate the status of the English language as it was written in the fifteenth century near the southern limits of the Northern dialect, in the N.E. Midlands, in the E. Midlands, and in the S. Midlands. The fact that compositions may be so accurately located by their dialectal peculiarities, even when the dialects are not preserved in their pure states, is evidence that England was still, in the fifteenth century, far from a homogeneous literary standard of usage.

For the student of the Middle English drama, however, the chief interest in these stanzaic versions of the life of St. Anne lies in the fact that the Minnesota MS. version furnishes a logical source for the much disputed Virgin group of the *Ludus Coventriae*. It contains all the material of plays VIII to XV with the single exception of the interpolated *Visit to Elizabeth* (XIII); and the similarities in dialect, content, and phraseology present convincing evidence that this poem is the source of the Virgin group of plays.

I

The Life of St. Anne

MS. University of Minnesota Z. 822, N. 81
(Formerly Phillips MS. 8122).

All þat haues lyking for to lere
Off prophetes sawes & storys sere,
   Herkens now to me.
A lytill tretice ȝe sall here   4   [fol. 185b]
Of anna & hyr doghter dere,   Invocation.
   Mary þat maydyn fre ;
How scho was born & in what land
Als seynt mathew yt wretyn fand   8
   In grew & þerfor he
Made it in latyn out of grewe
Als saynt Ierom þe doctour trew
   Witnes it suld be.   12

& forthermore als þe story says
It befel in our elder days
   In ierslum was it swa.
Þer wond a man of nobil fame,   16   Joachim of
& Ioachim þan was his name,   Jerusalem
   Born in þe land of Iuda.   was a
He was rytght wys in ylke a dede,   virtuous
& god ouyr all most gon he drede.   20   man.
   With other vertues ma
He was bath meke & mylde
& buxom boȝth to man & chylde,
   Noȝth wele qwhen þam was wa.   24

& for he lufd his god so wele,
He multiplied so his catele
   For sothe as I ȝow tell

Note: Initial letters in each verse have been rubricated throughout this MS. ; therefore initial *ff* is printed *Ff* for the sake of accuracy and to prevent confusion with *ff* which is not rubricated.

Unnethes lyued þe any slyke 28
Of gude lyuyng was none hym lyke
   Þat dwelled in Isrel.
As herde he kepyd hys awn shepe
Of other thyng toke he no kepe 32
   Nowther to by no selle ;
Bot he & other of hys housald
To kepe hys catell, for so þai wald,
   Full fayre be fyrth & fell. 36

Joachim divides his property into three parts.

& of þe frute þat god hym sent
He parted it with gud entent
   In iij partes als I say :
A party to gyf wald he noȝt spare 40
To þam þat in þe tempyll ware
   At serued god nyght & day.
Þe secunde part gayf he neuer þe lesse
To widows & childer fadyrlesse 44
   & other pouer at lay.
Þe thryd parte alway ordand he
To susten hym & hys meynyhe.
   Þis was all hys aray. 48

Joachim marries Anne, daughter of Agar, and they are childless for twenty years.

In þis wyse lede þat man hys lyfe,
& sythen þai did hym haue a wyfe
   When he was xxti ȝer.
Anna þan says þe boke scho hight ; 52
Scho was one of þe fayrest wyght
   Þat þan lyued ffer or ner.

[fol. 186a]

Agar doghter was þat virgyn ;
Comen scho was of dauid kyn ; 56
   Þerfore þai made gude chere.
At þe mariage was gret gamen.
Withouten childer þai leued sam
   All fully xxti ȝere. 60

They pray for a child.

Boyth day & nyght bisili þai prayed
& with a voyce bayth þai sayde
   To gret god on þis wyse :
If he walde of hys curtasy 64
Sende þam sum frute of hyr body
   To offer yt to god seruyse.

To gete þai prayede always
& went to þe tempyll on þer fest days,   68
  For help in prayer lyse ;
& at þe laste god þer prayer herde.
Bot herkyns fyrst how yt ferde
  Er þer frute myght ryse.   72

Apon a fest day þus ytt stode :   *They go to the temple to make an offering.*
Þe paryshyn to þe temple ȝode
  With many folk of kyn ;
Amang þaim þer als þai gan stande   76
Ylk man redy with hys offerande
  Dressed hym withouten dyn.
Þe bysshop þan hyght Isakar ;
Of Ioachym sone was he war.   80
  To hym fast gon he ryn
To offer þer ryght als other did ;
& so þis wonder hym betyd
  Er þai suld begyn.   84

Of his comyng was Ioachym agrysed,   *The priest refuses Joachim's offering because he is childless.*
For he hym & hys offryng dispysed
  & sayd on þis maner :
Oute of þis tempyll fast þu wende ;   88
Among gude men sall þu noȝt lende
  To make non offryng here,
Ffor gode has vised þam ylkane ;
& frute of þe comes þer ryght nane,   92
  Male ne famal sere :
& god cursse þam þat na fruyte beres.
Ioachym þan with wepyng teres
  Away went in were.   96

& for neghburs herd hys shame   *Joachim flees to the hills in shame.*
Þerfore durst he noȝth wend hame
  Bot to þe helles held pas ;
& all hys bestes with hys hyrdmen   100
He draue þam oure thurgh fell & fen
  To a uncouth place
Tyll he some xxti dayes iournay þithen.   [fol. 186b]
All fully fyue monethes dwelt he sythen   104
  Fra anna in þis cas

Life of St. Anne

Þat scho wist of hym in no stede
Whether þat he war whik or dede.
   Full lang thoght hyr þat spas.   108

Anne prays to God.

& as sho lay in hyr moste drede
Apon a day til hyr yherde sho yhede,
   Company had sho non.
Under a tre þat laureall hatt   112
In an herber on knes sho satt
   To god makand hyr mone.
A nest of sparowes saw sho þare :
Lord god, sho sayd, þin are   116
   Ylk best of blod & bone
Haues ioy of þe fruyte þat þai furth bryng,
And for I am bot a barayn thyng
   Fro me is gone my husband.   120

So for þu me no childer sent
My husband now away es went,
   Ded trow I best he be;
& whore to fynd hym wate I noȝt   124
Þat he to beryng myght be broght,
   Forþi full wo es me.
Þu knawes my will my god so mylde
Þat yf þow had sent me a childe   128
   It suld be offred to þe.

An angel appears to Anne and promises her a child.

With þat an angell come fra heuen
& spak to hir with ful mild steuen
   Þis worde under þat tre :   132
Anna, drede þow þe no dele,
For god has herd þi prayer wele
   & sothely I þe say
Þi brith in gods awn counsel is,   136
& it sall be to more & lesse
   Wonderful euer & ay;
Þerfore of his sande hald þe payd.
& qwen þe angell þus hade sayde   140
   He wanyst sone away.
Anna of þis sight was adrede
& fore his worde sho ȝede to bede;
   Þer in hyr prares lay.   144

Day and nyght praiand lay sho.
At last a maydyn sho called hir to
   & said, lufed þu me oght
So as þu sese me þusgate lye   148
Als a wydow full drerylye
   þu suld of me haue thoght.
Sho said : yf god þi wambe haf closed
Fro child beryng & þu haues losed   152
   þi husband, blame me noȝt.
At þat word anna thoght ryght yll.
Scho turnyd & lay wepand full styll—
   Of god sho sokour soght.   156

Þat tyme als anna lay in were   [fol. 187a]
A yhonge child þan gon apere   An angel
   To Ioachim on a hyll   appears to
                                       Joachim
                                       and
Þer he ys bestes kepyd wild & tame   160 repeats the
& sayd : syr, why gas þu noȝt hame   promise
   To þe wyf? For what skyll?   made to
                                       Anne.
He sayd, me lykes nothyng hyr game.
For xxti ȝere we haue bene same   164
   & it is noȝtht gods wyll
To sende us childre us aboute ;
Þerfore þe temple I was dryune oute,
   For shame þat lykes me yll.   168

Whareto þerfore suld I hame wende?
My neghburs for shame wil me shende
   Þis thyng so wel is kend.
Sen I was so fro þe tempel broght, 172
Here with my bestes þan haue I thoght
   All my lyfetyme to lend.
Neuer þe lesse ay whils I lyfe
Off my gudes I sall gar gyffe   176
   Be my awn seruandes hende
To poure men þat þer god þam dredes
& þat in þe temple synges & redes.
   Þer partes I sall þam sende.   180

When he had sayd so, þis gude man,
Þat ylke yhong child appered þan
   To hym a fayre angell

Sayd : Ioachym of þe blode of Iuda, 184
I am comen fro þi wyfe anna
& comfored hyr I þe tell.
Als I sayde hyr, I say þe here
þat scho sall bere a doghter dere ; 188
In hyr þe halygast sall dwell
& in godis temple fayrest þat fre
Blessed ouer all women sall be
And of all gudnes þe well 192

So þat all þis wyde world I wene
Sall say þer was neuer none swylk sene
Befor hyr far or nere.
Ane lyke to hyr sall neuer be none 196
Of woman kynde in blode ne bone
& þerfore with gude chere
Haste þe to hyr þi selfe to saue ;
Ffor in hyr wambe sal þu fynd hir haue 200
þat I haue sayde þe here
Goddes gudnesse, þat blissed sede,
& scho modyr withouten drede
Of þat blyssed byrth so dere. 204

<small>Joachim thanks the angel and makes a burnt offering. [fol. 187b]</small>

Ioachym thankyd hym in þat place :
& sen þow has broght me grace,
Cum sitt with me & ette,
And als þi seruand here blysse þu me. 208
He sayd, þan bathe seruaundys er we
Of god whas grace es grett ;
& herdly man lyfs none so gude
þat es of powere to se oure fude, 212
For invisible es my mete.
Bot what þow wald for ordan,
Offer it to god here in þis playn
& byrn it with grete hete. 216

He answerde & sayd on þis wyse :
To god dere I make no sacrifyse
Bot at þi comhandment.
þe angell answerde unto hym þer 220
& saide : goddes wille & it noȝt war
To þe wer I noȝt sent.

Þe beste lame þat he had he toke
& offerd it per als says þe boke 224
   Hertly with gude intente;
& als þe fyre was brynnand bryght,
In þe low þare befor his syght
   To heuen þe angell wente. 228

Þan Ioachim fell down in a sweyme. *Joachim falls in a swoon.*
Fra undron unto euensang tyme
   In hys prayrs he lay
So þat hys herdmen in þat stede 232
Wende all wele he hade bene dede
   & wakend hym son þat day.
Þe syght þat he had herde & sene
When he had told þam all bedene 236
   Fful fast þan conseld þai
To anna þat he suld hym haste
Ffor drede of god þat he lufd maste—
   Þus redd þai hym alway. 240

Ioachym wyste neuer what was beste
Bot fell oft doun & toke hys reste
   Als man þat had bene lame.
Þe angell appered to hym efte 244 *The angel tells Joachim to return home.*
& sayde: ryse upe, for I am belefte
   At kepe þe oute of blame;
Ffor god has herde ȝowr prayers bath.
Ryse up sikyrly, it hys no wath, 248
   To anna hy þe hame.
He rayse & tolde hys men þat tale.
Þa answerd þam with voce all hale
   And conseld hym to do þe same. 252

Iochachim hamward þan gan he draw
With hys bestes bot a pase ryght slaw.
   Ne xxti days he ȝode
& pastured þam all wele be þe way. 256
Þe angell to anna gune say, *The angel reappears to Anne.*
   Rys up now with myld mode;
Þi husband comes here in gude state; [fol. 188a]
Go kepe hyn at þe gylden ȝhate. 260
   Þan rase þat frely fode,

Life of St. Anne

    & hyr maydens þan be hyr side.
Ffull lang hir thoght scho gun abide
    In þat ȝhat als sho stode.   264

Joachim and Anne meet at the golden gate.

When scho hym saw scho was all blyth
& went agayn hym þan full swyth
    With hir maydyns infere.
Scho halsed hym fast about þe neke   268
& kyssed hym sayand, I ne reke
    On lyf, I haue ȝow here.
I was a wedow in my lyfe,
Now loue I god I am a wyfe;   272
    Lo goddes help ay es nere.
Barren I was & I ne wyst how,
Bot se I haue consawed now
    & þerfore make gud chere.   276

Hame þai went þan bath togeder
& many of þer kyn sone come þider
    For glad of þis tythyng;
So dede all þat þerof harde tell   280
Thurghowtt þe land of Israell
    Als fere as word myght spryng.
All made þai myrth þat þerof mende,
& qwen þe ix monethes was com to ende   284

Mary is born.

    Anna þat blystful thyng
Scho bare a mayden of hyr body.
To name þai called þat childe mary;
    Þer blyssed be þat beryng.   288

Anna of hyr doghter was full glade,
& Ioachym also gret lykyng hade.
    Ffull tenderly þai hyr fed
& wande hyr when scho was thre ȝere.   292

Mary is presented at the temple.

With other damsels þaym was dere
    To þe temple þai hyr led.
When þai unto þe temple war comen,
Þair best clothes with þam had þai nomen   296
    Þat þai suld be in cled
Ffor to make þar sacrafys
As in þar law was þan þe gyse,
    Þer god so sore þai dred.   300

Bot xv greces þan stude yt hegh
Þe temple or þai suld yt negh
 Standand bothe est & west;
To schyfte þer cloythes wyls þat þai ȝode   304
Sett mare þat frely fode
 Att grece fote hyr to reste.
Witoutyn helpe of erthly man
To þe temple allone scho wan,   308
 So gracyous was þat geste.
Þe bysshopes sone þat child þai fand
In þat temple allone knelande
 And wonder þam what was beste.   312

She goes alone up the fifteen steps and is found praying in the temple.

Þer xv greces so lang and brade
In þe honor of þe xv psalmes was made
 Þat þis childe wente up by.
Anna come þan & mary myste;   316
Whore scho sulde fynd hyr noȝt scho wyste
 Bot ran up hastyly,
& in þe tempell scho fande hyr þar
Kneland als scho a woman ware   320
 Prayand deuoutly.
Ylk man had wonder it myght be so,
Sayde yt may be tyll us and mo
 A mariage here of mary.   324

[fol. 188b]

Anna before þe pepyll most
Ffulfilled þan of þe halygost
 Oppenly þus scho prayde:
Lorde gode in trynyte   328
Þat ys & was & ay sall be,
 Of þe grace þu me prauayde.
I thank þe, lorde, bath lowd & styll,
For þu knawes ylk man hert & wyll   332
 & how our ennemys sayde
Offrand to þe we suld non make.
Now es it sene þat for our sake
 Þat lorde full law is layde.   336

Anne offers a prayer of thanks.

Ioachym, þat wele lyfand man,
& anna before þe pepyll þan
 To þe bysshopes of þe law

Mary is dedicated to God's service and left in the temple

Life of St. Anne

  Sayd both togyder upon þis wyse: 340
We offer up here to goddes servyse
  Oure child our god to knawe
  & to serue als we haue hith.
Þe bisshops wer glad of þat syght. 344
  Þer þai stod all on rawe
& merualyd þat so ȝohng a thyng
All hyr werkys to goddes plesyng
  So sone couth dresse & drawe. 348

When þis was done anna hame wente,
& Ioachym yhode hys bestys to tente
  Þer þai wer on þe felde.
Thurghoute þe lande of Israell 352
Als fare als þai hard tell
  Come þider & hyr behelde
& merualyd gretly of hyr dedys
How þat so ȝonge a chyld wald nedys 356
  Goddes werkes haue in welde,
For of hyr bedys was scho neuer yrke,
& als a woman þan wald scho wyrke.
  Be þat scho was v ȝere held. 360

Her manner of life in the temple.

Þus mary encresed more & more
Amang all þas vyrgyns þat þer wore
  In þe temple day & nyght.
On þis wyse ordard scho hyr tyme: 364
Ffro morne arly unto hegh prime
  To pray scho was full lyght;
& so fro primeward unto none
Sylk & purpur sewed scho sone, 368
  Couth none so wele it dyght.
 * * * * * *
 * * * * * *
  * * * * * 372

[fol. 189a]

Of all þe vyrgyns þat scho with lered.
Sythen an angell to hyr apperede
  At none ylke day be day
& fede hyr ay whils hir gud thoght; 376
Þe mett þat other men to hir broght
  To poure folke gayf scho yt ay.

In gude thewes was scho plentyuouse
& neuer wroght bot ay gracyuose 380
　So myk als I þow say
Þat all þat any seknes hade
& towched hyr þai myght be glade,
　For hale þai went away. 384

Whoso honoured hyr anythyng
Or haylsed hyr at hyr metyng,
　Als many on oft sythes did,
Scho thankyd god ay of þat doyng 388
& answerde þam to goddes louyng
　Als efte as yt betyde ;
& qwen any of hyr felawes
Legh or sayd any wanton sawes, 392
　Myldly wald scho þam bidd :
Þes damaysels þer sawes er noȝt gud,
Ffor goddes lar & ȝe understode
　Swilke dedes suld ay be hyd. 396

Þis vyrgyn gudnes sprang so wyde
Þat þer was neuer none on na syde
　Byfor hyr born, I wene,
So mylde in grace and all gudnes, 400
Ne sall be after hyr neuerþelesse,
　Euen lik to hyr be sene.
Ffor hyr gudnes & gret bewte
Abathar prest of þe lawe went he 404 *Abathar the priest wishes Mary to marry his son.*
　To þe bisshopes all bedene
& bad gret gyftys to haue mary
To hys sone þat was semely
　Weddid yf þai myght bene. 408

Be þat tyme was scho xii yhere olde,
& als þe lagh and custom walde
　All þe vergyns þat ware
In þe temple at þat full elde 412 *When Mary is twelve, the priests advise her to choose a husband. She refuses.*
Suld take þam husbandes þam to welde
　For nothyng suld þai spare.
& for mary suld noȝt be betrayde
Þe bysshops a gret consayll peruade 416
　In þe temple of les & mare.

Life of St. Anne

<pre>
         Of ysraell come all þe best blode
         Before þam all qwar mary stode ;
            Þe bysshops moneste hyr þare   420

         Þat scho sulde take hyr a husbande,
         Ane of þe best en all þat lande,
            Chese hyr sum gud manchilde.
         Þi frendes & ylke man þat here es   424
         Aredes þam elles for þi fayrnes
            Þat þu sall be begy(l)de.
         Mary answerde þam full sone :
         Late be, syrys, it may noȝt be done   428
            Þat I suld wax so wyld
[fol. 189b] To knawe a husbande noȝ ȝyt he me.
         I haue gyfne myn vyrgynyte
            To god at kep unfylde,   432

         & þerfore certys I sall assay
         At kepe in clennesse yf I may
            To hym maydenhede.
         One sayd þan : lang er þu was born   436
         Other vergyns dyd so þe beforne,
            Þer lyfys lely to lede
         In matremonie to fullfill þe law.
         Fore þe, damoisell, do so þe awe   440
            Elles comes of þe no sede,
         & perauenture some ȝohng man
         Ffor þi bewte sall begyle þe þan
            So sall þu lese þi mede.   444

Mary   Scho answerde hym þan full myldly
defends her
refusal to & sayd : seruay here ensempyll why
marry.   Als ȝe may wrytyn se.
         Abell þat cursyd kayn slogh   448
         Lyfs now in heuen with yoy enoght,
            And two corones haues he :
         One had he for hys martyrdom ;
         Another he had hym best becom   452
            Ffor hys vergynte.
         And Ely ravyst to heuen þan es
         For he keped hym in clennesse ;
            Swylk grace may god send me.   456
</pre>

All men had wonder þat þer were
Off mary wordes & hyr answere ;
  Gaynsay hyr couth þai noȝt.
Þe bysshop abaythar up ras þan ;   460 Abathar recommends that she be kept in the temple.
Into a pulpit he wan þan
  Als he wald preche þam thoght.
He command þat all folk suld be styll
To tyme þat he had said hys wyll.   464
  Þis mater forth he broght :
Þe foles of fayth to trow untrew
Sen þat þis tempyll was fyrst mad new
  & thurgh wyse salams wroght   468

Haues vergyns & maydens dwelt herein,
Som kyng doghters, comlyest of kyne,
  Þat ouerwhare war dwelland ;
Som byshops þat in our law wer gude,   472
& som of prestes, & som of þe best blode
  Þat was in all þis land ;
& qwen þai were at þe full age,
Þai were þan put to maryage   476
  In lele wedlak to stande.
Bot mary forsakyd now þat degre ;
Þerfor emang us I rede it be
  To kep hir here ordand   480

Þat scho with no man be dessauyd.
All other purpos sone was wayfed ;
  Hereto assent þai all,
& kest lotes þan als I ȝow tell   484 [fol. 190a]
Emang þe xii tribus of Israell   The twelve tribes of Israel cast lots for Mary.
  To wham mary suld fall.
On Iuda fell þat lote at laste.
Þe prest þan of þe trybe als faste   488 She falls to Juda.
  Befor hym ded he call
All men þat war unweddid þan
& oppenly byfor ylke man
  Charged both gret & small   492 The men of Juda are ordered to present rods at the temple altar.

On þe morne þat þai suld ald & yhyng
Euer ylkon to þe tempyll bryng
  Þe yherd of a vyne tre.

Þai went all hame þe yherdys to dight, 496
& Iosep, þat ald man noȝt lyght,
   Þat tyme no wyf had he.
Goddes byddyng wald he noȝt dispise
Bot dight hym a yherd on hys wysse 500
   Emang ȝong men to be
To bere hys yherde als all other dide.
& þat nyght thus gate yt betidde
   With þe byshop of þat countre. 504

God spak to hym als I say ȝhowe
& sayd: Isachar, I byde þe now
   Tomorne be tyme of day
Þe men with þe þer yherdes when þat þai er come 508
Unto my place of sancta sanctorum
   On þe autre þu þam lay.
Als þare offrand yow lay þam þare
& byd þe folke þat þai noght spare 512
   Þat day & nyght to pray.
On þe morne put þe yherdes in þe handes,
& in qwhilke yherde þis selkouth standes
   Gyf hym mary alway. 516

Mary is to be married to the man whose rod bears nuts.

Þis sygne & selkuoth sall be þere:
A yherde sall burgeon & nutes bere
   Befor ȝow in ȝowr syght;
& oute of þe heghest of þat wande 520
A qwyte douyfe sall þu se flyande
   Up into heuen ful ryght:
Gyffe mary to hym þat þis yherd beres.
When he had herd þis with hys eres, 524
   To do ytt he was ful lyght.
Þe bysshop hereof was noȝt afered;
On þe morne ylke man he gayf his yherde
   Saue on wanted a wyght; 528

Joseph has no rod and no token is shown.

& þat was Iosep witouten doute,
For he was all þe folke withoute.
   As he þerof ne roght
He stode & lened hym on hys croch, 532
For who hys yhered wald tak & tuch
   Þerof gayf he ryght noȝt.

Life of St. Anne

Neuerþelesse for all þe fayre
Oute of no yherede þat þan was þer 536
   Sygne was sene ne wroght.
To þe byshope þan an angell spake;
Bad hym þat yhered he suld up take
   And gyf it hym þat it broght. 540

Att þat worde up þe yherde he toke   [fol. 190b]
And faste aboute hym gon he loke
   Als hym thoght was gret nede.
He saw þat Iosep yherd hade none, 544
& to þe tempell hade he broght one,
   Fforþi to hym he ȝhede.
Þat yherd to Iosep þan gayfe he,
& spryngand began it son to be 548
   Wit nottes ful fayre to sprede.
A qwhite douyf þeroute als gon flegh
Þat wonder all þat þis syght þer seigh,
   Bot Iosep ȝyt had moste drede. 552

Ffor ferde þe byshop suld hym blame
Iosep couth speke no wrode for shame,
   Bot stode & lokyd myldly.
Þe bysshop & all þat hym behelde 556
Sayd: man, þou erte blist in þine elde,
   Fful wele es þe forthy;
Of god allone þu es chosen here
To haue þis damysell þat us es dere 560
   Att wede hyr oppynly.
He sayde to þam: for shame lat be,
What suld a yhong wench do with me?
   My banes er old & dry. 564
& god haues sent me childre also;
Þerfore wyfys will I haue no mo;
   Lat sum ȝong man hyr take.
Þai luf me lytell þat to hyr redes; 568
I had mare nede to byd me bedes
   Amendes for my mys to make.
Abathar þan to hym gon drawe,
Þe gretteste byshope of þe lawe, 572
   Bad Iosep thynk on þe wrake

God toke of satan and abyron
& þose þat felle þam thre apon
 For þai his sande wald forsake;   576

Þerfore luke þat þu be nott shent
Iff þu dispyes þis commandement
 Oure byddyng to fulfyll.
Iosep answerd þan on þis wyse: 580
Godes byddyng wil I noȝt dispise,
 For I am lowed & still
Redy at do þat ȝe commande.

The bishop gives Mary to Joseph.

Þe bishop toke hym þan be þe hand,   584
 Mary he gayf hym tyll
& bad hym lede with hyr hys lyfe
In lele matremony als with his wyfe,
 For certes yt was godes wyll.   588

Mary is given five virgins for company— their work.

& for hyr solace & hyr game
Ffyue virgnis sal be with ȝou same,
 Þe best in al þis place.
Iosep was noȝt contraryus   592
Bot led þam hame þan to hys huse,
 & þer within a space
He dight a fayre chambre belyue
Ffor mary and þas vergynis fyue   596
 Þat was so fayre of face

[fol. 191a]

Þat þai myght in þer disporte,
Bot most to make mary comforte
 He kest hym in þis case.   600

& unto ylk man Iosep sayde
Of mary þat he held hym payde
 & wele wold he hyr tente;
With hyr fyue vergyns to be hyr by   604
At kepe hyr fra euell company
 Þus þat hold man mente.
All þas v maydens had swilk merkys
Þat ylkone of þam wroght sere werkys,   608
 Swylke grace had god þam sent.
Þe name of þas v I vnderstande
Als we in þe boke þam wreten fande
 Herkens with gude entent.   612

Gentea & sophora hyght þe twa,
Sussanna and albigia,
   Þe fyfte hyght agabell.
Ilkon wroght sere werk als we fynde;   616
One wroght grene silk, anoþer Inde,
   Þe thryd whyte so her fell.
Þe forte wroght bysse; þe v wroght lyne;
& mary wroght werke þat was most fyne,   620
   All propure soth to tell
Ffor it was best wroght of entayle
Þai ordand it for gods tempell wale
   Þer þai befor gon dwell.   624

& for it was werk most of pryse
Passand all silke werke or bysse
   Þe damsels had dedeygne
Þat scho wroght propure more þan þai.   628
& so befell it apon a day
On of þam gon her pleyne
& sayd: kynges doghters all v. er we,
Lo scho werkys passand oure degre   632
   Þat scho may noȝt atteyne.
Þai sayd all fyue: þe soth es sene
Scho castes hyr for to be oure qwhene.
   Swylk falsed gon þai seyne.   636

The virgins become envious of Mary.

Þus qwene on skorne þai callyd hyr þer;
Bot mary writthed hyr neuer þe mare,
   Ful fast prayand scho stude;
& als þai spak her of all fyue   640
Ane angell appered to þam belyue
   Sayd: fules, ȝe can no gude.
Þis þat ȝe sp(a)ke so scornandly
Sall be fulfylled thurgh prophecy   644
   In mary, þat frely fude,
& ȝowr qwhene sall scho be algate
Passand all (q)whenes in ylka state.
   With þat þe angell ȝowde.   648

An angel rebukes the virgins.

Qwhen þe vergynis all v. hard þis
Þai wyste wele þat þai sayd of mys
   & mary þai hasked mercy,

Life of St. Anne

<small>The angel tells Mary she shall bear the light of the world.
[fol. 191b]</small>

    & scho fogafe þam ononc ryght;   652
Bot on þe morne appered in þer syght
    Þe angell all openly.
He sayd: mary, blyssed mot þu be,
Ffor lyght sall com fro heuen to þe   656
    & ryst in þi body.
In þi wambe ys goddes dwellyng made
Þat sall lyght þis world wyde & brade.
    Herof þas thoght ferly.   660

Mary thankyd god with myght & mayn
& yohode to hyr prayers agayne.

<small>Gabriel greets Mary and tells her she shall bear God's son.</small>

    Lo gabrell soth to say
On þe morne appered before hyr face   664
& said: mary full of grace,
    God ys with þe þis day.
Of all women blyssede be yhow
& þe frute þat in þi wombe ys now,   668
    Blessed be it ever & ay.
When mary had þis herde & sene
Scho thoght in hyr hert what may þis mene,
    For ferd scho qwake allway.   672

Þe angell sayd: mary, dred þe noȝth.
Þe grace þat þu so lange haues soght
    In god has fon it clere.
Be you sall consaue withouten syn   676
& bere a child þu clere virgyn,
    Ihesus is name is here.
He sall be gret & goddes son calde;
Hys fader sall gyf hym þe see to hald   680
    Of david þat is hym dere.
In þe huse of Iacob þan sall he lende
& regne in heuen withouten ende
    & in erth fer & nere.   684

Mary þan to þe angell sayde:
How suld þis thyng on me be layde
    & man knew I neuer none?
To þis þe anngell þan answerd he   688
& sayd: þe halygost sall light in þe,
    Umlap þe blod & bone.

On þe sall born be goddes awn child,
& so eliȝabeth, þi cosyne so mylde, 692
Sex monethes ys yt now gone.
Þai called hyr baran in toun & felde,
Now haves scho consaued in hyr elde
Of goddes gret grace allone. 696
Nothyng impossible may be forthy
To god; þerfore dred þe noȝth, mary;
Þu has consaued þy son.
Mary hym answerd with myld chere, 700
Goddes awn handmayden es me here;
Als he wyll be yt don.
Þe angell up to heuen fleigh þan,
& mary prayed als scho began 704
To god sittand in trone.
Þe angell ylke day br(o)ght hyr meet.
Within a whyle scho wox ryght gret;
Hyr gudnes wyst bot fone. 708

Leue we now mary in gude name
& speke of Iosep þat was fro hame
Lyfand in mykil thoght.
Yf he were alde & nothyng lyghte, 712
Þe boke says þat he was awryght
& trewerke allway wroght.
Als lang als he fro mary was
Neuerþelesse no day suld hym passe 716
Þat his seruand þan broght
To þe vergnis all þat þam sull fall [fol. 192a]
At ete or drynk or wirk with all
So þat þam lakkid ryght noght. 720

Be scho was fully fyftene ȝere
Scho had consaued þat derling dere
& þan it þus betid:
When hyr neyne monethes ware nere att ende, 724
Iosepe dreste hym home to wende,
At loke qwhat mary did.
Þe fyue vergnis at þer werke he fande,
& mary at hyr boke prayhande 728
Als fast scho myght bid.

Joseph returns home and finds Mary with child. He rebukes the virgins for deceiving him.

Scho rase up myldly hym agayne
& of hyr wambe was he noȝt fayne,
   Bot it myght noȝt be hid ;   732

For qwen he saw þat it was so grete,
All þe fyue vergnis fast gon he threte
   & lowd began to cry.
He fell done & thus gate he sayde :   736
What happ, lord, has þu for me layde ?
   So ald a man als I
Sall now haue more shame & more anger ;
Lord, lat me are lyfe no longere   740
   Bot dight me here to dy.
& damoyselles, he sayd, wo yow be,
Ffalsly have ȝe dessauede me ;
   So haue ȝe don mary.   744

The virgins defend themselves and say that only an angel has spoken with Mary.

Þe vergnis sayd to Iosepe þan :
Wayt ȝe wele to hyr come na man
   At wayt hyr with non ylle,
& we wyll witnesse þis allway ;   748
We partes neuer fro hyr nyght ne day
   Ne scho neuer lowd ne styll
Spake neuer with no man in þere wones,
Bot ylke day come an angell ones   752
   & fed hyr all hyr fyll.
So all þe mete þat ȝe hyr sent
To powre folke gayf scho it verement,
   Þis witnesse ay we wyll ;   756

Þerfore suppose none ille so sone,
Ffor we wate neuer how yt myght be done
   With hir any maner of syn,
Ffor other þan þe angell spake with hir none ; 760
& þerfore þe holygoste allone
   We trow light hir within
& þat has mad hyr wambe so hegh.

Joseph is not convinced and plans to steal away.

He sayd : damoiselles, ȝe er full slegh ;   764
   I trow ȝou not lefe ȝour dyn.
Ȝe say þan þe angell made hir with child ;
Nay, sum lyke an angell has hyr begiled,
   A ȝong man with sum gyn,   768

& I wende scho hade bene syker w*ith* ȝow.
What me ys best wate I noght now,
 I wax als heuy as led;
& I dare loke no ma*n* in þe face,   772
In þe tempyll no i*n* na place.
 For shame why ne were I ded?
He sayd þus sighand sythes fele
& sithen he thoght fro hyr to stele   776
 Into su*m* uncouth steed.
& als he þerto wald hym dyght   [fol. 192*b*]
Þe angell appered to hy*m* þat nyght,   An angel corrects
 Bad : Iosep, turn þi red   780 Joseph and bids him
& dred ye nogthyng of þis lyf   return to Mary.
For to take mary to þi wyf
 Ne thynke w*ith* hyr no shame.
Þe child þat scho sall bere i*n* hast   784
Scho has co*n*sayued thurgh þe halygast,
 & jhe*sus* sall be hys name,
Gret gods awn power sall haue
All hys folke fra syn to saue   788
 Þat ada*m* broght i*n* blame.
Iosep at morne he went belyue
To mary & to þis ve*r*gnis fyue
 & told þa*m* all þis same.   792

He thankyd god & was full glad,
Bot of þe suspecion he to þa*m* had
 He asked mary forg*a*yfnes.
*   *   *   *   *
*   *   *   *   *   796
 *   *   *   *   *
All þe folke þat dwelled þe*r* abowte   The people accuse
Had me*r*welle & ware in gret dowte   800 Joseph of beguiling Mary.
 & wondreth bor mor & lesse
Þat mary was so grete w*ith* childe,
& sayd yf þat scho ware begilde
 Iosep to blame most esse.   804

Þai wreghyd hym all for þa*m* yll thoght;
Syne before abythar þai Iosep broght
 Was byshop of þe lawe.

He charged hym fast of þat doynge 808
& how mary, þat blystful thynge,
   Wald any fleschly knawe,
Ffor on hyr wombe it es now sene.
Iosep swore fast & mad hym clene, 812
   To god gon witnesse drawe
Þat he neuer with wyll hyr knew ne wyst
So mekyll þat scho a man aues kyst;
   Þis was allway his sawe. 816

Þe bishop sayde, how consaued scho þan?
Thurgh þe or els sum other man
   Lost scho hyr maydynhed.
Iosep sayd, ȝe sall all wele wytt 820
Þat scho ys clene vergyn ȝytt
   Boyth in thoght & dede.
& many other prestes þat þare wasse
Sayd : so lyghtly sall þu noȝt passe, 824
   With swilke lyrtes us lede.
A maner of watyr þai had perfore
In þe tempyll was kepyd in store
   For thyng þat was in drede 828

Joseph drinks the water of purification and proves himself innocent.

Þat whoso ware of a thyng gilty
& drank þerof suld haue oppenly
   A gret spot in hys face.
Þai gar hym drynke þar he stode 832
Sythen seuen sythes about he ȝhode
   Þe awter in þat space,
& spot ne sygne couth þai fynde none.
Þe bysshop & prestes sayd þan ylkone : 836
   Þu ert blist in þis place,
Ffor we can fynd in þe no blame.
Þai callyd mary þan, bad hym go hame,
   Opposed hyr in þis cace. 840

[fol. 193a]

The bishop urges Mary to confess with whom she has sinned.

Sayd, sen Iosep has made hym clene of þe,
Tell me, þi bisshop, who yt may be
   Þu gos so gret withall,
Ffor fayrer yt es in schryfte to tell 844
Þe soyth how þat þis chaunce befell
   Þan gods wrake on þe fall.

Scho sayd : yf any unclennes
Of fleshly syn or wykkidnes 848
  Be in me, gret or small,
I pray to god he shew yt here ;
& als he wote þat I am clere
  Hys help hertly I call. 852

Þai wald assay hyr ȝyt neuer þe latter,   *Mary proves*
& did mary drynk of þe water   *her*
  Þat Iosep drank of before.   *innocence by drinking*
To drynk þarof had scho na drede, 856 *the water of purification.*
& boute þe auter sithen scho ȝede
  Seuen sythes withouten more.
When þai no signe in hyr face couth se,
Þe bysshop sayde : how may þis be ? 860
  & other wys men of lore,
Mary es wreyghed here wrangwusly.
Some says itt semes done for envy,
  Þat may þam rewe sore. 864

Lorde god, scho sayd, þu wote full wele,
Ffor yow my doyng knawes ylke dele,
  Þat man me neuer ȝyt knewe
& þat I lufed sen my childhede 868
At kepe to þe my maydenhede   *Mary*
  In clennes gude & trewe.   *forgives her*
Þe bysshop & prestes both old & ȝhyng *accuser and returns to*
Askyd mary forgyfnes of þer doyng, 872 *Anne, her mother.*
  Ffor sore it gon þam rewe ;
& scho forgayf þam euer ylke a man.
To Iosep þai lede hyre þan
  With ioy & myrth enowe. 876

& þer a whyle þai dwelte all same
& made mary desport & game
  All þat þai couth or myght.
To anna hyr moder sythen þai hir lede, 880
& scho þam all full frendly ffede.
  Ffor wersehyp of þat wyght
Þai sayde : anna, blysed be yow
Þat swylke a doghter born had now 884
  Þat þe halygast wald in lyght,

Ffor þe child þat sall of hyr be borne
Sall saue þe folke þat suld be lorne;
   Loved be he day & nyght.   888

Besyde Ier(usa)lem þis thyng befell
In galile in þe lande of Israell
   Þer mary was dwelland.

Cæsar Augustus inaugurates the headpence.

& aftyr a whyle þan was yt þus: 892
Þe kyng sesar augustus
   Gart ordayn thurghout his lande,
Ffor he wald all hys pepyll knaw
What nowmbre he myght to hym draw   896
   Yf þat hym nede sulld stand,
Þat þai suld pay for ylke a heued
A peny; þat nane behynd were leued
   He did cry & command.   900

[fol. 193b]

And þat ilke man in hys awne cyte
Suld pay † anowre, þan þer mone,
   Of payn of gret pyne
Als it before þat tyme was made.   904
With hym þan þe kyngdom hade
   Of sery syr Egryne.
When Iosep hade herd þe kynges cry,
He spake þan unto mylde mary   908
   & saide: leve doghter myne,
Me bus wende now bedlem unto
At pay þe als our neighboures do;
   Þerfore heygh we us heyne.   912

Mary sayde: I am at ȝowre wyll
To wende with ȝow als it hys skyll
   In bedlem for to dwell.

Joseph and Mary start to Bethlehem to pay their headpence.

Iosep toke his childer towo,   916
A ȝhong damysell & no mo
   O menȝhe soyth to tell.
He drest hym & trussed same al hys ger
And toke hy(s) asse mary to ber   920
   Full fayre oure fyrth & fell.
Hys ox drafe he als to þat entent
What tyme þat þer spendyng was wente
   Þe ox þat he myght sell.   924

And als þai welke fourth be þe way
Mary gon to Iosep say:
  Behold, syr, qwhat I se.
Two maner of folke es us before;   928   *Mary sees a vision of joyful and sorrowful people who will meet them.*
Þe tane makes ioy, þe tother wepes sore,
  Ayther in þer degre.
Iosep ȝhode hyr pland be þe strete,   *Joseph sees no people and accuses Mary of folly.*
Sayd: I se no folke þat us sall mete   932
  Ne noȝtht bot fewle of tre.
Leue doghter, ȝow begynnes to fone;
Þerfore I pray þe þat yow ryde one
  & latt swylk folys be.   936

Ane angell appered clede all in wythe   *An angel rebukes Joseph and interprets the vision.*
& sayde unto Iosep als tytte
  Be þe way als he ȝohude,
Bad hym speke noght so to mary   940
Ne call hyr wordes wordes of foly,
  For he saw hyr saw was gude.
A folk of Iewes sho saw þat muraned;
Some tyme were guide & now her turaned   944
  Fro god als þai wer wode.
Another folke of paenys scho saw
War some tyme ille & now þai draw
  To god with ioy full mode.   948

& so þe wordes þat grett god spake
To habraham, jacob, & to Isake
  Er now fulfyld indede;
Þe blyssyng þat god þam gaf & hyght   952
Sall be now done thurgh his grett myght
  & shewed in habrahams sede.
Þis & wele more þe angell sayde,
& Iosep anone eres þerto layde,   956
  Bot to þe toun wald hym spede.
& er þai come att any town   [fol. 194a]
He bad Iosep take mary doun;
  No ferer sul he hir led,   960

Ffor gret gode has hir tyme now sett
Þat scho sall bere withoutene lett
  *   *   *   *   *

* * * * * *
* * * * * *

& scho gods son of heuen.
Iosep sayd: anngell, bot may scho noȝt
Ffyrste untill a town be broght?
Þe anngell said with myld steuenen:
Þis certen scho may noȝt passe;
Bot here ys a cafe þat sumtym wasse
For lyons sex or seuen.

Now es Iosep to þe town wente
At bryng to mary has he mente
A medwyf yf he myght.
& þe boke says þat two he gatt;
ȝebell certes þe tone scho hatt,
Þe totyhr salome hyght.
& mary es went into þe cafe
& þe anngell with hyr to kep hir safe
& comfortht hyr day & nyght.
No lyght for darke myght þerto wyn,
Bot sone when mary was comme yn
Yt was all lemmad lygtht.

Ynto þe cafe ȝhede none bot þas two,
Bot of anngells come many one mo
Gret multitud to þam þer.
Thurgh þe myght of god þat es maste,
And also grace of þe halygaste,
Gods awn dere child scho bare
Witouten wembe of any syn,
& scho in þe byrth a clene vergyn
Before & after þar.
So with hym þer ys persons thre
& bot one god in trynnyte,
This sall we trow euer mare.

For Iosep was noȝt ful lyght of lym,
He rade & broght þe wemen with hym
Walkand ouer hygh & law.
So to þe cafe þai come at þe last,
Bot enter ne durst þai noght for gast
So gret light þer þai saw.

Iosep ȝohod to mary þan,
Sayd, here er two mydwyfs þat can   1004
   Of women preuetes knaw;
& mary smyled. Laghes þu, sayd he.
He saw a knaue child on hyr kne.
   Þan sayde he : I was ouer slaw,   1008
Bot certes, mary, I myght com ne are;
Neuerþelesse my counsels or þai fare
   Speke with þam boyth infere
& shew þam þi preuytes of þis dede   1012
Þat yow no mydicyns hereafter nede,
   Ffor þat wald cost ouer dere.
Mary bad call þam hyder bath.   [fol. 194b]
Ȝebell entyrd, þe thother thoght layth,   1016   *The midwives are astonished.*
   Bot stude out all inwere.
& ȝebell come & graped mary.
Lord god, scho sayde, mercy
   Þe syght þat I se here;   1020
Here hys a meruayll was neuer none swylke.
I felt hyr two pappes full of milke
   & a childe frely borne,
& wymbe of birth es here non sene;   1024
Scho moder es als a mayden clene.
   Þis was neuer sene beforne.
To tell salome scho was full yhape;
& salome sayd, bot I hyr graype   1028   *Salome is punished for her doubt.*
   I hald þi salk bot scorne.
When scho to grape mary was comen,
Hyr hend, hyr armes war all benomen.
   Allas, scho sayd, I am lorne.   1032
Ffull wele I wote I haue done mys,
For my mystrowyng all haf I þis
   Þat I lyfed in a drede;
& god þu wote I lufed nyght & day   1036
Women & chylder to help þam ay;
   Helpe now me in þis nede.
Gabrell bad hyr aske mary forgyfnes   *Christ heals Salome.*
And sayde, touche þe childe þat borne es,   1040
   Þu sall be hale gude spede.

Scho dyd sone als þe anngell bad
& was all hale; þan was scho glad
   & loued god of þat dede.   1044
These women went þan both bedene,
& all þat þai had herde or sene
   Þai told thurghout þe land;
& men & women trowed þam enew,   1048
For þai halden wer ayther full trew
   Boyth of tung and hand.
Þe grete multitude of anngels bryght
Þat had brogtht mary all þe lyght   1052

Angels sing Gloria.

   Mad yoiful lowd syngnand;
A sang þat hali kyrke falles unto
Es gloria in excelsis deo,
   Þat es to understand   1056

Ioy be to god þat neuer sall sees,
In heuen & also in erth pees
   To all men of gud wyll.
Þis anngell sang was herd ful fare   1060
So mykyll þat sere hyrdmen þat were
   Þat nyght apon a hyll
Wakand per bestes apon þe feld
Lukyd all up & þai beheld   1064
   A sterne standand full styll
Nerr þe erth & also hogely more
Þan euer þai saw any other before;
   Ffor ferde þai gaf þam yll.   1068

[fol. 195a]

An angel directs the herdmen to the Christ child.

Þe anngell sayde: hyrdmen, dred ȝow noȝt
Of þis wonder þat here es wroght;
   New tythand I ȝow bryng
Þat ys ioy to yow & to þe pepyll all, 1072
Ffor he ys borne þat saue ȝow sall
   Mankynd bath old & ȝyng
In a cafe under ȝhone fayre sterne
Whare ȝe sall se hym þer I ȝow werne; 1076
   Þis tell I ȝow to takenyng
In bedelem sall he funden be,
& in a stabyll withoute þat cite
   Es made now hys rystyng.   1080

Life of St. Anne

Þer in a cryb sall ȝe fynd hym ly
Betwyx ane ox & a asse myldly
  Apon a lityll hay.
When þis was sayd þe anngell went;   1084
Þe herdmen has þer harnes hent,
  To bedlem toke þer way.
Be þat tyme had myld mary bene
So lange in þat ylke cafe I wene   1088
  Yt was þan þe thyrd day.
Iosep sett mary on hys asse
& toke hyr child als he swedild wasse;
  To bedlem fast went þai.   1092

Bot when þai come bedlem unto   *Joseph Mary find no lodging except in stable.*
So mekyll folke þer at do
  Þer hed penys to pay þare
Þat all þe ynnes in þe ton were tane;   1096
So Iosep myght gett herber nane;
  Fforþi hys hert was sare.
At þe touns ende bitwix twa walles
Fand he made both crybbes & stalles,   1100
  For uther bestes standyng ware.
He tok myld mary doun full softe
& layd hyr child in a manger o lofte;
  Þis was bot symple fare.   1104

In þat place als þe story says
Ware þai all herberd thre days,
  For better myght þai noȝt do.
Þe ox and þe asse boyth Iosep fest   1108
At a manger als hym thoght best
  & gayf þam hay at ette.
On þat same hay he layd þat childe
Whils þat he dryst for mary mylde   1112 *The beasts kneel to Christ.*
  A stra couche for hir sett.
Þe ox & þe as þai bath knelid doun
& honored þat child with breth & soun;
  Þis was a meruyll grett.   1116

Þe hirdmen held forthe ay þer pase.   *The herdmen honour Him.*
At þe laste þai come unto þis place
  Þer þai were herbard all.

Life of St. Anne

When þai fand as þe anngell sayd, 1120
Þai honored þat child & held þam payd
   Þer he lay be þe wall.
When þai had done þai went þer way
& lefte þe childe liggand on þe hay 1124
   Bytwene þe bestes in þe stall.
Þe boke says þat hay fra bedlem
Sant Elan broght to Ierslem;
   Se þer ytt men sall. 1128

[fol. 195b]

The temple of Apollo falls.

& in Rome þe same tym befell
Þe lordes & ryche men þat þer gun dwell
   A gret temple gart make.
Þe werke þai wroght was gud & fyne 1132
In honour of gode apolyne
   Þat was a deuel ful blake.
When it was made þai askyd hym faste
How lang þat ylke tempyle suld laste 1136
   Sum taken of hym to take.
He gayf þam to answere þare
Unto a mayden a childe bare;
   He sayd it suld neuer slake. 1140

Þai held þis soyth & noght lesse
& called yt þan þe tempyll of pesse
   To last withouten ende.
Bot þat same sononday as says þe boke 1144
Þat cryste was borne it all to shoke
   Wele wers þan euer þai wende.
Þe folk of Rome wyst wole þerby
Þan was fulfyllyd þe prophecy 1148
   Of crystys beryng & kende.
& þerof afterward garte þai wyrke
In honour of mylde mary a kyrke
   All þer mysse to mende. 1152

Many mo wondyrs war shewed þat nyght
Þat cryst was borne to proue þe ryght
   Þat he was god and man.
At þis tyme leve wyll we. 1156
Bot þe vij day of hyr natyuyte
   Mary þat blyssyd woman

Life of St. Anne 31

Hyr child into bedlem scho bare.
Þe viij day to circumsicid hym þare.   1160   The circumcision.
  To se hym many one ran.
Iosep frendes comen to do þat ded;
Þe fyrste blod god for man gon bled
  Þe boke says it was þan.   1164
When þai had done as þame awe
& with þe child fulfylled þe lawe
  Þai named hym þer ihesus
As þe anngell had hym called beforn   1168
Ere euer he was consaved or borne;
  Þe boke bers wytnes þus.
Bot after xxxij days
A wyse man of þe law þan says: 1172
  Mary tak tent to us;
With Iosep frendes bus ihesus fare
Unto þe temple be offyrd þare,
  & allway do þus þe bus.   1176
Ffor our law bids þus ouer all thyng
Þat ylke a woman eftyr hyr childyng
  Ffourty day sall scho
Hyr husband bed allway forbere   1180   The Purification
& fro other dedes þat myght hyr dere
  Þe tempyll þan cum to.
And eftyr sall scho puryfyed be
In token of clennes & chastite;   1184
  On þis wyse sall ȝe do.
A pare of dowuys or a turtyll ȝe take   [fol. 196a]
& go with hym offryng to make
  Er ȝe take ryst or ro.   1188
Þe pryste of þe tempyll hyght symon;
So gret age was fallen hym apon
  He was a C & x ȝhere.   Simeon sees Christ.
When he of ihesus comyng harde;   1192
At þe tempyll ȝate þiderwarde
  To kepe hym with gude chere
& toke þe child in hys armes two
& to þe auter wit hym gon go   1196
  Hys folowyd infere.

He sayd: now leve þi seruand, lord, in pees,
Ffor both myne eyne withoutyn lesse
 Has sene my saueour here, 1200
Lyght to all folke for soyth to tell
& yoi to þe pepyll of Ysraell
 Thurgh god ordand & dyght.
Þe ald man bare þe childe as he walde, 1204
Bot þe child þan gouernd þe halde
 & sayd to hym wele ryght.
Symeon said, me lyst leue full ylle
Forþi let me dye when it ys þi wylle, 1208
 Lord, sen I of þe has syght.

* * * * * *
* * * * * *
 * * * * * 1212

Þe masters and doctours of þe law
Be sere prophecies gon þai knaw
 Þat he was cryst, god son,
Ffor of hys byrthe men spak ful wyde 1216
& mervelyd gretly on ylke a syde;
 & so þai euer mare mon.
Mary & Iosep þerof ware fayn
& went to bedlem þan agayn, 1220
 Drest þam þerin to won.
Bot gabriell neuer more part fro hyr,
& Iosep for he yll myght styr
 Wit þer frendes most were fon. 1224

When ihesus was fully two ȝere
Thre kynges war dwelland in contreths sere,
 Fful connand men of clergy.
& by a sterne þai saw all thre 1228
How þat a ȝhong child borne suld be
 & callyd kyng of jury.
To seke þat child þai haue all thoght
Unwyttand ylkon of uther wroght 1232
 Thurgh þare astronomy.
& als god ilk man tyme has sett,
At þe water of cayres ylkon þai met
 And shipped þer redely. 1236

Three kings go in search of the Christ child.

When þai had ilkon understand
Þat þai were all boun to a land
  & all to a dede
Þer war þai all thre glad of uther   1240
& went forth ylkone uther brother
  Als þe sterne gun þam lede.
Att þe last unto Ierslem comme þai,
& þer þai askyd wysmen alway :   1244
  Qwhare ys þat lord in lede
Þat hys now borne & jewes kyng?
We saw ys sterne in þe est shynyng
  & we towene oure mede   1248

Comys with ryche gyftes hym to offer.   [fol. 190b]
Þe Jewes wer all gryued of þat propfer
  & went with gret dispyte
To tell kynge herode how þat þai sayde.   1252
Þan was he wode & wele were payde.
  He did call þam thre als tyte
& askyd þam what þai wald bemene.
Þai sayd all thyng as þai had sene ;   1256
  Þan had he sorow & sythe.
He sayd for 3owre tythyng god reste
& comand at serue þam of þe beste
  To drynke boyth red & qwyte.   1260

Herod asks the meaning of the visit of the three kings.

In þis men tyme herod dide call
Þe wysest men of þe Jewry all
  To wit whare criste was borne.
Þai sayd all in bedleem Jude   1264
Als 3e may in oure bokes se
  Thurgh prophetes sayd befforne.
Ane sayd yn bedleem Jues land
Yf 3ow for lityll pris stande   1268
  & men thynke on þe skorne
Oute of þe sall sprynge & sprede
A duke þat sall þe pepyll lede
  Of Israel þat was lorne.   1272

Herod's counsellors tell him that the King of kings is born.

We fynd wryten als þat a maydyn myld
Sall consavefe & bere a childe
  In clene vergynyte.

Life of St. Anne

Þe prophetes says he sall be so gret	1276
On his fader ryght hand sal be hys set	
In heuen in þe heghest degre;	
& of all lordes he sall be lorde	
& bryng in ane þat were a dyscorde	1280
His folke & make þam fre.	
Besyde bedleem in þe land of Jury	
Sall he be borne syr sykyrly	
Þat kyng of kynges sall be.	1284
He sayd, es it soth, wote ȝe wele?	
Þai answerd, ȝa, lorde, ylka dele	
& more yf ȝe take tent.	

Herod plots against Christ.

Herod sayd þan with some wyle,	1288
Bus me loke þat lad to begyle	
& elles hald I me shent.	
Þe thre kynges did he call forth þan.	
He sayd : yf ȝe wyll seke þat ȝhon(g) man	1292
Þat ȝe are while of ment	

  * * * * * *
  * * * * * *
   * * * * *   *1296*

With ryche offerandes unto hym wende.	
Þus feyned he hym þer a fals frende	
And thoght þat child to sla.	
Þai held hys tale trew and gude	1300
& toke þer leue all thre ande ȝhode,	
Bot afterward fell yt swa:	
One sayd alas, whare ys þe sterne	

The star disappears from the three kings.

Þat suld us all boyth wysse & warne	1304
To þe chyld how we suld ga?	
Another sayd, wa worth ȝhone deuelles lym,	
Ffor sene we went to speke wyth hym	
The sterne ys past us fra.	1308

[fol. 197a]

Þe thryd sayd, to god I rede we pray	
Þat he wald to wysse us þe way	
Sende us þe sterne agayne.	

The star returns in answer to their prayer.

Unnethes had þai þat prayer made	1312
Þat þai þareof all gude syght hade	
Ffor soyth þan ware þai fayne.	

When þai say ytt stand and reste,
Þai sayd & be þare clergy keste 1316
  Trewly withowten trayne
Þe huse þat ȝhon sterne standes abouen,
Þar hys þat lorde of grett renown ;
  Us þar no ferrer ffrayne. 1320
& when þai come unto þe place
Þare þe sterne stynt of hys pace
  Þai entred & ware noȝt drade.
Iosep & mary in þai fande 1324
& þe child on hyr kne syttande.
  Þan ware þai blyth & glade. *The three kings present their gifts.*
Þai toke þan oute of þer tresore
& knelyd all thre þe child before 1328
  With gude countennance & sayd :
Jaspar gayfe hym gold to hys offryng
In taken þat he was verray kyng,
  Ouer all kynges power had ; 1332
Yelchar ensens unto hym offerd
In taken swilke thyng hym proferde
  Þat he was god verray ;
Baltyȝar offerd hym myr myldly 1336
In taken þat he was man & sulde dy
  When gret god dight ys day
Man sawle þat was thrall to make it fre.
Þus knew þai hym with þer offerandes thre 1340
  Kyng, god, & man alway.
Mary thankyd þam þan with myld chere
& þer als þai knelyd all infere
  Þe childes blyssyng had þai. 1344

When þis was don, hamward þai went.
All thre to herode þan haue þai ment
  Þer way trewly at take *An angel warns the three kings against Herod.*
To telle hym of ihesus as þai hym hyght ; 1348
Bot an anngell appered to þam þat nyght,
  Bad, slepe noȝt, syrs, bot wake ;
Wendes noght to herode for nakyns thyng,
Ffor he es fals of hys sayng. 1352
  He haytes ȝow for ihesus sake ;

Life of St. Anne

  Bayth ȝow & hym he thynkes to sla;
  Þerfore anather way hame ȝe ga
    To passe fals herodes wrake.   1356

  Þai rase & thankyd god with myld mode
  & hamward anoþer way þai ȝohde
    Als þe anngell þam command.
  Þe water of taars when þai were past   1360
  Þan were þai glad & heghed þam fast
    Ylkon to þer awen land.
  Bot efter þam fast enqwerede,
  & als sone als he was of þam lered   1364
    Þat þai ware passed þat strand,
[fol. 197b]   Þe same schype þat þai past ouer yn
  And other allso þan did þai byrne,
    All þat hys men þer fande.   1368

  Ffor wa almost herode wod was
  Þat þai so gatte fro hym suld passe.
Herod orders the slaughter of the innocents.   He called hys consell hym nere
  & ordand all þat land thurgh outte   1372
    Within bedleem & þare abowte
  All þe childyr of twa ȝere
  & yf þai war a half ȝere more,
  Lordys or lauedys, what ouer þai wore,   1376
    Sla þam all don infere.
  Of payne of lyfe & lym he bade :
  So sall I best venge me of þat lade
    & on no noþer manere.   1380

  Bot gret god of hys grace alsone
  Þat wote all thynge or yt be done
    Herof sett remedy.
An angel warns Joseph to flee with Christ to Egypt.   He sent to Iosepe an angell bryght   1384
  Als he lay slepand þe same nyght,
    Bad hym ryse hastely
  & take þe childe & hys modyr hende,
  Bad hym faste into Egyp wende   1388
    & dwell þer prevely
  Unto I wyt þe for to say ;
  For herodes sekes þi child alway
    To sla hym sikyrly.   1392

Iosep rase up þan sone I wys
& sayd : lorde god, what lyf ys þis ?
In what place may I dwell ?
I am ald & my banys er sare ;   1396
Now bus me wende I wot neuer qwhare
Bot als I hard þe angell tell.
Here wend I haf lyfd with my frendes,
& now herode all togider shendes ;   1400
Curst be he with brek & bell,
Ffor may I myself neuer so yll welde
Yt bus me trauell now in my elede
Ffull fare ouer many a fell.   1404

He cald þan on hys childer two
And hys ʒohng damsell, bad þam go
To trusse & all playn.
Mo þan two oxen had þai noʒt ;   1408
Hys other hernays full sone was broght
& layd all in a wayn.
Mary with her child on an asse satt
& Iosep another for hymself he gatt   1412
To go, for he was noʒt bayn.
When þai had on þis wysse trussed,
Þai went be nyght, for þai ne dursted
Be day for dred be slayn.   1416

So wald þai noʒt walke in apert
Bot went ouer mowntayns thurgh desert
Þat no man suld þam knaw.
Fra herodes towns þai gonn þam dresse,   1420
And held ay forth þe wyldernesse ;
Bot wyld bestes noʒt þai saw.
Herodes men has fast childyr slayn,
Soukand & spayned þay spared ryght nan   1424   144,000 children are slain.
Nowther of heigh no lawe ;
So þat þai slow in bedlem lande   [fol. 198a]
A Cxl and foure thowsande.
Þis was a sory thrawe.   1428

Off þis ylke nombre þat were inward
Childre of herodes þat war noʒt sparde,
Ffor two was slayn ful eueyn ;

Herod commits suicide and is succeeded by Archylaus.

Because of ihesus toke he þus brake, 1432
& sene þai dyede for god sake
Þer sawles er all in heuen.
Herode had eftyr sorow jnogh,
Ffor with hys knyfe hymselfe he slogh; 1436
He hade hym þat none sall neuen.
Effter come hys son archylaus
& regned, þe boke beres wytnes þus;
So sett gret god þer steuen. 1440

The hardships of Joseph's flight.

Iosep with all hys fayre menȝhe
Wendes furth thurgh þat wyld contre,
For þai durst noȝt abyde,
Na for hete wyst þai noȝt what was best; 1444
And plase saw þai nane in to reste
Bot a cafe þer besyde.
Þer toke he down mary so swete
& ihesus went furth on hys fette; 1448
Bot out of þat cafe wyde
Come þer wylde dragons many one.
Allas, sayd mary, my child bes slone;
Grett god help hym þis tyde. 1452

Ihesus ȝode fourht emang þam all,
& to hys fett fast gonn þai ffall
& worshypt hym on þer wyse;
Lyons & lebardes com hym aboute, 1456
& þai gon hym lowe and lowte,
Noȝt stirred till he had ryse.
Iosep & hys thre childre stode
Apon þe wayne full myld of mode 1460
So sare þam gon þai gryse.
Ihesus sayd, moder, dred ȝow noght,
& Iosep, of þe bestes haue ȝe na thoght;
Þai com for oure seruyse. 1464

Wild beasts honour and obey Christ.

Iosep & hys menȝhe war þan all blyth
& come doun fra þe wayn ful swyth,
Þerto yf þam thoght layth.
All þas wyld bestes for ihesus sake 1468
Mad þam desport als þai couth make,
Dragons & lyons bath,

Life of St. Anne

So mykyll þat had þer ennemyse bene
Þai ffor þam all appon þat grene 1472
   Þai sulde do þam no skath.
Iosep sayd þan, lorde, blyssed be yow
Þat swylke a child haues sent us now
   Samwyse us fra all whaht. 1476
Þan was fulfyllyd þe prophecy   *Prophecy is fulfilled.*
Þat danyell sayde and jeremy
   Of ihesus full lange beforne,
How dragons sall do þe honor 1480
& lyons & lybardys for þe socour
   Lowe hym for uther store.
When Iosep had rest hym þer a whyle
He sayd, Egyp ys hythen many a myle; 1484
   I wald fayne we wer thore.
Mary on hyr asse agayn he drest;   [fol. 193b]
Þe lyons & liberds wald þer noȝt rest
   Bot folowed þam euer more. 1488

Þus went þai furth on þer (j)aurneye
Ouer hilles & dales fully dayes thre,   *Mary must rest and eat.*
   Ffand þai thurogh hegh gate.
Mary sayd þan hyr burd rest efte, 1492
For febyll hyr strengh was hyr ner refte
   Þe weder was þan so hatte.
Under a tre þar owmbre was;
Iosep toke hyr doun of hir asse 1496
   Þat semely þer under scho sate.
Þe tres was fayre & wonder hegh;
Mary luked up, þer on scho segh
   Heng many a full fayr date. 1500

Iosep, scho sayd, & grett god wald,
Of ȝhone fayre fruyte whyne myght I fald
   Ffor us & oure menȝhe.
He sayd: leue mary, leue þi dyn; 1504
Here es no man may þerto wyn
   Þat hys so hegh a tre.
I haue mar toght, als god me saue,
Whar I myght any watter haue 1508
   To drynke our bestes & we.

I wald we þeroff had our ffill,
With þi þe dates hang here full styll
  All þis seuen ȝher for me.   1512

Ihesus went up & don and playd,
& how mary & Iosep sayde
  He herd & at þam logh.
Moder, he sayd, or ȝe hythin gang   1516
Of ȝhone fruyte yf yt hegher hang
  Ȝe gett þerof ynogh.
He sayd þe tre, yow make þe boun
& to my moder here bow doun   1520
  I bid þe ylke a bogh.
At hys byddyng sone downe yt ȝhode ;
To ete þerof whyls þam thoght gude
  Iosep dates to hym drogh   1524

And sayd : now fayre we wele me thynke ;
Bot how þat we sall do of drynke
  Þerof no red I can.
Ihesus bade þe tre stand up agayne ;   1528
To hys byddyng þe tre was bayne,
  Als he was fyrst stod þan.
He bade oute of þe rote spryng
A well with water most plesyng ;   1532
  Ffor helpe of woman
Þer was a well er Iosep wyst
Cold & gude þat sloken thryst,
  To drynke full fast þai ran.   1536

When þai had eten & dronken wele
& ryst þam in þat place sum dele,
  Ihesus to þat tre sayd :
Ffor yow has comfort my moder here   1540
With other trees þat me ere dere
  Þi place hys now preuad
To be in pradysse for euer mare.
With an anngell sone was þare   1544
  & a braunche of gon brayd
& bare it & sett yt in paradys,
For fruet þat es of gret prys
  Þeron sall be dispayed.   1548

When þis was don als I ȝow say
Iosep heghed hym on hys way
   Als fast as he myght truse.
Ihesus on mary kne he satt,   1552
& be þe way Iosep noght forgat.
   He sayd : leue son ihesus,
Þer mountans er so hegh & grett
& þe sone scaldes us nere for hete   1556
   Þat shynes so hate on us ;
May we noght sauely leve þes douns
& walke here by ȝe se gude touns ?
   For owmbre lat us do þus ;   1560

Ffor and we ouer þe montanys merke
Seuen & thrytty lang day werke
   To Egip get we or mare ;
He sayd, ȝe shorot (?) þam all ways.   1564
& ihesus byght hym, within thre days,
   Iosep, ȝe sall be þar.
He bad Iosep before hym loke,
& Egyp hylles als says þe boke   1568
   Als son before þam ware.
Iosep hurkyld up þan & smylde
& sayd, þis es a blyssed chylde,
   Mary, þat þu us bare.   1572

Jesus shortens the journey to Egypt.

Be þat tyme drew yt nere to nyght,
Bot tyll a cyte þai com full ryght
   Þe boke says hat sotryne.
A lytell fra egyp þat cete was,   1576
Bot ferrer þan þat nyght wald þai noght passe,
   Þai had na gude wyll thyne ;
So þai wer kynde þer with no man.
At þe last to a wydow hows þai wan   1580
   Whore herber was gude & fyne ;
& þat nyght þer þai toke þer reste.
Þai were refresshed wele of þe beste
   Boyth with gude met & wyne.   1584

They take lodging for the night.

Up in chamber þis menȝhe lay ;
Þer bestes stud under þam & ete hay ;
   Bot word went of þam tyte

A child visiting Jesus is pushed downstairs and killed.

Þat many of þe chldyr of þat cete 1588
Come on þe morne ihesus for to se
　He was so fayre & whyte.
& als þai þe stayre up wente
Ane of þam another hente 1592
Þat mast was leef to flyte
& to þe erth doun hym keste
Þat hys nekbon þer all to breste.
　Y[lk]one gon other wyte. 1596

Ane after another þan hame þai ȝohode
To þe childe frendes howse.　þai wer wode,
　Sayd þer child ded suld be.
Þai askyd þam how & in qwhat stede 1600
Þat þar childe suld þan be dede.

Jesus is accused of the child's death.

Þe childer bad cum & se.
Ȝyll spyrde þam als who dyd þat thyng;
Þe childer sayd, syrs, a ȝong fundelyng 1604
　New come to þis cete.

[fol. 199b]

When þai fande als þe childre sayde,
Up unto þe chambre gon þai brade,
　Sayd þai suld dye all thre. 1608
Of þe wyset of þam þan spake one
& sayd, ȝowr child our child has slone;
　Þerfore ȝe sall here dye.
Ihesus stude still before þam all 1612
& answerde no word gret ne small,
　Þerof was gret ferly.
Iosep & mary bathe togedere
Sayd, soun, we er com hydere 1616
　To dwell þu wote wole qwy;
Fforþi son help us in þis nede
Sen we er all clene of þis dede,
　White us here oppenly. 1620
Ihesus before þaim answerd þan
& bad : go we furth ilke man,
　Speke with hym þat ded lys.
Þe men had wonder all of þat tale, 1624
& þider þai folowed hym out all hale.
　Ihesus bad þe child up rysse.

He sayd : þu, ȝeon be þi name,
Es I oght of þi ded to blame   1628   Jesus proves himself innocent.
  Er kest þe don on þis wysse ?
Speke oppynly here before all men
So þat þai þe soythe wele kone
  Þat þai me noȝt dyspysse.   1632

Þe sat up and spake gude spede.
He sayd, lorde, ȝe wate noȝt of þis dede
  Ne none of ȝhurs thoghght.
He lay doun dede as he dyde are.   1636
So, syrs, saide ihesus, what wyll ȝe mare ?
  Þis wekednes neuer I wroght.
Now tell us, child, þan who yt dyd,
Ffor certys hys dede sall noȝt be hyd.   1640
  Ihesus said he wald noȝt.
Yt suffys ynogh to þam & me
Þat we þerof noght gylty be
  Ne hym to hys ded broght.   1644

Þer men stode all þan als þai ward made;
Answer to ihesus none þai hade,
  Bot þai made dowl full faste.
Mary sayd þen unto ihesus :   1648
Son, sen þis child com hider for us
  To se þe was his caste;
Allowe hym þerfore for hys gud wyll
& lat hym noȝt þus ded lyg styll ;   1652
  He makes hys frend agaste.
Now moder, he sayde, at þi byddyng
Ffull bleythly þan will I do þis thyng ;
  Hys lyfe sall langer laste.   1656

Ihesus before þam in þat stede   Jesus restores the child to life.
Sayd, ryse up, ȝeon, & be noȝt ded,
  Ffor þu sall lyfe agayne.
At hys biddyng þe child up rase.   1660
Hys frendys þat wer befor his fase
  Wer þan all glad & fayne
& dyd hym worshyp & gret honour,
& sayd, þis hys oure saweour   1664
  Sall save þis world al playne.

Life of St. Anne

[fol. 200a]
  Thurgh oute þat cete þis worde son wente,
  & ȝeon frendes grett presandes sent
   To þam was noȝt to layn.   1668

  Þus þai visite þam dayes sere
  And did þam dwell þer all þat ȝere
   With ioy & myrth enogh.
  Be þan ihesus was thre ȝere ald;   1672
  He wex full fast both wyse & bolde
   & fayr of hyd & hew.

  Þat cete of sotryne was lang & wyde,
  & þe tempyll of Egyp stud be a syde 1676
   Full of þer godes untrew.
  Mary & ihesus soyth to say
  Went þam þider apon a day;
   Few folke hys power knew,   1680

The false gods fall before Jesus.
  Bot when þai com within þat place
  All þas fals godys be þar face
   Ffell doun & myght noȝt stand.
  Þe dowke of þat cyte, affredoseus,   1684
  Hard som tell þat yt was þus.
   Þe best knyghtes of ys land
  He toke with hym & som þider went.
  Þe prestes of þe tempyll wande haf ben hent 1688
  Þer godes for he so fand
  All had gret wondyr how yt myght be.
  He lokyd beseyde & mary gon se
   With hyr son in hir hand.   1692

  Þe duke trowed þer gods þan war fendes.
  He sayd to all hys knyghtes & frendes :
   Bot þis child gods son ware
  He had noght rasyd ȝeon þat was dede 1696
  & sithen gart our godes in þis stede
   Ffall don for all þer ffare.
  Ȝe se wele he garte þam bow;
  Þerfore I rede we on hym trow   1700
   & leue þer fendes euer mare
  Þat we noght wregh ne falles noȝt jn
  Als dyd kyng pharro for hys syn,
   Ffor þat wald smart us sare.   1704

Life of St. Anne

How he pursued ȝe hard well tell
Moyses and þe folke of ysraell *The city is converted.*
  To þai com to þe see.
Yt stode on ayther syde us as a wall   1708
On to þe tyme þai war past all,
  Sythen drounde hys men & he.
Þai sayde þe dukes consell was gude,
& loved all gode with hert and mode   1712
  Thurgh oute þat gret cete
Þat had þam swylke a prophet sente
Oute of ysraell þam to tente
  Ffro fendes & make þam fre.   1716

Þe lordes & all men þat þar was
Prayd mary & ihesus þai suld noȝt passe
  Bot dwell here wils ȝe wyll.
In þat cete had þai gret werchype,   1720
And thurgh oute all þe land of Egype
  Þer durst nane do þam yll.
Bot so befell yt withouten dowte   [fol. 200b]
Ihesus for to play hym he went oute;   1724 *Jesus goes out to play.*
  Hys moder at home was styll,
And fyue ȝher old he was þat tyde.
He went to þe see syde
  & childer come many hym tyll.   1728

And as þai playd þam on þe sand
Ilke child made hym with hys hand
  A podell with water þerin
& with closed it wonder wele   1732
So þat þe water neuer a dele
  Suld þerout passe ne ryn.
A prest son of egypt tempyll þer ore
Whar ihesus cast doun þe goddes befor   1736 *A priest's son disturbs Jesus' play and is killed.*
  To hys podell fast gon wende,
And spitously he brake ihesus game.
Þe childre hys felows sayd þan same
  Þerof þat he dyd syn.   1740

Ihesus sayd, se withoute gylt
How þis child my game has spilte.
  To hym þan sayd he mare:

Life of St. Anne

Þu deuel son, seed of wykkednes,	1744
Wit*h*outen grace and all gudness,	
Þi brau*n*ches er baran & bare ;	
Þe rowtes of þe er old, cold, & dry.	
At þat word fell he sudanly	1748
Benomen ryght als he ware.	
Ih*esus* all lyggand þe*r* hym lefte	
& to þe*r* game agayne ȝode efte,	
Ffor hym wald þai noght spare.	1752
Ih*esus* toke clay, wi*th* water yt weted,	
Sythen byrdes þe*r* of he countyrfeted	
Ffull propurly to þer paye.	
A yew come forby & saw wele how	1756
& sayde : child, þu suld noȝt wyrke now ;	
Yt ys our sabot day ;	
Þe*r*fore þu sall by for þis dede	
Unto þi frendes I sall þe lede.	1760
Toke hy*m* be þe hand alwaye ;	
Hame to Iospe sone he hy*m* broght	
& sayd, se what ȝowr child has wroght	
Expreyse agayn our laye.	1764

Jesus causes clay birds to fly.

Iosep on hys heued þan ih*esus* smate ;	
He sayde, þu sulde be wi*th* us algate,	
Ffra wanton childe*r* draw.	
Ih*esus* sayd þan, sen I am blamed	1768
Ffor clay & ȝe þam byrdes has named,	
Fle furth sparows on raw.	
At þat worde sone þai toke þer fleyght.	
Þe jew was wonderd þan of þat syght ;	1772
Ffor shame couth no ma*n* knaw	
Es here þe same thyng þ*at* he made ;	
Chasty hym þat he bowred noȝt so brad	
To wyrke agayne our law,	1776
Bot wente & tolde hys frendes alsone	
How ih*esus* þat yhong child had done	
Þa*n* had þai gret mervayle.	
Be þan þe p*r*este hys son has myst ;	1780
Þe childre þat of þat doyng wyst	
Told hy*m* fra top to tayle.	

Hys frendes assembled þan togyder; [fol. 201a]
To Iosep hows þai went all thyder 1784
  & sayd : gud man, all hayle,
ȝour childe þat standes before us here
On better maner bus ȝow hym lere
  Elles all ȝour frendshyp wil fayle. 1788
He cursed oure child apon þe sande
& þer lefte hym dede lyggande;
  Þis was a wykyd dede.
Teche hym noȝt to curse childer so, 1792
Ffor to blysse þam sulde he tytter to;
  Þat wer wele gretter nede.
Fforþi bot ȝe þis mys amende
To dwell here with hym we ȝow defende, 1796
  Bot fast ȝe hyther hym lede.
Iosep blamed ihesus þar oppynly;   Joseph complains
Sythen went he forth unto mary,   to Mary of Jesus'
  Bad hir scho suld take hede 1800   conduct.

Ihesus, hyr ȝong son, better to tent
Elles wyll he gar us all be shent
  & into pryson be tane.
Þe folke er in poynt agayne us ryse, 1804
For a child þat ded yonder lyse
  Þan make þai all þis mane.
Byd hym swylke maners þat he leue
Or elles hys lyfe þai will hym reue; 1808
  Þan war our ioy all gane.
Mary sayd to hym þan with wordes myld,
Swete son, what trespast yhone childe
  On þe sand þat he ligs slane? 1812

Moder, he sayd, he ys worthy   At Mary's
Hys dede, for he brake spitously   request, Jesus
  Þe handwarke þat I wroght.   restores the
Ma son, scho sayd, I wald full fayne 1816   dead child.
Þat þe child war on lyfe agayne,
  To ded elles be we broght;
Þat gettes us ennemys & we er demed
Out of þis land ilkane be flemede, 1820
  Ffor shame þat wold I noght.

Ihesus wald noȝt hys modyr wreght
Bot sayd, to gett hys frendship blyth
 Hys socour sall son be soght.   1824
Unto þe dede childe þan ihesus ȝode.
Hys frendes ylkone about hym stode
 With hevy herttes & noȝt lyght ;
& ihesus put hym un þe bake   1828
& with hys fote þis word he spake :
 Ryse up, þu woryde wyght,
Ffor yow arte noght worthy I wys
At come unto my faydyr blysse   1832
 Whar yoi and ryste ys dyght.
Þe child rase up þan verrament
& hayme with hys (f)rendys þus he went ;
 Þai war glad of þat syght.   1836

A child who strikes Jesus falls dead.

Has ihesus wente home þan be þe stret
Another jew child þat gon he met,
 & on hys brest he hym smate
Sythen ran away when he had don.   1840
Ihesus unto þat child sayd full son :
 Stand, sone, stynt of þi grate ;

[fol. 201b]

Þou smate me & I noȝt trespaste.
Þus pleynde he hym & toke witnes fast   1844
 Þat raysed no debate.
Þe child at þat worde ded fell doun ;
Ilke man gon þai to other rowun—
 Ihesus is of gret state.   1848

Þe frendes of þat ded child þan aghte ;
To Iosep & mary fast þai raghte
 & þis challenge þam kest :
Ihesus, ȝowr sone so wode and wylde,   1852
Ryght now has he slayne our child,
 Bad þam loke what war beste ;
Ffor certys hys dedys us mykell deres.

The people complain to Joseph.

Iosep toke þan ihesus be þe eres,   1856
 Sayd, þu kan haf no ryste ;
Lo what þai wittnesse all on raw.
Ilk man sayd wele war þam þai saw
 For þai wold haf yt dreste.   1860

3yt askyd þai more whare þai hym had
And sayd : for soth we er all drade
 3our hawn child he no3t esse,
Ffor he werkes wounders on many wyse   1864
& in þis cete makes grett maystryse
 Hys werkes bers witnesse.
Mary answerde unto þam þer :
God wote wele þat I hym bar ;   1868
 Als oures we sall hym drysse.
& ihesus sayd, bot my fader wyll ware,
Swylke werkes ne wroght I neuer mare.
 Here of wondred mare & lesse   1872

& sayd : for fader, moder, & brother
Herdely yow sall do another
 Or here þu sall no3t dwell,
Ffor þou dos thyng was never arevsed.   1876
Als many as ihesus þar acused
 To be blynd þam befell.
Mary sayd, ihesus, son, lat swilke be.
& he sayd, moder, soyth þai se   1880
 Þer alken dampnacoun of hell.
Þan made þa(m) dole & wer sary,
Bot ihesus at prayer of myld mary
 Heled þam all soth to tell.   1884

Jesus' accusers become blind, but he heals them at Mary's request.

& þat same day als says þe boke
Ihesus hys way unto þe feld toke
 & saw a flat of whete.
Off þas fayre eres he gederd some ;   1888
Sythen hame agayne fast did he come.
 Þe glene was no3t full gret
Bot sone he hong yt ouer þe fyre
& Iosep childre in þer atyyre   1892
 Þerof some gart he ette.
Iosep sayd þan, þis is gret skorne ;
Can þu no3t knaw other mens corne ?
 Þerfore wald ihesus be bette.   1896

Ihesus sayd, Iosep, wryth 3ow noght.
Þe flate þat I þe corn fra broght
 Ffra now furth sall do þis :

The miracle of the grains of wheat.

Als many whete cornes als here er, 1900
Als many bussheles þan sall yt ber
　　Ylke ȝere & neuer on mys.
[fol. 202a]　Þa lorde þat aw it þan sall have þat;
Þis grace þan grant I unto þat flat 1904
　　Euer more to bere I wys.
Josep sayd: ihesus, blessed be yow;
Fforgyfe me þat I haue trespast now,
　　Þerto, son, lat us kys. 1908

Þus þai dwelled in egype lande
In þe cyte of Sotryne, I understand.
　　At a blist anngel byddyng
Þe tempyll with þer fals godys bydene 1912
Ihesus gart fall & made all clene,
　　To god turned old & ȝhyng.
An angel directs Joseph to return home.　& so yt befell apon a nyght
To Iosep appered an anngell bryght. 1916
　　He sayd: wake of þi slepyng;
Wake þi child & mary alsa
& wende agayne to þe land of Iuda
　　& make þer ȝowr dwellyng, 1920

Ffor þai er ded now euer ylkane
Þat wold þe child & ȝow haue slane;
　　Þerfore hau(e) ȝow no drede.
Sone on þe morne when yt was day 1924
Iosep drest hym to wende hys way,
　　Toke leve at all þat lede.
He trust togyder swylke als he hade
& sayd, þus was neuer old man bestade 1928
　　Þat þerof had na nede.
He sett mary & hyr sone on an asse
& toke ane for hymselfe ordand wasse,
　　Went all furthe, gode þam spede. 1932

When þai were in þe hegh way sett,
Iosep spyrde of ylk man þat he mett
　　Thythandes of þat contre;
He goes to Nazareth.　& many told hym wele enogh 1936
How þat kyng herod hymselfe slogh.
　　He askyd qwho kyng suld be.

Life of St. Anne

Þai sayde all, archilaus, hys sone;
& Iosep dred hym nere þerto wone;   1940
  To naȝareth forþi went he;
Þer had he frendes & herytage:
By þan was ihesus sex ȝer age;
  All war glade hym to see.   1944

& mykyll of þat folke þat Iosep knew
Mad þam myrthes ouer ylke day new,
  Bot most for ihesus sake;
Ffor þai wald of hys mervayls here   1948
& also of hys gude techyng lere,
  Ensample of hym take.
Bot when he hard þat ryst and pes
Was in bedleem withowtyn lesses,   1952
  Iosep gan hym redy make
& þitherwarde went, þe sothe to tell.
Bot in þe way þis chaunce hym befell:
  By a wade in a slake   1956

Outlawes & thefes welke in þat lande.   *Captured by*
Þis custom had þai all ordan(d)e   *an outlaw*
                                           en route to
  For stryfe amang þam þer,   *Bethlehem.*
What day robe þat þai went oute   1960
Ylk man suld haue hys day aboute
  Þe pray qwhat euer yt war;
On other wyse wald þai noȝt skyfte.   [fol. 202b]
He þat fell þat day hys hede up lyft,   1964
  About hym fayst gon stare.
He saw Iosep and mary come.
Ffelawes, he sayde, ȝe sall non nome,
  Þis hys myn war it mare.   1968

He sayd, stand, stand, for ȝe sall noȝt passe.
Man & best, all þat þare was,
  Tyll hys home he it led.
Hys dwellyng was be þat same wodside   1972
Þare thoght he þam all þat tyde
  Iosep was neuer so drede.
Þe thefs wyffe scho toke þam in
& sayde, leue, syr, yt were gret syn   1976
  To leve þer folke unclad.

Life of St. Anne

I rede on no wysse þat ȝe þam spoyle
Ffor drede ȝe fall in fowler dowle ;
 Þus allway scho hym rade.   1980

Þe thef hade a childe ȝhong
Was blynde & also had no tong,
 No fote apon to gan.
A bath of erbes was made for yt ;   1984
Mary prayed hyr sone þerin myght sit
 A qwhyle fyrst, noȝt full lang.
Þe thef wyfe when scho ihesus se
Scho sayd to mary it so suld be   1988
 Ffor soyth elles did scho wrang.
Whyls ihesus in þat bath was done,
A fayre bed made scho hym sone
 In a byrn þam emang.   1992

The outlaw's child is healed.

When he was bathed he was wele payde ;
In a fayre bede þai hym layde
 To ryst þat frely fode.
Þe thyfe wyfe withouten lette   1996
Hyr lamed chyld in þat bath scho sett
 Whyls hyr toght gude,
& sone to hys modyr spake
Out of þat bathe scho suld hym take.   2000
 On two fette þan he stode
& loked on hyr with eyn full bryght ;
Scho was full glade of þat syght.
 To tell þe thef scho ȝode   2004

And sayd : syr, trow to my tale ;
Our lamed childe es now hale
 Ffro hys hede to hys hele.
Cum se, for here in we haue   2008
Hym þat þis world fro syn sall saue,
 Ihesus, þis wote I wele.
Þai went to þe bed þar ihesus lay
& seys hym swet þen alway.   2012
 He sayd, se what I fele ;
Þe swettest salbour þat euer feld man
All þat fro ihesus face come þan
 Þai keped yt ilke a dele   2016

Life of St. Anne

And in a syluer boyst þai yt dyd.   *The box of precious ointment.*
When ihesus wakynde yt þus betyd;
 Þai askyd hym boyth mercy.
He fforgayfe þaim, þan war þai glade.   2020
Ffull sone þai sold all þat þai hade
 & folowed furth infere.
So went þai with ihesus fro home   [fol. 203a]
Unto tyll þai to a cyte come   2024
 Was in þe land of Jury.
Of ihesus comyng þer godes wyst faste;
Þai fell doun & þe tempyll braste,
 Þerfore war Iewes drerry.   2028

In þat cete was þan hunger gretto
& also mekyll defawte of mette,
 Ffor corne was þer so der
So þat þe gudman and hys wyfe   2032
Had no thyng wher with to lede þer lyfe,
 Þer gud was gone so ner.
Bot þat bouste with þat swete so gude   *The ointment is sold to a harlot.*
When ihesus slepyd þat fro hys face ȝode   2036
 In hys hous when þai were
& þat a gentyll woman boght
To pop hyr with, for scho thoght
 To make hyr face swet & clere;   2040

Thre hundreth penys scho gayf þerfor,
& yt was worth full mykell more;
 Bot þat ne west þai.
Þis woman leyfe in lechery,   2044
Ffor scho ne warned no man hir body
 To take men outher nyght or day.
Þus scho did to þat intent,
Scho hard wele tell & word wyde went   2048
 Ihesus, godys son allway,
He suld be borne of a woman.
Bot who suld be hys fadyr þan
 Þat couth no man say.   2052

Þat woman fayne wald scho haue bene,
Bot on a thowsand fald so clene
 Of god was ordan & dyght.

The ointment converts the harlot— Mary Magdalene.

> To þat entent hyr syn scho wroght 2056
> Yf all yt served hyr of noght,
> Bot efter yt helpyd hyr ryght.
> Ffor efter scho had ones enoynt hyr face
> With þat oynment þat so precyus was, 2060
> Scho was neuer alf so bryght;
> & swylk a grace broght hir within
> Scho had neuer efter wyll to do syn,
> Þat swette had swylke a myght. 2064

> Þis woman name was mary magdelen;
> Of hyr boust was scho full farynen,
> To hyr þat was full swette;
> & of hyr dedes þat scho had done 2068
> Scho went & of þam shrayfe hir sone,
> Ffor hir syns sore scho grett.
> With þat oyntment so precyus
> Scho come to symond leprous huse, 2072
> Þer with oynt ihesus fett
> & of hir synnes askyd scho hym mercy.
> He forgayf hyr þar appynly,
> Þe story bers wytnes þer. 2076

> Þus dwell þai in þat cete þar;
> Sythen unto bedleem gon þai fare
> With þar frendes ffor ever mare.

[fol. 203b]

> Iosepe had þore boyth kyn & kyth, 2080
> Ffor he was of þe hous of dauide
> & als of hys menȝe.
> Be þan was ihesus ȝeres seuen.
> Þe prestes of þe tempel com soth to neuen 2084
> & outher frendes hym to se.
> Þai conseld mary & Iosep also
> Þat ihesus suld unto þe skole go.
> Blythly, sayd þai, wyll we, 2088

> & ȝhede to þe scole with hym infere.

Jesus is sent to school and slays his master.

> Hys maister come þat suld hym lere
> And .a. b. c. for hym he wrate
> & toke it to ihesus & bad hym say a. 2092
> Ihesus sayd, tell maister or þu ga
> Ffyrst what es .b. algate,

Life of St. Anne

And I sall tell what a. es þan.
Þe master was a dispitous man;   2096
   Ihesus fortene he smate;
& ded smate hym & slow hym sone.
Ihesus rase up when þat was done
   & ȝede hame by þe gate.   2100

When Iospe hard þis he was yll payd
& to mary sone he sayd:
   Þi child I will ga fra hym.
He dos so many a wykkid dede   2104
Some hasty man forþi I drede
   Þerfore sum tym sal sla hym.
Mary sayd: Iosep, dred ȝow noȝt;
He þat hym heder sent and broght   2108
   On na wyse wyll forga hym,
& he wyll kepe hym boyth day & nyght
Þat na man gettes of hym swylke myght.
   To hys kepyng I be tak hym.   2112

Þe word hereof þan went full wyde
Bot so another mayster was þer besyde,
   & ȝache was his name.
He spake to hym & was yuel payde.   2116
Why gare ȝe noȝth lere ȝow child, he sayd,
   Me thynke ȝe er to blam.
He begyns fast to manstate at draw;
Ffor þi lat lere hym of moyses law   2120
   & oþer letture for sham.
And Iosep sayd: who can hym lere?
I knaw no man nowþer fer no nere
   Can wysse hym wele fra ham.   2124

Ȝache sayde: ȝys, als god me saue,
Wyth oþer dyssiples þat I have
   Ffull wele can I hym teche.
Ihesus hard hys saw wele & fyne   2128
& sayd: þou can of worldes doctrine;
   I now bath proue & preche,
& in yhour haues þu als connyng
Þat I before þe law haues knawyng   2132
   & further ȝit can I reche;

Joseph again complains of Jesus.

Jesus has a new teacher.

Jesus astonishes all with his wisdom.

Life of St. Anne

Ffor of ȝow wayte when ȝe wer borne
& I wote wele & lang beforne.
 All mervayles þan of his speche   2136

[fol. 204a] & sayde, swylke wordes herd we neuer ȝyt
Of philopher ne of prophette
 Als he shewes sad & sere.
Þus sayd þai all & of þam demes   2140
Þe child es elder far þan hym semes ;
 He spekes of many ȝere,
Ffor he menes of Noye fflode.
All men þat þer abut hym stode   2144
 War þan in full gret were,
& ȝache sayd : Iosep, I am adrade,
Ffor ane disciple wend I here haue had
 Now hafe I mayster here.   2148

Who gat hym or bare hym or gaf hym at sowke ?
Ffor so bald wordes in no mans bowke
 Was neuer in Israell.
He ys grett als god for all our dyn,   2152
Or elles an anngell spekes hym withyn ;
 I can no noþer tell.
Ihesus sayd to þam bath alde & ȝhyng :
Ȝe mervayle for I am so ȝong a thyng   2156
 & spekes wordes ȝow thynghke ful fell.
I say ȝow þat I wote certanly
When ȝe wer born & qwhen sall dy
 & whore ȝe sall ay dwell ;   2160
& here of yf ȝow thynke mervayle,
I say ȝow þis & sall noght fayle
 A mervayle two so sare ;
When I fro þe erth ys lyft on lofte   2164
Þe oyngtyng of ȝowr kyng al softe
 Sall fayle als neuer war.
Þus met he als þe prophtee says
When þai hym on þe crosse sall rayse   2168
 Þe fioles þat þai had þer
With ountment to oynt kyng withall
Suld be all voide both gret and small
 & sees foreuer mare.   2172

Life of St. Anne

Þe Iewys & pharaseus when þai þis harde
Als þai war mad men all þai farde
   & sayd, qwhat deuel ys þis?
Yt semes als þis ȝong child war wode,   2176
Or elles he can ouer mekell gude
   Euen lyk a god of blys.
Bot Iosep had þer besyde a frende,
Another maister curtas & hende   2180   Joseph's friend undertakes to teach Jesus.
   & mek withouten mys.
He sayd to Iosep and mary mylde,
Qwy wyll ȝe noght take me ȝour child,
   Blythely will I hym wys   2184

Tyll tym he grewe & ebrew couth
& als speke latyn with hys mowth
   & ȝyt oþer seyens mo.
Sen he es of so fayre stature,   2188
Þe folke of Israell wald hym honoure
   Ffor hys comyng to an fro.
Mary & Iosep boyth þan togyder
Assent wele ihesus suld go þider.   2192
   To þe maister hus went þai two,
And has he gon þer aboute loke   [fol. 204b]
Ihesus was war sonne of a boke;
   To yt fast gon he go   2196

& opend it sone with hys hande.   Jesus explains the law and the prophets to his teacher.
Als tytte before hym wreten he fand
   Þe gret poynt of þe lawe;
& prophetes of þe halygaste.   2200
He undid þam lest & maste
   As he red þam on rawe.
All þe dyssiples þat war þeryn
Whils ihesus red mad þai na dyn,   2204
   To here fast þai draw.
Þe maister prayd hym to rede more forþi,
And ihesus rede so gracyuosly
   Þai stood of hym gret awe.   2208

To Iosep hous went he belyve
& sayd: þu gude man & þu gude wyfe,
   Tak home ȝour child agayne.

He ys þe wysest of all place, 2212
Ffor he ys full of gods grace
  Þerof may ȝe be fayne;
& of god has he all þis wytt.
Ihesus sayd : full sogth ys ytt ; 2216
  My wysdom, myght, & mayne
All togyder verrament
Of my fader hyder sent
  Ffor soth es noȝt to layne. 2220

Jesus restores the dead teacher.

& for þi gude worde & þi dede
Yf I þerto haf litell nede
  Sych harte I thar to lak.
My fyrst maister þat me so smate 2224
Sall ryse fro ded to lyfe algate ;
  Þis do I for þi sake.
Byfor þai all þer in þat stede
Þe maister fechid þat was dede 2228
  Hys sorow & syte to slak.
Of his lyfe was he glade & blyth
& thankyd ihesus full fele syth,
  Gret louyng of hym gon make. 2232

When þis was don als I ȝow say,
Ihesus went out into þe way.
  Before hym þer se he stand
A child þat hewes wod in þe strete, 2236
& with hys ax had he hurt his fette ;
  He stod full fast bledand,
Ffor all þe taas of hys ryght fote
War euen of & help no bote 2240
  Of no man nowre he fand.

Jesus heals a wounded child.

Ihesus toke up þan all hys taas
& to þe hurt child furth he gas
  & blyssed ys hurt with hys hand. 2244
Withouten wemb was he þan all halle.
Ihesus sayd : gyf yow neuer taylle
  Bo(t) go agayn to þi werke
& thynk on me here efterwarde. 2248
Þe Iewes þat þis thyng saw & harde
  Bad ilkan other herke

Life of St. Anne

& sayd, se qwhat þis child dos here. [fol. 205a]
Sum sayd he was cryst, god son dere, 2252
   Þat myght swylk maistris werke;
& sum sayde, he sall noȝt come ȝytt;
When Moyses comes, all men sall wytt;
   Hes dedes bes noȝt so derke. 2256

Sone on anoþer day yt befell
Mary sent hyr mayden to þe well
   To fech water clere.
Ihesus herd wele hys moder speke 2260
& wyst wele þat scho hyr pot suld brake,
   Forþi folowed he hyr nere.
Bot als scho ȝede þe folke emang
Þe mayden hyr pot brake in þe thrang. 2264
   Scho went hame with yll chere
& talde mary all hyr unhape.
Ihesus broght wayter ham in hys lape;
   He said: moder, haue water here, 2268

& bad þe damysel þat scho suld fett   *The miracle of the water pitcher.*
All þe skarthes of þe broken pott,
   & scho did so belyve.
Ihesus made it hale son on ane 2272
Þat sygne of brekyng couth þer se nane,
   Nowther man ne wyfe.
Mary kyst hyr swete son þan
& sayd: blyssed be þu þat so gate can 2276
   Kepe us fro sorow & stryfe,
& blyssed be god withouten ende
Þat swylke a gracyus child wald me send;
   Swete son, wele mote þu thryfe. 2280

In bedleem ȝyt befell yt so
A gud man suld to hys gardyng go,
   Iames alfey so he hyght,
Wortes & herbes to take þer yn. 2284
Als he to shere þam suld begyn
   A nedder of hym had syght
& tanged hym yll on hys ryght hand.
He sayd, allas, full lowde cryand. 2288
   Þan hard ihesus þat swete wyght

  & to Iames belyve he ȝede.
  He sayd, bot I haue help gud sped
   My hand bes lost þis nyght.   2292

Jesus heals the adder's bite.
  Ihesus bad hym in trowth be trew
  & þan apon hys hand he blew;
   Yt was all hale þus sone.
  Þe nedder þat tanged him in þat sted   2296
  For hys trespas als tyte was ded
   Þat he to Iames had done.
  All Iames frendes þat saw þis thyng
  Had gret wonder of þat doyng   2300
   When þai saw þer so sone
  Þe nedder thus dede withoutyn strake
  & sayd, no man may swylke maistris make
   Bot gret god son in trone.   2304

  Also befell yt in þat same ton
  Þer was a wryght bar gret renown
   Of a full gude werkman.
  A maister thakker of þe hus þat same tyde   2308
  Was hys neghbur nere besyde.
   Unto hym spak he þan

[fol. 205b]
  Ffor to make hym a sotyll warke.
  Þe wryght alsone had takyn hys m[a]rke   2312
   On hys note fast began;
  When he hys werke togeder suld sett
  Ane tre was shorter þan þe fyrst mete.
   Þan gunne he curse and band   2316

  & sayd, allas, þis werke ys loste;

Jesus lengthens a beam for a workman.
  Now bred me paye all þat yt coste,
   Þat I may do full yll.
  Ihesus come walkand hym allone   2320
  & harde þis wryght makand ys mone;
   He sayd: gud man, be styll;
  Wylke ys þat short tre my lefe brother?
  Take þe ton ende, gyfe me þe tother,   2324
   & draw with gud wyll.
  Ihesus hys ende a fote oyt drewe
  & sayd, now es yt long enewe;
   Go lay þi merke þer tyll.   2328

At ihesus byddyng þat tre he drest,
Þan was hys worke wele of þe best.
   Þerof full fayne was he
& sayd, swylk connyng myght neuer man con   2332
Uther þan cryst, gods awen dere sone.
   So sayd all þat yt se
& loved hym forþi bothe nyght & day.
Ihesus went aftyrward out to play   2336
   With childer gret plente.
Unto a fayre medow þai ȝod full ryght
Whane þe sone shane hayte & bryght;
   Þer thoght þam best to be.   2340

Ihesus hys wyld turnes noȝt forgate;   *Jesus sits*
He lepe up & on þe son beme he sate   *on a*
   Oppenly befor þam all.   *sunbeam.*
Þai sayd, do we als he haues done,   2344
& styrt up, bot þe sone fayled þam son;
   Forþi ded don þai fall.
Some brake hys shulder & som hys arme
& sum hys leg, sum had more harme,   2348
   & sum ys neke in sonder small.
Ihesus sat styll, noȝt styr hym lyst.
Gude men when þai þer childer myst
   Come þider hame þam to call.   2352

When þai ihesus saw on þe sone so sytt,
Þai went ner hand out of þer wytt
   Ffor dole of þer childer ded
& sayd, lowde cryand on hym ylkane,   2356
Oure childer has þu shent and slane
   Ffor þai trowed at þi rede.
Ihesus sayd: gud men, speke noȝt so gret;
Þai wald my dedes allway conterfett;   2360
   Þat wroght þam all þis qwed.
Ffor ȝe suld not my moder blame
He bad, ryse up childer & gos hame;
   Lys no langer in þis sted.   2364

At ihesus byddyng þai ros up þan;
All hale with þer frendes hame þai ran;
   Þai thankyd god specially.

Life of St. Anne

Joseph returns to Nazareth.

Ffro tyme þat Iosep herd þerof telle 2368
Lenger þer wald he noght dwelle
  Bot dryst hym thyn hastely.
He dyrssed togeder all þat þai had;
Ffor he was feble, hys childer he bad 2372
  Tent ihesus wele & mary.
So went þai furth ouer hyll & heth
Tyll þai come agayne to nazareth;
  Þer hoped Iosep best to be. 2376

He admonishes Jesus.

When þai to nazareth come war
Iosep byfore myld mare þar
  To Ihesus þus he sayde :
ȝow erte xij ȝere ald, god wayte, 2380
& drawes full fast to mans state,
  Tyme war þi playes wer layd;
Fforþi do now no wanton dede
& put me on myne eld in drede 2384
  & make þi moder yll payd.
Ihesus sayd þan Iosep unto,
I wote my selfe best what I sall do.
  He went oute þan & playd. 2388

& fore he had bene þar fore
Þe schilder obayte hym mykkyll mor
  To be in hys company.
All þat euer of hys comyng hard 2392
Fast þai drew unto hym ward
  & welcomd hym þer forþi.
When þai were semblyd a wele gret rowt
Þai went þe cete þan wythowte 2396
  Tyll a grene fayr & dry,
& þer som at bares þai ran
& som to lepe also began
  Who myght get þer þe maistry. 2400

Jesus again leaps on a sunbeam.

Bot ihesus alson tuckyd up hys skyrt
& one þe sonnes beme up he styrte
  & lepe furth a gret lepe.
He sayd, lepe now hereto for shame. 2404
Þe childer hys felows wend do þe same :
  Bot þai myst ate fyrst stepe,

Ffor þai fell doun & þer lymes brake,
Sum leg, sum arme, sum schuder, sum bake 2408
Þerto so fast þai threp.
So harmles myght na child thyn go ;
& als one brake hys neke in two
Was mast schrew of þat hepe. 2412

Þis ylke shrewed child þan hyght Iudas,   Judas,
Symon skarate son he was,   among
  A rych man & a Iew.   others, is
   killed
He & odyr gudmen of þat ton 2416 trying to
   imitate
To Iosep hous son mad þam bon   Jesus.
  At mak plant of ihesu.
Þai sayd, ȝowr son þe cheldyr ha shent ;
Chasty hym & better als ȝe hym tent 2420
  Or sare yt sall ȝow rew.
Iosep lay þer all at male esse,   [fol. 206b]
Sayd mary suld þat mys amese
  & mend þat þai all knew. 2424

Ihesus wyst wele þat þai were gon
Ffor to make playnt on hym ylkon ;
  Ffor þi whils þai þer stude
He made þer childer all hale up ryse, 2428
Saue anely Iudas ded styll lyse,
  & with þam home he ȝhode.
Bot when þat mary saw ihesus come,
Lo, scho sayd, ȝhonder er childer some 2432
  All hale of bane & blude.
What þai suld say þan noȝt þai wyst ;
Bot when þat þai þe ded child myst,
  His fader was nerhand wode 2436

& sayd to mary & ihesus infere,
Whare es my son ? He es noȝt here.
  Sum sayd styll he lay.
Mary for hys lyfe þan ihesus prayde : 2440
A wyst ȝe, moder, to hyr he sayde,
  What he sall do som day
Unto ȝour selfe & sythen to me,
Ouer all þis wrold lady to be, 2444
  Ȝe wald noȝt for hym pray ;

  & better to hym ware to lyfe noȝt;
  Ffor ihesus of hys doyng þer thoght
   How he suld hym betray.   2448

Jesus restores Judas to life.

  Bot now at ȝowr byddyng he sall noȝt dy,
  Ffor hym bus fulfyll þe prophecy
   Þat prophetys of me has talde.
  He bad hys frendes go þan to þe stret,   2452
  On lyf agayne sall ȝe hym mete;
   Þan had þai joy manyfalde.
  Emang þam was þer a Iew wysest
  Had a child þat luyfed ihesus best,   2456
   Ffor he was wyse & balde.
  Þai dred so sare hys company
  In pryson þai put þar child forþi
   & set hym in a stranghalde.   2460

  So when þe Iew had þusgate done
  On a day ihesus went þider sone
   Þe child & þe hus to se;
  & ihesus sayd, child, what dos þu þar?   2464
  He sayd, for I lufyde ihesus company mar
   Þan childer of þis cete.
  Ihesus bad þat þe child luke oute;
  He sayd he myght not withouten dout.   2468
   Þan, bad he, put þi fynger to me.

Jesus frees an imprisoned child.

  Þer was bot a hole als says þe boke
  & by þe fynger out þe child he toke,
   Þus harmles yhen paste he.   2472

  When hys frendes hard þat yt was so
  & saw þar child with ihesus (?) go
   Þai sayd & were agaste:
  Bot we our child ys lyfe refe   2476
  Ihesus company will he notȝ lefe
   Swylke lufe þai to hym cast.

[fol. 207a]

  Som of þam bad þam lat þam allayn
  So þat oure childer be noght slane,   2480
   Lat þam play with hym fast.
  To ihesus gyderde þai þan so many
  Unhes at hame was þer lefte any;
   & so befell it at þe last   2484

Life of St. Anne

Þe childer assentyd þam emange
Unto þe wod þat þai wald gayne
 Ruttes for to gedyr þer
& hew þam mittes & braunches grene 2488
To bryng home with þam all bedene,
 A commen game als yt war.
Þer was a child boythe wyse & balde,
Þe emperon son & hyght arnalde, 2492
 Gret state emang þam bare.
He lufyde wele ihesus compane;
All other childer to þe wod for he
 With ihesus þan did he fare. 2496

& qwen þai wer to þe wod come all
Ihesus bade þam all bothe gret & small
 Noght parte, bot go infere
Ffor dred of dragons and bestys wylde. 2500
Þe childer all þat þis saw þai smylde
 Gret skorn ryght als yt wer.
Þai had noȝt gon thene ouer a myle
When þer come to þam within a whyle 2504
 Lyons & lebardys full sere.
Þe childre for ferd away þai rane;
Up into a gret krukyd tre þai wane
 Stode ouer a ryuer. 2508

To ihesus wald þai do no skayth,
Bot lyons, lybardes, and beres bath
 Ffolowed þam to þat tre
& shoked it so þe soyth to tell 2512
Þat þe childer in þe ryver fell
 & drowned þat was pyte,
& some of þe wilde bestys swam & slogh.
Þe foster come rynand & wele wyste ynogh; 2516
 All þis doyng he se
& went and tolde þer frendes ylkone
How wyld bestes hase þer childyr slone,
 Bot ihesus na harme had he. 2520

Þe emperone son in þat stede
How þat arnald hys schild was ded
 He sorowd on ylka syd.

Jesus and other children go to the woods to play.

Wild beasts attack and kill the children.

	To mary þan þai went furth full sone	2524
	& told hyr all howe ihesus had done;	
	Þe wonder þerof went wyde.	
	He bad hyr gold full gret plente	
	To helpe hys child of lyue myght be.	2528
	Mary wald noȝt abyde;	
	Scho sayd, to þe childer wele ȝe kene.	
	Þe emperour toke many armed men	
	& to þe wod went þat tyd.	2532
	Ihesus wyst wele þai wald to hym come,	
	Forþe of þe wyld bestes slo he some	
	Olyue lefte lyons two.	
	Qwhen þe empour was come to grene,	2536
	He saw ihesus lyons & hym betwyne	
	On onather syd go.	
[fol. 207b]	Ffor ferd þan durst þai come no nere.	
	Ihesus spake to þam all on far,	2540
	Sayd, syrs, why stand ȝe so?	
	Þe bestes þat has ȝowr childer slane,	
	Lo qwhare þai lige here ded ylkan;	
	Will ȝe þat I sla mo?	2544
	Þai durst Not go to hym a fote	
	& als þe emperour wyst yt was no bote	
	With ihesus for to stryve,	
	Bot cryed, qwhare es our childer, qwhare?	2548
	He sayd, at ȝone tre take þam þare	
	& led þam home be lyve.	
	Þe emperour did fech a wayn als gast	
	& all þe ded childer þer in þai caste;	2552
	Ffor þam morned man & wyfe.	
	Ihesus with þe lyons up and done,	
	& þe empour men unto þe toune	
	Þe wayne begynnes to dryve.	2556
Jesus restores the dead children and puts dead beasts in their places.	So went þai home & sare þai wepe,	
	Bot ihesus mad þam sone at slepe	
	All þat wer with þat wayne.	
	He ȝod to þe childer þat þer was ded;	2560
	He toke þam oute & put in þar sted	
	Þe wyld best þer agayne	

Life of St. Anne

& couerd it as it was before.
Þai woke sone & went with hert sore   2564
  To ton ouer þat playne.
Bot arnold & hys felaws all
Played with ihesus at þe ball;
  Þerof wer þai wele fayne.   2568

When þe wayne was come þe cyte myd
Þe emperour did cry & ylk man byd
  Cum tak þer ys awne child.
Þi come & wend on þer childer to loke;   2572
Bot þar wer when þai þam out toke
  Qwarters of best wyld,
Of lyons & libardys þat ihesus slew.
Þan had þai care & sorow ynew   2576
& sayd þai war begyld.
Bot we helpe of myld mary
Euer more may we be sary;
  At þat worde mary smyld   2580
& sayd: gudmen, be noȝt adred;
He þat ȝowr childer fro home has led
  Bryng hame agayn wele may.
Ffor scho wyst wele hyr son ihesus   2584
Wald noȝt leve þer childer þus,
  Þat gart hyr so gat say.
& has þai stode spekyng þer lukyd sum
& saw ihesus with þe childer come   2588
  Before hym in þe way
With glad chere faste syngand
& ylkon a grene branche in his hand
  Euen like a somyr play.   2592

Þe emperour & all men in þe strete
Ffell doun þer before ihesus fete;
  As lord þai gon hym low
& sayd, blist be þu & þi dame,   2596
For þu es comen in godys name;
  Ihesus, gods son, aret þow.
Þai bed hym gold & rentȝ full fayr
& þe emperour sayd, þu sall be myn ayr   2600
  & wed my doghter now.

[fol. 208a]

The emperor wishes Jesus to marry his daughter.

Ihesus sayd to hym : swete syr, late be ;
Þer sall none part my moder & me,
   Þe thar non other trow.   2604

Þe emperour & all men þat þer ware
To ihesus durst þai þan say no mare,
   Bot let hym do als he wold ;
& mary toke hym & hame wente.   2608
Þe emperour to þam gret presantȝ sent
   Boȝth met & drynke & gold.
All þat euer was of Iosep kyne
& dwelled þe cyte þar withyne   2612
   Of ihesus war blyth & bolde.
Bot so befell yt in þat same ȝer
Corne in þat cyte was þer so der
   Ffor hunger þai dyed thyk folde ;   2616

& mykyll of þe folke·war at myschyefe.
Grett derth of corn did þan all grefe
   & gart þam fayre ryght yll.
Mary þerfore made gret murnyng   2620
& thoght sett some bote of þat thyng.
   Scho called ihesus hyr tyll
& sayd : my swete son, thynk wele how
Emang Iosep best frendes er we now   2624
   & thynkes to dwell her styll.
Sen þai haue swylk faute of corne,
Helpe þat þe pepyll ne be not lorne
   & þus for hunger spyll.   2628

Jesus relieves a famine,

Ihesus þan to hys moder sayde :
Sen Iosep frendes wald be wele payd
   & thank ȝou for þis dede
& for ȝe wyll, moder, þat be so,   2632
Unto þe feld þon wyll I go
   & help þam in þis nede.
Thre whete cornes he toke sone
& thre of barly withouten hone,   2636
   Wald he haue no mor sed.
Before þer folk þis corne he sew
& sayd, I wald þe heyward blew
   To repe þis corne ȝe ȝede.   2640

Þus made he þan a new harvest,
& þe folke þai suld noght rest
 Bot werk fast ylke a wyght.
All þat myght croke or sekell bere   2644
Went þat corne to repe & schere;
 Spared non þat wer of myght;
To do þat hervest fast þai rane
& many a cart & wayne þane   2648
 Ffull of corn ham þai dyght.
So was þat cete refresshyd wele
& all þat cuntre euer ylka dele
 Lovyd ihesus day & nyght.   2652

Bot als he welke þer up & down   [fol. 208b]
Mykyll of þe folke in þat town   and performs other miracles.
 He helpid & gaf þam met,
Se mekyll þat with a laf of brede   2656
A thowsand of pur folke in þat sted
 Had all yonw at ete.
Þe croked & lame he made so ryght;
Þe blynd also he gayf þare syght,   2660
 & temples don did he bete
With þer fals gods & mad all clene.
To god þan turned þai all bedene
 Þe folke bath small & grett.   2664

When þis was done soyth to tell,
Ihesus wald þer no lenger dwell
 Bot went yheyn soyth to say.
And mary hys moder at hame styll was;   2668
& also Iosep myght noȝt þem passe,
 For þat tyme selke he lay.
Bot Iosep come sone withowten flyke
Unto a cete men calles affryke;   2672
 & þat cete þat same day
A lyster stude þer hym agayne
& sayd, wyne es þu ȝong swayn,
 & whider ert þu on way?   2676

Ihesus answerd þan als hym thoght
& sayd: whyne þat I am rek þe noȝt,
 Bot þis ton come I tyll

Jesus meets a lyster and agrees to work for him.

Ffor to seke thyng þat hys loste 2680
& pay þerfore more þan yt coste.
  Þat, sayd he, was no skyll.
Bot ihesus ment it be mans kynde
How he for þat syn suld be pynde 2684
  On rode tre on ane hyll.
Þe lyster sayd, lat swylke worde be;
Þe es better lere a crafte with me
  & dwell here with me styll. 2688

Ihesus answerd, what crafte hys itt?
He sayd: son, þu sall lere to lytt;
  Ffor þi come with me swyth.
Ihesus sayd blethly þat he wald. 2692
Hys wyfe when scho gon hym beholde
  Of ihesus was glad & blyth.
Scho sayd: swete son, withouten doute
Þu may noȝt now all day ryn oute 2696
  & fro þi werk go lyghtly,
Ffor þe bus besy be here at hame.
He sayd blethly in goddes name
  No maistris wald he kythe. 2700

Þe lyster sayd: son, be now ware,
Ffor our bischope abyathare
  Thre rych clothes sent me to.
Ane bus be blew, a noder rede, 2704
Þe thyrd grene, ylkon in ser lede;
  Be leve luke þat þu do

[fol. 209a]

& make gude fyres under all thre,
Ffor tyll our neghburs wend will we 2708
  An erand boyth I and scho,
& gar þam bule be we come agayne.
Ihesus sayd þat he walde full fayne
  Elles suld he be by þat bro. 2712

Jesus leaves his work to play.

Þe dyer & hys wyfe out went,
& ihesus haues þe thre clothes hent
  & kest all in a lede.
He made gret fyre þer under gude spede, 2716
& sythen out all þe dore he ȝede;
  He bade no lenger in þat stede.

Þe childer of þe strete out did he call
& played þer with þam at þe bawll;   2720
  Þai welterd all ars ouer hede.
Þe lyster spak þan: ryse up þu dame,
Yt hys gude þat we ga hame.
  Scho sayd: syr, so I rede,   2724
Ffor ȝe lefte at hame a wanton childe
And lyghtly may ȝe be begylede
  Yf ȝe dwell fro hym lang.
Þai heghed þam hame withouten dyn,   2728
Bot when þai fand noght ihesus yn   *The lyster returns.*
  Þai lest wele of no sang.
Qwhen þe clothes in a lede þai fand
With fyre & water full fast buland   2732
  Ffor dole þer handes þai wrang.
Þe lyster wepyd als he wer wode;
Ihesus come in þan als he stude;
  He sayd he sulde hym hang.   2736

Ladd, he sayd, why did þu þus?   *He threatens Jesus.*
Þu has ffordone both þe & us,
  Þat sall þu by full dere.
A gret fyre brand at hym he kest;   2740
Yt stode up & floryst þer of þe best,
  A fayre tre als it were.
Ihesus sayd: mayster, be noȝt wroght;
Yf ȝe of my servys be lothe,   2744
  A byd speke with me here.
I sall boyth our worships salve;
Loke qwhat colour þat ȝe wyll sawe
  & draw yt out with gude chere.   2748

Þe lyster ȝode to hys ledd full tyte   *The cloths come out properly dyed.*
& drew a cloth he wend war whyte,
  Bot yt was scarlet bryght.
A nodther cloth þan out he drew,   2752
& yt was one of þe best blew
  Þat euer he had of syght.
He drew þe thryde & yt was grene;
A god, he sayd, what may þis mene?   2756
  Þe clothes er full wele dyght.

Child, þou sall lere me more to draw
& dwell styll here als my felaw;
 Þu seruys a gayne þe ryght.   2760

[fol. 269b]
Jesus leaves the lyster.

Ihesus sayd nay, þat wald he noght,
Bot bad hym tech furthe als he had wroght
 And laue it with no man;
And als of þi mystere   2764
Ne of no nother nedes me to lere,
 Ffor of all thyng I can.
Þus toke he þer hys leue and went.
Þe lyster þan þe clothes hame sent   2768
 To þe byshop how or he blan.
All meruayld gretly þat þer ware
And sayd, swylke colours saw we neuer are
 Ne half so wele lyt þan.   2772

He told þam ryght als yt was
& how þe child fro hym gon has;
 Þan hade þai meruele all.
Bot als ihesus went thurgh þe strete   2776
Mekyll of þe pepyll gon he mete
 With vessels gret & small.
To fech þam water þai come þat while
Att a well was þen thre myle,   2780
 Ffor nar haue none þai sall.
Ihesus wente with þam sothe to say
& euer he spyred þam be þe way
 How þat thyng myght befall.   2784

Þai sayde it was euer a wary sone,
Ffore ane of þe rychest man of þat ton
 Aught it withouten doute
& sald þerof water full dere,   2788
Ffor þer was none þe ton so ner
 Of all þe plasses þer aboute.
Ihesus sayd þan it were no syn
To make water nerrer þe ton to ryn   2792
 At bere bothe ship & shout.
Som sayd þan do þat thyng may none
Other þan grette god sone allone;
 Ryght so sayd all þe rout.   2796

Life of St. Anne

When þai unto þe wele were comen
& ilk man had hys mesure nom(e)n　　　*Jesus brings*
　To pay þai war ryght fayne　　　　　*water to a*
Unto hys seruant þat þat well aght.　2800　*dry town.*
Ihesus in hys lappe water raght,
　Went ham with þam agayne.
A bown affryke þan stode a hyll;
Ihesus sayd þer þe folke untyll: 2804
　Wald noght, syrres, ouer þis playne
Twa stremes of water ryn ryght wele
And serve þe town ever ylka dele
　Withouten peny or payn? 2808

Þai sayd all, ȝa, withouten drede,
& it were a grete almosse dede
　Who myght gar it be done.
Ihesus bade þan þe folke abyde; 2812
He ȝode to þe hell þai stode besyde,
　Hys water he kest down sone.
Ihesus bad two stremes þat tyde　　　[fol. 210a]
Ryn to þe toun on aither syde; 2816
　Þai did so withouten hone.
Ieron called he þer þe tane,
Þe toþer water þan called he dane;
　Þus had þai all þer bone. 2820

Man & woman all þat þer was
Prayd ihesus þan he suld noȝt pas
　Bot wende with þam to woun.
Þis thyng was sone emang þam tolde, 2824
Agayne hym boyth ȝonge come & olde
　With grett processyon
& sayd ylkone: we wate wele now
Þat in gods name comen es yow, 2828
　Gods son of gret renown,
& oure saueour sall yow be als.
Þer tempils full of gods so fals
　Þai stroyed & bet all down 2832

& sayde: þis ys a kyndnes grete,　　　*Jesus*
What sall we do þe for þis ser benfete?　*prophesies*
　Lefe lord, will þu us tell?　　　　　*his death.*

	He sayd : in god trowes stedfastly	2836
	& qwen ȝe se þe prophisy	
	Ffulfilled þerwith ȝe dwell,	
	With my dedes yf ȝe now wele thynke	
	Ȝe sall here efter gyfe me to drynke	2840
	Gall & full soure aisell.	
	All at þis word þan thoght gret shame ;	
	Ilkon fro ihesus þan stale þai hame	
	Þat tyme it þus befell.	2844
He goes to Jerusalem.	Ffro thyn to Ierslem þan went ihesus,	
	& þat tyme in þat cete was yt þus :	
	Þer dwelt þe wysest men	
	& most conand in all clerge	2848
	Þat was in all þer Iewrye	
	Ouer whare lyfand þan.	
	With þam thoght ihesus dispute þe law	
	At se by clarge yf þai couth knaw	2852
	Whar criste was born & qwhen,	
	How þat þai suld not be excused	
	Þe law wrangfully yf þai used	
	& noȝt hym for oure criste kene.	2856
Joseph and Mary go in search of Jesus.	Bot mary thynkes lang scho ihesus myst,	
	& qwhore to fynd hym no thyng scho wyst	
	Ne whiderward he was rone.	
	Ffor þi unto Iosep scho spake	2860
	& sayd þe way þat þai bud take	
	To seke ihesus þer son.	
	Iosepe sayd þan, I hope he be	
	With oure frendys in þis contre,	2864
	Hop I he sall be son.	
	Þan sayd mary, we wyll go loke.	
	Ayther of þam an asse þai toke,	
	Went þider þer þai suld won ;	2868
[fol. 210b] They hear of his miracles.	Bot thurgh þe contre als þai hath past	
	Þe pepyll tald how ihesus helyd faste	
	Mykyll folke of sere seknesse,	
	& blynd men how he gart þam se,	2872
	Croked & lame all hale mad he	
	So gret was hys gudnes ;	

Of men & women deulles catched he oute
& mad þer templis clene all aboute   2876
   Of fals gods mar & lesse.
Bot mary & josep er wrath als wynd,
Ffor þi myght nour of ihesus fynde;
   None couth tell war he hys.   2880
At þe laste into jherusalem come þai,
& preuely þer spired þam allway
   Yf ihesus was oght þare.
Bot tythandes of hym hard þai non talde,   2884
Ffor he couthe be ay when he walde
   Invisibele euerhay ware;
& so apon a day yt stude
Mary & Iosep to þe tempil ʒode   2888
   Whare þer clarkes gedyr war.
Þai lokyd & ihesus syttand saw
Emang þe doctours of þe law
   Apposand þam sad & sar   2892

& with hys argument gretly þam newd,   *They find Him disputing with the doctors in the temple.*
Ffor ylkon of þame he conclude
   Euen in þer awn sayng;
So þat all þas þat myght hym here   2896
Had wondyr whare swylk a child suld lere
   To be so wysse of doyng.
Ffor shame nerehand þer wytt þai loysed
When ihesus answerde or apposede,   2900
   So gracious was hys spekyng.
& so a gret doctour þam layd
A buke befor ihesus & prayd
   Hym red þerof som thyng.   2904

Ihesus oppend þat buke with hys hand
& son before opon he fand
   Of þe prophete Isaye.
Lo, he sayd, ʒe docturs dere,   2908
Of myselfe now fynd I here
   Wretyn a soth prophecye:
Þe halygast on me es lyght
& enoynt me þerfore with ryght   2912
   & sent me oppenly

To preche þe folke heuen how þai sall wyn
& caytyfs & wreches of þar syn
   Fforgyfnes þat askes mercy ; 2916
& als of gods gudnes to teche
Of grace & meknes for to preche
   To all þat wyll do wele,
& days of vengeaunce at shew þam tyll 2920
Þat er synfull and thynkes do yll
   To ponnysh þer dedes ylka dele.
When ihesus had red þe buke he fold
& gayf yt þe docturs agayn to hold ; 2924
   To ihesus þan did he knele ;
Þai war so wondred of hys wytt
Ffor shame myght þai no langer syt
   Bot stale away wyth unsele. 2928

Ihesus saw mary & Iosep sone ;
He went to þam withouten hone.
   Scho sayd : swete son ihesus,
What ayld þe & why dyd yow so ? 2932
Lo, þi fadyr & I wyth mykyll wo
   Has soght þe hedyr þus.
He sayd : to seke me noȝt ȝow nedes,
Ffor wyt ȝe wele in my fader dedes 2936
   All way be me bus ;
& moder, ȝe wot I am sent þerto.
Mary sayd, at þi wyll ay yow do ;
   Bot now come forth with us. 2940

Ihesus went with þam withawten lett
& served þam boyth als þe sugett
   By þe way als þai ȝede.
Ihesus, son, thynk one þi selfe, 2944
Ffor ȝow passes ouer ȝe ȝheres twelf
   Lyke now to do mans dede.
Help mary, þi moder, for I am noȝt,
Ffor whyls I myght allway I wroght 2948
   Us both to cleth & fede ;
Bot certes now may I wyrke no more
Ne noȝt wele ga for faynte and sore
   Bot yf sum man me lede. 2952

Life of St. Anne

Ffor þi to nazareth bryng me ones ;   *They return to Nazareth.*
Þar thynke I rest my ald bones
   Unto my lyfys ende.
Mary sayd : son sall ȝe come thyder ;   2956
My son and I boythe togyder
   Sall ȝou makess amende.
At nazareth war þay þan full sone,
& Iosep in hys bed was done ;   2960
   He fare þan sone wende.
Ffor febyll & faynt he began to grone ;
How nere hys ded was west þer non
   Bot ihesus þat all thyng kend.   2964

Bot Iosep frendes come hym sport to make
& broght wyne & spyces for hys sake
   Yf he war seke bestade ;
Bot þai made gret dole in þat sted,   2968
Ffor one of þar childer was dede,
   A frend þat Iosep had.
Mari hard þam sore for hym murne ;
Scho thoght þer sorow sone to turne,   2972
   Fforþi hyr son scho bad
Þat þe child myght leve agayne ;
& ihesus said he walde full fayne ;
   Þan war hys frendes al glad.   2976

He went furth fast unto þat stede   *Jesus restores a dead child.*
Þer þe gude mans child was dede ;
   He lukyd on hym þat ded lyse.
He was a neghbour þe alther nexst ;   2980
& ihesus touchyd hym on þe breste,
   Bad, þu ded child upryse
& lyf, for yow sall noȝt dy ȝhytt.
Ilke man wondyr þan in hys wyt   2984
   Þat he wroght on swylke wyse.
Ffra ded to lyfe he hym raysyd ;
Þerfore he was ful mykyll praysyd
   Als lorde of gret pryse.   2988

& als he went hamward be þe strete   [fol. 211b]
A blynd man þan gon he mete ;
   His frendes about hym stod,

He heals a blind man.

Ffor hys comyng alway þai spied.
When ihesus come þe blynde man cryed,
  Leve lorde, do me sum gud.
He sayd, what wyll þou of me crave?
Lorde, my eyne syght walde I haue
  Yf þu wald frely fode.
Ihesus bad hym stand up and luke;
He saw als sone as þe buke;
  With ihesus hale furth he ȝude.

2992

2996

3000

He heals divers diseases.

Oythyr sek men broght þai hym also
& men traueland wyth deuels two
  Out of þer wyt war clene,
All bunden wer þai broght byfor hym.
Ihesus bad, come out, þu delves lym;
  Be fro for þe folke al bedene.
At hys byddyng þe wycked spirytȝ
Come out, þan had þe men þar wythytt,
  Both hale & sownd þai bene.
& ihesus sayd: þas deuels blake
To wildernes þer flyght to take
  Neuer mar thar efte be sene.

3004

3008

3012

All þat wyll euer on hym trowe,
What euele or seknes þat ȝe haf now
  Ȝe sall be hale þus sone.
Þe pepyll turnyd þan unto hym fast
& prayed god lang hys lyf suld last
  Als he shop son & mone.
Bot some of þe trybes of ysraell
So tyte als þai hard here of tell
  & how ihesus had done
To Iosep & mary sone went þai.
Bot Iosep bedredyn þat tyme lay
  Ffull febyll þat west bot frone;

3016

3020

3024

The people ask Mary who Jesus is.

Ffor þai to mary þai spak, I wys,
& sayd: yow dame, whays child es þis
  Þat ded folke mau þus rays
& sawes þe pepyll þat on hym trowes?
Es þu hys moder & þis þi awowes?
  Tell us tytt qwhat þu says.

3028

Scho sayd: for sothe hys moder am I,
& als god lykes turght hys mercy 3032
  Myself suld I noȝt prays;
Bot of my body certes I hym bare.
Þai sayd: blyssed be þu euere mare
& so be he alw(a)ys, 3036
Ffor now þan wote we ylkon wele
Hys power comes of ylka dele;
  Loved be god nyght & day
Þat haues us swylk a prophet sent. 3040
Mary þer wordes wyth gud entent
In hyr hert held scho ay.
Bot Iosep drawes to dedward fast;
Hys tyme es come; he may noȝt last; 3044
  Þat hym bus wend hys way;
Þus made he in Nazareth hys endyng. *Joseph dies.*
Mary broght hym to fayre beryng;
God haue his sawle þat best may. 3048

Now haue ȝe harde how Iosep endes [fol. 212a]
& grauen was þer emang hys frendes
  In Nazareth als ȝe here;
Bot mary eftyr hym scho dwelt þer syne 3052 *Mary lives with her mother, Anne.*
With anna, hyr moder, & with Emeryne
  Þat boyth ful sisters wer.
Of emeryne was borne be cryste
Elyȝabeth, þe moder o Iohn baptyste 3056
  Þat was gods derlyng dere;
& of anna was borne sykyrly
Goddes moder of heuen, myld mary,
  Blyssed be scho fer & nere. 3060

& sone when Ioachym dede was *Joachim dies and Anne marries Cleophas.*
Anna was wede to cleophas;
  And a doghter had scho þare.
Þe secunde mary þai called hyr so; 3064
Þe childe was wede to alpheo,
  & James alphet scho bare *After his death she marries Salome.*
& Iosep, hys brother; so two scho had.
Bot when cleophas was so bestrade 3068
  Þat he myght lyfe no mare,

Life of St. Anne

  Anna þe thryde tyme wedded suld be
  Unto ane husband þat hyght salame,
   Þis was a ferly fare.   3072

She has a daughter, Mary, by each husband.

  Þe thryd mary with hym had scho,
  & ʒebedee was þat chyld wed to,
   A wysman of lyffyng.
  Scho bare two chylder wele men weste,   3076
  Iames ʒebedei & Iohn Euangeliste ;
   Þis was a blyst beryng.
  & þerfore als þe story standys,
  Anna scho had thre husbandes   3080
   & bare thre marys ʒhyng.
  Þe chylder þus of þere two marys
  Ffolowed þe thryd in gods seruys ;
   Þus bade þai cristes commyng.   3084

  So with anne & all þat progene

Jesus is head of the house.

  Dwelled mary styll in þat cete,
   In naʒareth a gret thraw ;
  & ihesus was in þar company ;   3088
  Bot for he was wyse & most myghty
   Þai stode of hym gret aw,
  So mykyll þat þai wald no day ete
  To þai had dyght for hym hys sete   3092
   Als he lykyd hegh or law.
  No bred to ete wald þai none take
  Unto he blyssed yt & efter brake,
   & sythen þai gayf on raw ;   3096

Next him is Mary.

  & when þat ihesus was oght fra home
  Mary in hys stede scho come,
   & all þat menʒhe he blyste ;
  For scho was gude & full of grace ;   3100
  Þerfore next ihesus in þat place
   Held þai hyr þan þe beste.
  Bot ihesus he ʒode whore þat he wolde,
  Ffor þan was he fyften ʒer alde   3104
   & to gret doyng hym kest,
  For man & woman of sere seknes
  He helyd þat trowed on hym mor & les
   & deluels out of þam kest.   3108

Life of St. Anne

So was hys dedes gretly alowed [fol. 212b]
& mykyll of þe folke þat on hym trowed   Jesus heals many.
   Sayd þat wer seke bestade
Myght þai bat touche hys cote heme 3112
Þai suld be hale without̄en weme
   Of what yuel þat þai hade.
So gret vertu out of hym sprang
Þat mykyll folke trowed yt þam emang 3116
   With stedfast trough & sade;
& by þat moheson many a man
Solde and gayfe þat þai hade þan
   & folowyd hym with hert glad. 3120

Þai held yt so trew þat he þam techid,
For in all places euer he þam prechede
   Of þe kyngdom of heuene,
What yoy & blys þat þai suld haue 3124
Þat walde þer saules ffro syn save
   More þan any tong couth neuen.
Bot als þai folowed hym on a day
A leperous man sat be þe way, 3128
   To ihesus with ful myld steuen
*   *   *   *   *   *
*   *   *   *   *   *
   *   *   *   *   * 3132

Ihesus sayd, man, tell me þi tale.
What wyll þu? Lorde, he sayd, be hale
   Yf þat þi wyll ware.
& ihesus sayd: I wyll hale þe nowe. 3136
Be hale & trewly on me trowe;
   Þu sall be seke no mare;
Bot go now, schryfe þe to þe pryste
& after to god þan alther neste 3140
   Als moyses bad al bare.
Þe man did all as ihesus sayde
& was all hale; þan was he payde
   & folowed ay furth his fare. 3144

Ȝytt bade ihesus he suld no man tell,
Bot mykyll þe more how yt befell
   He told in ylka place;

& þe folk trowed hym wele enoghe.
Forþi to ihesus þe more þai droghe
& besoght hym ay of grace.
So þer was a lorde hyght Centurio
& unto ihesus þan sayd he so
Efter þis a lytell space :
Lord, my son full seke he lyse ;
Help hym & make hym hale to ryse
I pray þe in þis case.

Ihesus sayd, I come alsone
To hele þi childe withouten hone.
Centurio sayd : noȝt, nay
I am noȝt worthy me so bonetyuose
Þat þu suld entyr within my house ;
Fforþi do noȝt bot say
& I trow hale he sall be þane,
For in oure law am I swylke man
Þat so mykyll do I may :
To knyghtes þat under me er I wyse
Wylk of þam all I byde do þis
He dose yt sone allway.

[fol. 213a]

& whilke of my seruands þat I bide go
He rynnys & dosse my will also
What sall be done & howe ;
Þerfore, lorde, yf þi welles be
Þi byddyng suffys enogh to me.

*   *   *   *   *
*   *   *   *   *   *
*   *   *   *   *   *

Here may ȝe se mek hert bow,
For so trew trowth in Isaraell
Als I here now centureo tell
Ffand I neuer ȝyt als now.

Jesus heals a centurion's son.

Þerfore sayd ihesus centurio untyll :
Gude man, it sall be als þu wyll ;
For þu in trowth es trew.
Þi child sall þan be hale als faste
& in þi trouth yf þow wyll laste
It sall þe neuer more rew.

3148

3152

3156

3160

3164

3168

3172

3176

3180

3184

Hys saruandes hyghed hame þat stound
& fand hys child both hale & sound. 3188
 Þam made þar myrth enowe ;
Þai fell down & kyst ihesus fette
& sayde, þis passes state of prophete.
 For gods son þai hym knewe. 3192

Fra thyne to galile ihesus ȝode,
& als he past furth be þe se flode
 Two brether þer he saw ;
Peter, andrew both in a bote 3196
Wer fessheres & went þe soth I wote
 Fysshe for to take & draw.
Ihesus sayd to þam : comes, folowes me,
For fisshers of men þan sall ȝe be 3200
 & lay þis crafte full law.
Þai forsoke bath shyp and nete
& folowed hym fourth withoutyn lette
 Of his lare mare to knaw. 3204

Jesus goes to Galilee and chooses six disciples.

Bot als þai went furth forthermar
Another bote saw þai þam before,
 Thre wer þerin I wene,
Ȝebedee & als hys childer two, 3208
Iames & Iohn euangelist, was þer no mo ;
 Of fysshyng had þai bene.
Þer netes for old wer alto bryste
& þai mad þam agayn & dreste. 3212
 Bot ihesus with wordes full clene
Sayd to þaim two, folowes me belyve.
Þer fader & nettes all lat þai dryve
 & folowed hym boyth bedene. 3216

Bot forther in galilee als ihesus went
He met a man of full trew intent,
 & phelipp þan es his name,
Ffor he was borne in bethsayda 3220
& þat same cete come he fra,
 For þer was he at hame.
Ihesus bad hym, folow me now.
To hys byddyng sone did bow 3224
 Lett nouther for bleth no blame

Bot folowed hym furth als uther dyd.
With petir & andrew was it so betyd
  Þai & mo did þe same. 3228
So tyll a ton þai soth to wyt
& þer saw ihesus a toller sytt,
  Mathew hys name it was.

[fol. 213b]

Ihesus spake to hym on þis wysse: 3232
Come, folow me & fro þin þu ryse
  In mendyng of þi trespas.
Mathew lefte son all þat he hade
& folowed hym furth with hert glade 3236
  To what place he wald passe.
Þus had he sex onward o twelfe
Þat he had chosen chife for hymselfe
  Of þe dissiples þat he has. 3240

Bot in kaane of galele þare besyd
A gret brydell was dyght þat tyde
  With many men of menȝe
Thurgh ane archityclyne, a gret lord, 3244
And als þe boke beres gud recorde
  Most mayster of þat cete.
Bytwene whame þat brydell suld bene
Haue I in boke noȝt wretyn sene; 3248
  Þerfor lat I þam be.
Bot myld mary was prayd to be þer
& oþer women þat hyr cosyns war
  For gret solempnyte. 3252

Jesus attends a marriage and turns water into wine.

Als sone so archityclyne had understand
Þat jhesus was þar in þat land
  He prayd hym to þe brydall;
& he drest hym sone thyder to come; 3256
Of hys dyssipelys þan broght he sum—
  Þai come noȝt with hym all.
Bot because ihesus þat was þan his gest
Þai were wele serued ryght of þe best 3260
  With wild foule gret & small
& other dayntes full gud & gret.
Bot als þai wer in myddes þer mette
  Þis farly þer gun fall: 3264

Er þai had ettyn þai wantyd wyne.
Þe seruanteȝs had þan sorow & pyne
  & gretly marned þai all
& sayd, allas þat þai war borne;   3268
Our lorde honour & ours er lorne,
  For wyne what sall we say?
Mary herd how þai sayd & whatt;
Scho sayd to ihesus þer he satt: 3272
  Son, þer wyne es away.
To hyr agayn þusgat sayd he:
Woman, what es þat to þe & me?
  My tyme es noȝt þis day.   3276

Scho sayd: ȝys, for honour of þis fest
& also, son, at my beheste
  Kepe þaim fro velany.
Þan west scho wele do somqwat he wald;   3280
Fforþi þe seruandȝes to hir scho cald
  & bad þaim prevely,
What so þat my sone byddes ȝow do
Luke be leve þat ȝe ga þer to   3284
  & do yt sone & smerthly.
Sex gret water pottes stude þar
Þat for purificacon ordand war
  By þe law of Iewry.   3288

Ihesus sade þe seruandeȝs untyll,
Full of water þas pottes ȝe fyll;
  & qwen ȝe haue so don
Ffyll oute of þe lykour þat in þaim er   3292 [fol. 214a]
& to architiclyne ȝe itt bere,
  Pray hym drynk þerof sone.
Þe seruandȝes did ryght als ihesus bad
& filled þe peces with hert full glad,   3296
  Wald þai no langar hone.
Þai bare yt in & gaf to architiclyne.
He sayd: syre spous, whyne come þis wyne
  For hym þat syttes in trone?   3300

Ffor be my taste full wele me thynke
Þat I drank neuer are so gud drynke
  Sen I to man was wroght.

þe seruandtȝes wyst wele ynoghe 3304
Wheyn yt come, for þai yt droghe,
  Bot þe spous wyst it noȝt ;
& has used ȝyt euer more
To serve þe best wyne euer before 3308
  It drynke whils þaim gude thoght ;
Sythen wers when men had dronken wele,
Bot þis hys þe best assay and felle
  Ffor soth þat now es broght. 3312

They recognize the Christ.

Þus haue ȝe ȝemed gud wyne till now
For spous, spyrs þi seruandeȝs how
  Þis best come in hande.
Bot how ihesus made yt when þai whyst 3316
Hys comyng þider ylkon þai blyssyd
  & his fett kist kneland.
Son hys disciples ylka man
Trowed wele þat he was godes son þan 3320
  Be þat ferly þat þai fand.
Þis was þe fyrst myracle of all
Byfore Hys dissiples in þat hall
  Þat ihesus did in þat land. 3324

Ffor þis fayre myracle & oþer mo
Mykell folke gonn with ihesus go
  To what place als he ȝed,
& whore he welke thurgh any strett 3328
Seke folke drest þam hym to mette
  Þat of hys help had ned.
Croked & lame bath þai to hym led
& som þat lay bedredyn in þer bed ; 3332
  & he withouten drede
All þat euer wald trow one hym
He made þaim hale in lyth & lym,
  & þat þai folowed hym gud spede. 3336

Bot als þai went to Ierico warde
A blynd man satt be þe way & harde
  Mykyll folke walkand forby.
He spyrde som what myght be mene, 3340
& þai sayde Ihesus nazarene
  Com be þat way sykyrly.

To cry full lowde þan he begone
& sayd, þow ihesus, dauid sone, 3344
Of þis blynd haue mercy.
Som men þat ȝode ihesus before
Blamed hym & bad hym cry no more,
Bot he þe faster ay did cry. 3348

When ihesus com forgayn þat stede [fol. 214b]
Þer þe blend man satt to beg hys bred Jesus heals
& hard hym so cry & rare, a blind man.
He bad byfore hym he suld be broght; 3352
Bot als he come ȝyt he sesyd noȝt
To cry he wald noȝt spare.
He sayd, what wald þu I did fore þe?
Lorde, noȝt bot make me for to se 3356
Yf þat þy wyll ware,
Ffor þu may do yt of þi gret myght.
Ihesus sayd, þu sall haue þi syght.
Bad hym se, sayd he na mare, 3360

& þe trew trouth man sall þi salve.
He lovyd god & sayd, now I haue Many
Myn egh syght fayre & clere. believe on
Ylke man he told how yt betyd 3364 him.
& folowed hym furth als oþer dyd,
Hys dissiple als he were.
Thurghout þat land boyth old & ȝyng
All þat harde of Ihesus doyng 3368
Trowed on hym boyth fer & ner.
Ihesus lefte þaim in a cete,
Toke þaim þat suld hys postils be,
Went furth by a reuer; 3372

& als he went byfore allone
Behynd hym come petyr & jone
& oþer apostils yll payd.
For þai sayde ilkon als þai ȝode, 3376
Emang us all bere we no gude
Na for us es noȝt pervade;
Þis es to us a full hevy lyffe
At forsake catell, childer, & wyfe 3380
Or walke yll þus arayde.

Jesus tells his disciples what their rewards shall be.

& nothyng es us hyght in certayn
What we sall haue þerfore agayne.
  Fforþi to ihesus peter sayd: 3384

Lorde, þai þat all þis warlde forsakes
& to þi techyng trowes & takes
  & walkes with þe allway
Þis sympil lyfe with þe to lede,   3388
What we sall haue þerfore to mede,
  Lefe lorde, wyll þu us say?
Ʒe þat þis warld for me refuse
& my techyng wyll trowe & use   3392
  Ʒe sall won with me ay.
Bot specially say I unto ʒow twelfe
Þat ʒe sall sytt ryght with my selfe
  & deme þis world on domes day.   3396

Ʒa & all þat euer forsakes & leves
Ffor my lufe landes, rentes, & greues,
  Catell, corn, & men,
Wyfs & childer, syluer & glode,   3400
Þai sall haue þerfore a hundreth fold
  I wot wele whore & qwhen.
And als þai sall haue þe blys of heuen
Whare joy ys more þan tung may neuen   3404
  Or eye may se or ken.
Vnto þat gret blys he us bryng,
Ihesus of wham es made þis thyng,
  Þerto says all amen.   3408

[fol. 215a]

You have now heard Christ's story as John the evangelist wrote it.

Now haue ʒe harde yf ʒe take hede
Of ihesus mykyll & hys chyldhede
  Þat he did in his yhouth
Tyll tyme he come into mans state   3412
Als saynt Iohn euangelyst it wrate,
  For next hym best he couth;
& als þe boke says who yt drew
Ihesus þe fyrst of all in grew   3416
  Made yt with hys awn mouth.
Ffor he was all relygyus þan
& þat tyme religion fyrst began
  Þerof thynkes som sel couth.   3420

Life of St. Anne

Bot saynt mathew eftyrward wele & fyn
Out of grew turnyd yt in latyn
  & had þus in doyng
At þe prayer of bysshopes two,   3424
Cromassi and Elydon men called þai so,
  Twa gude men of lyfyng.
& for all þis ȝyt es þer some
Þat says it es apocrysome   3428
  & none autentyk thyng.
Bot þer es nathyng done thynk me
Þat yt by possybylyte
  May be of gods wirkyng.   3432

& sen he become man for our gude
& touke als we haue flessh & blude
  In mary mayden wemlesse,
Thurgh kynde of man þan burd hym nedes   3436
In hys ȝong age do some child dedes
  Has saynt paule beres wytnesse.
For þus he says & yt so betyd,
When I was child, child dedes I dyd   3440
  & als a child wyt es;
& when to man stat I was broght
I voyde my child dedes & þan wroght
  Als a man dos neuerþelesse.   3444

Þus ihesus wroght on þis same wysse
& also mad he mo maystryse
  Emang þe Iewes so kene
Þat þai suld trow in hym yf þai wold   3448
& als god sone hym ken and holde
  For myracles þat wer sene.
Bot for þai hym & hys refusyd
Ffra pyne þai sall noȝt be excused   3452
  On domysday als I wene.
Þus es þis made for mans lernyng.
God graunt us heuen at our endyng;
  Says all amen bedene.

      Explicit Tractatus Bonus.

St. Matthew later wrote the story in Latin. It is called apocryphal.

II

The Life of St. Anne

MS. Trin. Coll. Camb. 601
(English Poets R. 3. 21).

[fol. 221a]   Incipit Vita Sancte Anne matris Sancte Marie Virginis

Invocation.
     O blyssyd Ihū that art full of myght
     The ground of vertu and of all goodnes,
     Qwykyn my derkenes and send me som lyght,
     Ffor in the ys verray sykernes ;   4
     Be my comfort and streyngth my febylnes
     In that I wold take on me for to wryte,
     Mekely besechyng thy grace to endyte.

Confession of weakness.
     Ffor in my sylf ryght well I undyrstand   8
     My wytte but sympyll and lak eke of connyng,
     Ffull vnabyll to take suche thyng on hand,
     Weyke of spyryt and febyll in doyng
     Sauyng oonly by the gret supportyng;   12
     Wherfore good lord now make I my request
     To quyte me lyke as hyt pleseth the best.

     Gret foly were and also presumpsion
     In hym that ys both naked and bareyn   16

The results of a collation of the poem on the life of St. Anne contained in MS. Chetham 8009 with that in Trinity College, Cambridge, 601 (R. 3. 21) are given herewith. Variant spellings have been neglected, but an effort has been made to give all variant readings contained in the Chetham MS. version of the poem. My thanks are due to the Librarian of the Chetham Society, Mr. Charles T. E. Phillips, who made a copy of the poem contained in the Chetham MS. The variant readings are taken from this copy, which has been collated with photographic reproductions of twelve of the twenty-two pages of the MS. This collation revealed only two errors of consequence. The accuracy of the copy, therefore, may be accepted with confidence. Incipit Vita, etc., *is omitted*.

     6. For *is omitted*.   8. . . I ryght wel . . .   10. . . suche a thyng . . .   15. Also *is omitted*.

As in makyng to lak discrecion
  Where nothyng ys to harde were to constreyn;
The trouth to sey I wyll be to yow pleyn,
I am vnpurueyed and in nowyse sure   20
Safe my good wyll feyne wold I put in vre.

Thus half in feare, somdell in cowardyse,
  Whyche ys in man a gret displesure,
Sore I am troubled many sondry wyse—   24
  Nothyng acordyng vnto my plesure,
  But euyn clene contrary to my desyre.
I wold be sory truly to offend;
Natwithstandyng to labour I entend.   28

Ffrom heuen cometh helpe ys an old prouerbe,   *The author looks to heaven for help.*
  Wherfore I wyll take now to me corage.
God yaue vertu both to stone and herbe
  Whiche be vnresonable as in parage;   32
  He were to blame and also gret damage
That hath hys wytte ioynyd to reson
But yef he occupy well hys seson.

Hyt ys a vertu to rede in storyes   36 [fol. 221b]
  And holy seynts lyfes to translate.   *The value of reading and translating saints' lives.*
Hit causeth to be in the memoryes
  Of well disposyd pepyll in good state—
  To theym where grace ys nothyng desolate   40
But by perseueraunce theym to apply,
Sore repentaunce puttyng awey foly.

Ffor he that ys repentaunt as I rede
  Mercy to hym cannot be denyed.   44
Gentyll Ihū hys owne body dyd sprede
  Ffor all synners on the crosse belyed
  And of the cruell iewes defyed;
Wherfore take me now vnto thys good hede,   48
He neuer faylyd creature at nede.

He that for helpe lyst mekely to hym call,
  He ys redy to euery good entent.

22. . . and sumwhat . . .   25. . . to my . . .   42. Sore repentant . . .   46. . . lyed . . .   48. . to þat . . .

   To let, I wyll nat what soeue*r* befall;   52
    I wyll kepe forth my p*ur*pose as I ment.
   More hardynes the good lord hath me sent
    A gret dell then I had at the begynnyng;
   I trust hys grace shall bryng hit to endyng. 56

   To be rebukyd, lo, I were to blame
    In myn owne mynde for doyng my dewte.
   Of ve*r*tuous labo*ur* cam neue*r* yet shame,
    Ffor idylnes ys nought in no degre   60
   The moder of vyce ys I am in suerte;
   Therfore I wyll besy me to spede
   And call aboue for help when I haue nede.

The three great virtues: mercy,

   In hym ys me*r*cy; in hym ys pyte;   64
    Beware ye cruell herts mercyles!
   Remember hym well; take good hede and se;
    Put clene fro you yowr froward crewelnes;
   Ye shall repent hit to sore els dowteles, 68
   Ffor man wit*h*out me*r*cy mercy shall mys;
   He shall haue me*r*cy that me*r*cifull ys.

[fol. 222*a*]

   Bethynk yow well on thys noble story
    Of pore lazar and diues in yo*ur* mynde— 72
   How ryche he was and now ys so sory
    Because to lazar he was so vnkynde.

pity,

   Ffor lak of grace he was to blynde
   In worldly ryches wi*th*outen pyte;   76
   Fforeue*r*more therfor dampnyd ys he.

   O noble ve*r*tu callyd pyte
    That art so gret in the hygh court aboue,
   Well ys hym that endewed ys wi*th* the 80
    Whyche came downe clerely for ve*r*rey loue
   Ffor worldly ioy neyther to heve ne shoue.
   Neue*r* man yet red in holy scripture
   A peteous man dampnyd, thys am I sure. 84

---

52. . . what so befalle. 53. I wyll kepe forth myne entent.
58. . . to do my dute. 61. Ys *is omitted.* 62. . . to proceed.
75. . . pe*r*de he wase blynd. 78. . . I callyd petye. 81. Which camest doune for very pure love. 82. . . nether heve . . .
83. . . rede yet . . .

O per*f*yte charyte whyche are wi*th*outen pere, — charity.
   Thow art best werthy forto haue the thre
And to be worshyppyd ferre and nere,
   Ffor all ve*r*tues byn groundyd apon the, — 88
   Ffeythe and hope of thy consanguinite.
He that these iij lacketh ys but clene shent;
Wo shall he be that hath hys tyme so spent.

I lowly make now me peticion — 92 Petition to 'masters.'
   To all masteres that thys shall here or rede,
Submyttyng me to yowre co*r*reccion,
   Ffor vnconnyng my symple penne doth lede
As a voyce in feare and eke in drede; — 96
Thys ys the fyrst and eke the begynnyng
Besechyng yow of yowr good supportyng.
     Explicit prologus.

O Blessyd Anne aboue p*r*edestinate, — [fol. 222*b*]
   Chose by the godhede of hys gret goodnes — 100 Tribute to St. Anne.
To be moder of that inuiolate!
   Most glorious vyrgyn, grounde of mekenes,
   Moder to the secund pe*r*son pereles
Abydyng styll in pure virgynyte — 104
And euer shall in pe*r*petuyte!

Most dere brethern, thys day to vndyrstand,
   As hit apereth by the story,
We halow and worshyp in eue*r*y land — 108 Exposition to the audience.
   Of seynt Anne chefe the festfull memory,
   Whyche ys departyd and ys in glory
And hath forsaken the carnall pryson
Of the body to the soule a dongeon. — 112

Thys gloryous Anne, happy, full of grace,
   Ys caryed vp most worshipfully
To the hyghest of seynts in that place

---

85. A parfet man which whith ou3te art*e* pere.   86. . . to haue degre.   87. . . both fe*r* and nere.   88. For all rownd are gronddyd on the.   91. . . hys tym mysspent.   92. . . mak my peticyon.   93. . . se or red.   99*a*. Explicit prologus et incipit vita b*e*ate Anne Matris Marie.   100. . . thy gret goodnes.   107. . . by the historye.   109. Of sent anne the festfull memorey.

With the seruyce of aungelles truly 116
   Vnto the euerlastyng company
Of patriarks and prophets old;
   She ys comyn with ioyes manyfold.

Of whom she hath takyn hyr begynnyng 120
   And hyr flesshly habite by trewe discent
That god shuld send so by hyr forth bryngyng
   Vnto hys peple—thys was the entent
   Of the pure godhede sothly by assent— 124
By the frute of hyr wombe redempcion
And vtterly distroy discencion.

Why Holy Church worships St. Anne.

Therfore oure modyr, all holy chyrche clere,
   Of thys holy matrone doth both ioy and syng, 128
Cardyd and holdyn vp both fer and nere
   By hyr suffragys, and that in euery thyng;
Wherfore with all deuocion yeuyng
   In preysyng of hyr gret laude and thanke, 132
Ffor of oure wele she was the verrey banke.

[fol. 228a]

She ys forsoth that blessyd hygh erthe syne
   Of the whyche the heuynly potter hath made
Of the most swete shoure of hys dewe dyuyne; 136
   The pot of oure hope whiche shall neuer fade
   The son of god conceued vs to glade
In oure nature hath brought forth incarnate,
Whyche of the hygh influence was create. 140

She ys the goodly felde circumspect
   With floures of the heuynly bames,
Of whos swetnes the verrey preelect
   Diffuse odours clene withouten blames, 144
   Hath wellyd out with hys fragraunt floures
Of lyfe by the costes so louyngly
Of all the world to comfort feythfully.

117. Unto the everlastyng lyffe trulye and companey. 141. . . . in circumspecte.
143-145. Hath wellyd oughte wit hys flagrant flourys swete
    Deffuse oþer witouten blamys
    Of whose swettnes the very swetnes.

And in thys felde the spouse of vyrgyns all 148
   Hath medled hys myrre most delycious
With hys swete flauoures, whyche byn ethrall,
   Hath tempred with the swetnes precious
By the infinite power glorious 152
Of hys most excellent diuinite
The bitternes of oure sore mortalite.

Blyssed Anne, whyche in operacion
   Of oure redempcion ys gone out 156
Lyke as the rote hath dominacion
   Of the tre and the braunches rounde about,
   Of whom the heuynly rodde withouten dout
Ys comen out that most blyssyd virgyne, 160
Seynt mary, thys derk world to enlumyne;

St. Anne is mother of the Blessed Virgin.

Whyche, gret with chylde, hyr owne begotyn son,
   The hygh almond of the most dyuyne floure
Hath brought forth to sease oure dyuysion; 164
   Of whos swetnes dayly and euery houre
   The ioyfull refeccion and sucoure
Ffedeth the aungellys in heuyn aboue
And men in erthe of verrey pure loue. 168

Of bethlem, forsoth, that nobyll cyte   [fol. 223b]
   Of Dauid Anne ys gone out sycurly
And come out of the hygh rote of Iesse,
   Whos blyssyd chyld, that holy seynt mary, 172
Cryste hath brought forth and borne most perfytely,
Whyche the captiuite had turnyd clene
Of Iacob and all comyng of hys strene;

St. Anne is of the city of David and stock of Jesse.

And also the most harde durabyll wall 176
   Of oure old auncyen enimyte
Betwene god and man clerely ouerall;
   And by the mene of hys natyuyte
God in hys manhode of hys gret pyte 180
Hath distroyed oonly of hys grace
And ordeynyd hath vs to hys hygh palace.

---

150. Wit hys swete flourys which bene eternall.   154. The bytternes. . .   168. As men . . .   170. Off Anne dauyth ys gonne ouȝte sekyrly.   177. . . . auncyent diuinite.   178. By god and . . . 182. . . . hyȝe place.

How gloryous, how worthy and dere,
    Ys thys modyr & eke how precyous   184
To be takyn with hyr solempne prayere,
    Whyche hath brought vs a moder most famous
Of oure redempcion verrey ioyous
And in hyr includyd the testament   188
Of the hygh heritage by consentement;

Praise St. Anne as mother of the Blessed Virgin.

Wherfore we ought to preyse thys holy Anne,
    Modyr of thys most holy virgine,
With all worshyp that may be had or canne.   192
    And with the holy pryuylege diuine
    She has begoten hyr that ys most dygne,
Wheryn she passeth other moders all—
More happyer and in especiall   196

Of suche a chylde to ioy the priuilege
    Truly that shuld hyr owne maker begete;
And of all other, the trouthe to allege;
    Therfore ioy thow and be glad in thy fete,   200
    Thow happy modyr, before other grete
In conceuyng and bryngyng forth also
Suche oon that hath sesyd all oure wo;

[fol. 224a]

By whom the aungeles haue theyr gladnes,   204
    And the ryght wisemen haue theyr perfyte grace,
And synners forouer foryeuenes
    By meryte of thys modyr in thys cace,
    Of the modyr of cryst, owre chyef solace,   208
Euer styll abydyng virgyn pure and clene,
And euer shall; she ys oure parfyte mene.

The name of Anne to say hyt ys but grace;
    Ffor whyche, dere brethern, ye shall vndyrstond   212
She ys of grace full of the hyghest place
    In whom the herytage most surely doth stond
    Of oure fadyr Iacob, lowsyng the bond

---

183. How glorious and how worthy . . .   184. . . full precyous.
188. And in hyr meludye . . .   191. Most *is omitted*.   193. Diuine *is omitted*.   196. . . and more in specyall.   199. . . tyll a lege.
202. In contayning . . .   203. . . hath I seasyd . . .   205. . . ryȝttuouse men . . .   206. And the synnerys . . .   211. Hyt *is omitted*.   212. For why . . .

By hyr most ennobelyd magnificence, 216
Puttyng awey clene all vyolence.

The twelue sonnes of Iacob veryly *St. Anne occupies a place with Jacob and his twelve sons,*
   Support the ground of the fundacion
Of the holy place of Anne truly. 220
   They lyste hit clene by hygh elacion,
The most noble regale formacion.
Ezechias and Ozias also, *with Ezechias and Ozias,*
Whyche byn bryght shynyng with other many mo 224

As precious stones incomperabyll
   In the felyshyp yeuyng theyr beames;
And in the hous of the modyr stabyll
   Regale of god hath sent out hys stremes 228
   With so crestyons shynyng and lemes
No tong can tell how meruelously
Of the hygh influence copiously;

Among whom Iudas and Leui do shyne 232 *and with Judas and Levi.*
   Before all other there most myghtyly;
Of whom the kyngdom and presthode by lyne
   Of the same pepyll ys gon out truly.
   The corner stone Cryst hath bound hem surely 236
Togedyr as two stone walles most sure
In the blyssyd Anne, modyr clene and pure.

In hyr holsom formacion only [fol. 224*b*]
   She ys that most clere materal copious 240
Of the hyghest beldyng to magnyfy;
   Of the kynrede of whom god gloryous,
   The fadyr all mighty most precyous,
Ffouchesafe to make a syngler place new; 244
Of the glorious modyr and vyrgyn trew;

Of hys owne only begoten son dere, *This is St. Anne's Day.*
   Thys day, dere brethern, most specyally
In honour of thys matrone ferre and nere, 248
   Most worshipfull and blessyd entyerly,
   As we haue seyde before, now veryly

---

218. Treulye the . . .   229. With so crafty schenyng lemys.
233. There *is omitted*.   237. To god as . . .   248. . . fer ne nere.   249. Most blyssyd and worschipful interlye.

	And in thys day togedyr we byn come	
	We stedefastly beleue both all and some.	252
Joachim is husband of Anne.	Out of thys world she ys depertyd clene;	
	And worthy hit ys yet neuertheles	
	To laude and preyse hyr housbond by som mene,	
	Blyssyd Ioachym, the man of nobles,	256
	And of the most parfyte hygh holynes,	
	Whyche were both oon flesshe ioynyd parfytely;	
	Of whom procedyd euyn naturally	
	The most blyssyd and glorious virgyn.	260
Parentage of Mary.	As god wold haue hym in oure worshippyng,	
	Fforsoth the storyes shewyn by dyuyne	
	That the most clere and parfyte begynnyng	
	Of thys worshipfull virgyn, forth comyng	264
	Out of the stok of Dauid, veryly	
	Allwey styll pure, yeuyng lyghte feythfully	

Virtues of Joachim and Anne

Vnto thys derk world most prosperyously.
   Hyr fadyr Ioachim neuertheles,   268
And Anne forsoth, hyr modyr eke truly,
   Of worldly goodys lackyd none doubtles;
   They were mighty and puissaunt in nobles,
Of erthely thyngs so gret influence   272
Passing all other ferre in excellence;

[fol. 225a]

But yet were they more myghty a gret dele
   Of proud vertues euydently
As for theyre worldly ryches yet and wele   276
   In the encresyng toke none hede onely.
   Hyt was a thyng they set but lytell by;
But rather iustly ioyed in vertew,
Lawfully to lyue, all vice to eschew;   280

Ne theyre appetyte was so mykell
   In the ioy of thys world to folow here,
   But more a gret dele redy to fulfyll

251. . . to god we be . . .   256. . . the man of gret noblenes.
258. Both *is omitted*.   261. . . in oure worschiping to redres.
263-66   That the most clere and perfet hygh holynes
         Blyssyd Joachym the man of noblenes
         Which wer one fleche joned perfetlye
         Com ouȝte of the stok of Davyd verely.
281. Nor yet per haptyte . . .   283. Redy *is omitted*.

The heuynly lustyse that bothe ferre and nere 284
They besyd hem where that the pepyll were
And labored bothe sore in studying
In the law of god wit*h*out quarellyng.

Ffor the whyche they lyued in the pepyll of god; 288
But moche more studiously they were;
And in theyre deuocion was to gret od,
Passing all other of that same pepyll clere;
In theyre lyuyng they were wit*h*outyn pere, 292
Whyche brought forth of theyre most noble kynrede
Most shynyng sterre coueryd wit*h* the godhede;

Whyche of hys pyte hath brought forth a boose
Of the thorny pepyll, yet notwit*h*standyng 296
The fadyr and modyr wit*h*outen gloose
Of thys most holy pure virgyn beyng
Were clene wit*h*outen thornes hauyng;
But yet of theym byn they com rese*r*uyd, 300
By godds speciall grace p*r*eserued.

The iewes be lykenyd to thornes   The Jews
Ffor theyre obstinate froward crokydnes;   likened to
They may be callyd thorny, well ywys. 304   thorns.
Fforwhy? The thorne ys bareyn and fruteles;
So in theym ys nomaner of goodnes
But byn p*er*seueraunt in theyre errour,
Fforsakyng clene the heuynly socour. 308

Also they cam bothe verrey felolbly   [fol. 225*b*]
All of one wyll in p*er*fyte charyte.   The
They were ioynyd togeder lawfully   marriage of
In the nobyll cyte of galyle— 312   Joachim and Anne.
The contrey callyd ys nazareth parde—
Where Ioachim, the fadyr, was borne sure,
And Anne the modyr in Bethlem so pure.

And for they were bothe vnto god so iust, 316 They share
And all men as well, wit*h*outyn fable,   their
Ffor in hym was theyre verrey inward trust,   wealth.

284. That *is omitted*.   285. That *is omitted*.   295. . . . hath
brouȝth forth a rose.   302. . . we lekenyd . . .   306. . . no
man of goodnes.   311. They joyned wer to god lawfullye.
315. So pure *is omitted*.   316. . . to god . . .   317. And to all
men . . .

To the tempyll of god nothyng varyable
　　To nedy pylgryms eke bothe ferme & stable　　320
Yeuyng two partys of theyr propre goodes
By oon assent and with ryght good modys;

The thryd part to theyr owne vse reseruyd,
　　Wheron they lyuyd bothe temporally　　324
And were susteynyd and so preseruyd.

They are childless for twenty years.

　　Ffortosey bareyn they were both truly
　　About the seson of yeres twenti.
The tempyll of god where that they hauntyd　　328
Deuoutly praying there god worshipped

Sertayn dayes, as they were wonyd to done,

They pray for a child and promise it to God's service.

　　That they myght bothe deserue and in that case
Som worthy frute to god—thys was theyr bone—　　332
Of theyr owne flessh bryng forth withyn a space,
A son or a doughter onely by grace;
And whan that they had made theyr solempne avowe
There as they were in godds seruice howe　　336

What maner chylde soeuer they shuld begete
　　By godds yefte besechyng inwardly.
Aftyr thys Ioachym hys wo was grete,

Isacar rebukes Joachim.

　　Heryng the rebuke that so vnkyndely　　340
　　Of Isacar, the bysshop, thretyngly
As fortosey he callyd hym bareyne:
There ys no frute brought forth betwene yow tweyne

[fol. 226a]

In Israell; and when he thus had seyde　　344
　　Anon both sory and eke confusyd
Went forth hys wey and was euyn dismayed,

Joachim flees to his flocks.

　　Nat to hys howse as he somtyme vsyd
　　Ne to hys wyfe—he was clene abusyd—　　348
But to hys shepards sothly he went
Tyll bettyr tydyngs to hym were sent.

An angel promises Joachim a daughter

And the pyte dyuyne dyd recomfort
　　Hys greuous anguysshes and hys gret peyn.　　352
An aungell from heuyn downe to hym resort,

---

320. Eke *is omitted*.　　328. That *is omitted*.　　332. Sum
worschip frute . . .　　337. What maner of chylde they schulde beget.
339. Att thys . . .　　350. Tyll better tydyng wer to hym sente.
352. Hys grevuos anguesschis . . .　　353. . . . to hym dyd resorte.

Life of St. Anne

    Bothe syght and spekyng made hym ve*rr*ey feyn,
    And promysyd hym a mayden soue*r*eyn
    Of hys begetyng truly to be born   356
    To releue all that were but clene forlorn.

who shall become mother of the Son of God.

    Sothly that a me*r*uelous dignite
    Of the chyld pronouncyd by the aungell
    Shuld opynly be knowyn in all degre,   360
    And also a me*r*uelous clerete befell;
    The aungell of lyghte sent there for to tell
    To Ioachym, the fadyr, wi*th* gret lyght
    The aungell dyd appere to hym in syght;   364

    And to hym declared of that virgyne
    That shuld be borne, callyd the ve*rr*ey lyght,
    Comyng forth of the heuynly lyght to shyne
    So mickyll thys holyest virgyn bryght,   368
    Modyr to com and chose by godds myght
    To be the modyr of all holynes,
    Whyche that was born sure in clene pe*r*fytenes

    Of the most holy couple lawfully.   372
    Therfore forsoth of ryght hit most nede be
    That of all good the best ys she suerly;
    And of all holy the holyest ys she;
    Of bareyns frutefull virgynyte.   376
    And the most habundaunt frutefulnes
    Whyche shuld be born clere in parfyte goodnes,

    As a good tree bryngeth forth a ioyfull floure
    And of that floure a ve*rr*ey frute of lyfe.   380
    The furst were good, parfyte in eue*r*y houre*r*;
    The secund bettyr ferre wi*th*outen stryfe
    That blyssyd vyrgyn modyr, mayde, and wyfe
    At the last of these best incom*p*erabyll,   384
    Whyche bryngyng forth was most alowabyll

    That co*m*meth of a good fadyr and modyr.
    The commyng of the most blessyd virgyne
    Mary ys bettyr passyng all other   388

[fol. 226*b*]

354. . . mad hym verely to fayne.   357. . . that was clene forlorne.   361. And *is omitted*.   364. . . evyn to hym in sy3te.   375. And of all holyest . . .   379. . . frute or fleure.   384. But the last of thes both incom*p*erable.   387. . . of that most . . .

> Of whom the chylde that she brought forth most digne,
> As fortosey that blessyd frute dyuyne
> Of hyr wombe, ys good chyef aboue all thyng,
> Ffor he was verrey lord of all and kyng. 392

Excellence of the Blessed Virgin.

> Thys holy vyrgyn of these good commyng
> Ys bettyr and best of all hyr kynrede,
> Borne in the house of hyr fadyr beyng
> And by the space of iij yere in dede 396
> Brought forth and kept with aungells by theyr rede;
> Hyt ys beleuyd theryn no dout ys;
> To lytell and moche the trouth cannat mys.

> Also the trouthe techyng that hyt ys thus 400
> Known playnly by informacion
> And ys proued moche truer vnto vs;
> Ffor to make a trew declaracion,
> Ther ys none hath suche dominacion 404
> Insomoche ther can be nothyng so trew:
> She chaunged oure sorowes vnto ioyes new;

Angels keep Mary.

> That from the begynnyng she was kept sure
> With holy aungeles allwey hourely— 408
> Thys holyest virgyn that was so pure—
> Fforsoth, for they had knowlege certeynly
> Of hyr gret power to com so myghtyly;
> Aftyr allmyghty god aboue all clene, 412
> They knew she shuld of heuyn and erthe be quene.

[fol. 227a]
Genealogy of Anne.

> Begynnyng of the holy euangell
> Sheweth by tretyng aftyr mathew.
> The boke of the genology doth tell 416
> The nobyll discent; how that they came a rew
> Lynyally, the playn trouthe for to shew,
> Of Ihū cryst, the son of Dauid kyng,
> Son of Abraham, soforth downe commyng. 420

> And so forth the verrey pleyne Omely
> Of dyuerse tretyse ys drawyn oute;
> Therfor mathew euaungelist holy,

396. . . thre yere per being inded.   407. . . so sure.   409 thys holy . . .   418. Lenally the playne trough to schew   420. . . forsoth doune comyng.

Wrytyng the booke clerely without doute, 424
And besyd hym to bryng hit aboute
Of Ihū crysts generacion,
Makyng pleynly the declaracion,

And callyd hym the son of these above; 428
By other promyssys made certeynly
Whyche was done of verrey speciall love.
To these two cryst made repromyse onely
Long before thys to Abraham truly, 432
And seyde that all the pepyll in thy sede
Shal be blessyd on erthe with the godhede.

And also to dauid forsoth he seyde:
Of the frute of thy wombe shall syt on thy sete. 436
Abraham brought forth Isaac to eyde,
And Isaac Iacob he dyd begete;
Thys foloweth forsoth the trouth for to trete
The manhode of crysts generacion, 440
Whyche that he toke for oure sauaceron.

Mathew from the begynnyng of the promyse
That ys to Abraham, remembryng
The most noble progenitours and wyse, 444
Whyche lyneally procedyng doth bryng
Vnto Ioseph a verrey chosyn thyng,
Housbond of the blyssyd virgyn mary,
Of whom was borne swete Ihūs sycurly. 448

Whoso beholdeth and redeth onely [fol. 227b]
The hystory pleyn of the euanngell
In crysts most noble genology
All of habundaunce renneth as a welle 452
Downe vnto Anne, as the story doth telle
That she shuld be a verrey chosyn merke
Of lawe and grace forto fulfyll thys werke;

By whom ys seyn that the gret dygnyte 456
Of all mankynde in cryste shuld floryssh new;
And of hyr wombe forsoth hyt ys to se

429. Made *is omitted*. 433. And sayd all the people of thy sede,
436. . . schall be set on thy fet. 439. Thys folowed forth . . .
454. Chosyn *is omitted*.

Mary is the white cloth of Holy Church—its meaning.

She brought the floure forth; chyeff of all vertew.
Long before thys, whyche nedys most be trew, 460
The holygost seyde that of holy chyrche
A whyte clothe was made all oure wele to wyrche.

Ffiguryng of thys whyte cloth she hath made
Of whytenes the colour incomperable; 464
Hyt ys the same the whyche shall neuer fade.
The holygost spake of most laudable
That blyssyd virgyn euer veritable;
She ys the whyte clothe and syndony 468
That brought vnto all synners remedy

Whyche was most pure; and that she solde
And toke a gyrdyll to the Canane.
The snowy whytenes passeth manyfolde 472
Of thys syndony betokeneth purete;
And the virginall clennes to beholde
In the whyche the blyssyd modyr Anne
Abydyng styll whyche that she weued thanne. 476

The vndyrstandyng of thys Canane
Ys he that loueth wonder feruently;
So dyd the good lord in hys mageste.
She was the self and eke the same truly 480
That she toke to the gyrdell certeynly;
And for the gyrdyll what that hit doth mene,
Certys hyt ys the virgyne pure and clene.

[fol. 228a]

She was gyrdyll to the most louly lombe, 484
The secund persone of the trynyte,
When that he was withyn hyr blessyd wombe.
The most feythfull trew louer yet was he
That euer was; of hys gret pyte 488
He suffred peynes and oppression
Euyn wyllyngly for oure transgression.

When the modyr of good, blessyd mary,
That day she sprang in our nature humayne 492
And brought hyr forth in forme temporally

---

459. Chyeff *is omitted*. 460. . . which must neds . . . 470. Which þat . . . 476. . . with þat sche . . . 480. He wase the selffe and eke the sonn truly. 482. That *is omitted*. 484. Sche was gyrdyll to the most holy love. 487. . . . wase sche.

Out of the palace of hyr wombe certayne
   To the redempcion of mankynde playne
Whyche she solde to god, the fadyr aboue,   496
And in that virgyn was nothyng but loue.

Hyt well appereth the son incarnate
   Of the fadyr all myghty made shuld be ;
Pryce of the modyr clene i*m*maculate   500
   And that *p*recious virgyn mary fre
   Shuld appere to those in captyuyte
Clene to delyu*er* hem out of thraldom
By hyr gret goodnes and blyssyd wisdom.   504

Whereof the holy aungell from god was sent
   To show vnto the fadyr and modyr
Of thys most holy vyrgyn the entent
   That shuld be borne excedyng fer all other,   508
   Of oure feythe to be the guyde and rother,
Shewyng to hem hyr name and eke hyr lyfe ;
Hyr comyng pleyne to seasyng of all stryfe

Also pronounced hyr in the tyme com*m*yng   512 Gabriel greets Mary.
   The modyr of the son of god to be ;
To whom the gret aungell seyde accordyng,
   Gabraell, when he gret hyr on hys kne,
   When she was come to full age in the gre   516
Of maryage spousyd certeynly
To holy Ioseph, but nat carnally

Ne coupled by carnall affeccion—   [fol. 228*b*]
   The conneccion was ve*r*rey heuynly—   520 The heavenly marriage of Joseph and Mary.
The godhede toke holely direccion ;
   Natw*ith*standyng hit was lawfully
   Aftyr the course and forme vsually,
There was no sensuall part that greued ;   524
Hyt was all godly and so hyt preued.

Sothely aftyr thys salutacion
   Holy and worthy sent fro the hyghest
To suche a virgyne of p*r*obacion,   528

497. As in þat bargayne wase . . .   516. . . . to fulfill the . . .
522. . . . wase dunne lawfully.   525. Godly *is omitted*.

Excedyng all other both most and lest,
She was the verrey modyr of behest
To thys world that hath brought feythfully
The tresure of oure fynaunce fynally;   532

Mary was predestined to be the world's comfort.

She was the vessell of eleccion
Chosyn by the deyte gloryous
To bere hym that shuld make redempcion
Ffor all mankynde, shent and dolorous.   536
The aungell seyde to hyr gracious:
The holyest that euyr was or shal be;
Thow blessyd virgyn, shal be borne of the;

He shalbe called verrey godds son.   540
She was kept therfor most souerenly
In kepyng of aungells that seson;
They wallyd hyr clene round about surely.
Suche obseruaunce they dyd, and gret cause why: 544
They knew ryght well she shuld bryng forth the kyng
Of aungellys passyng all erthely thyng;

And a gret whyle before that she was borne
Hyr name was knowyn, hyr lyfe and dignite,   548
To bere hym that shuld were the crowne of thorne;
Preuyded by the blessyd trynyte,
She was predestinat, and none but she,
To be the worlds verrey chief comfort   552
By hym that shuld out of hyr wombe resort.

[fol. 229a]

But vnto thys maner of kepyng most sure,
That ys fortosey heuynly and aungelike,
Was gret in the fadyrs hous and pure;   556
But more excedyng ferre and autentyke
In the holy houshold of god nat lyke;
Whyche for to speke of ys incomperable,
No tong can tell how delectable.   560

Mary dedicated to God.

Of whom forsoth she was offryd vp pleyn;
In the temple bothe fadyr and modyr
To god presentyd hyr there both tweyn;

537. . . to hyr glorious.   543. Round *is omitted*.   552. Verrey *is omitted*.   555. That ys to say . . .

Life of St. Anne

And he receuyd hyr and none othyr, 564
Whyche passeth before all the other;
Natw*ith*standyng the other was ryght good,
Thys ys ve*r*re bettyr, whoso vndyrstood.

God that hath takyn hyr to hym self truly, 568
He hath kept hyr of hys inly goodnes;
By hys holy aungelys besyly
He hath p*rese*ruyd hyr full of mekenes
Euyn as hys owne sanctuary pereles 572
Hys owne dere son whyche was most pure and clene
Of god and men to be the ve*r*rey mene.

When the fulnes of tyme and the seson
Preuentyd before by tyme p*re*fynyte, 576
God sent hys son whyche passyth all reson,
Made of a woman w*ith*out lawe to quyte
And theym redeme that lost were by delyte,
By the lawe ageyne that were oppressyd 580
Lowsyng theyr bonds that had transgressyd.

Also thys mayden of god thus elect *Her manner of life.*
And p*r*eelect abode and dwellyd styll
In the temple of god to hyr most dilect; 584
And she also set holyly all hyr wyll
The plesure of god onely to fulfyll,
The woshipfull tempyll of god to preyse,
In that she myght the honour for to reyse. 588

That w*ith* hyr worthiest most p*r*ecious [fol. 229*b*]
Parfyte feyre speche inly delectable,
Holy, blessyd, and eke mellyflous;
That she myght therto be ryght acceptable; 592
That he that strong kyng Dauid & stable
Of the rote of whom she ys descendyd,
As the trouthe before ys comp*r*ehendyd;

Hyt is red in the psalme of Dauid pleyn; 596
Thow, good lord, part of myne enherytaunce.
Fforsoth forsaken was she now certeyn

566. . . the tod*er* . . .   567. Thys ys fer bett*er* who hyt
und*er*stod.   569. . . . hys only goodnes.   573. Most *is omitted*.
582. Thus *is omitted*.   584. To hyr *is omitted*.   590. Feyre *is
omitted*.   593. That strong kyng . . .   594. Of the lyne of
whome . . .

Life of St. Anne

    Of fadyr and modyr clerely in substaunce
        And there betakyn to godds vsaunce,   600
    Commytted to hym truly for to plese
    And the old sorowes sothly to appese.

    And how she lyuyd from that tyme forth
        Or how in the tempyll she behad hyr,   604
    Hyt ys nat possyble to sey forsoth
        To any man that euer was nygh or fer.
        To thynke or devyne all but veyne hyt were;
    Hyt passeth to fer all mannys reson;   608
    No tong can tell how she dyd that seson.

    And all feyre speche that can be thought truly
        Shall fayle; hit hys in comprehensible;
    And all the coniecturyng eke sothely   612
        Vanyssheth and ys clere impossible,
        To mannys reson clene insensible,
    Ffrom the face of hyr superhabundaunt
    Vertues innumerable extendaunt.   616

    Of thys virgyns most excellent grace
        In the conspect of the hygh mageste,
    Of hym whyche chase hyr for hys restyng place
        Preuuydyd by the parfyte Trinite;   620
        The mayde, the lyfe, the tyme when hit shuld be;
    Wherfore to yeue hyr dew laude and preysyng
    Accordyngly hit passeth all connyng.

[fol. 280a]

Joachim and Anne apostrophised.

    O happy Ioachim, therfor ioy thow   624
        And be glad that thus hast deserued
    To be callyd the verrey fadyr now
        Of suche a chylde; ioy thow thus preserued.
    But thow, Anne, that art also reserued   628
    Ioye now togedyr long tyme happyer
    Then Anne the modyr of Samuel fer.

    Thou hast brought forth the heuynly myrrour chyeff
        And the parfyte lyly of chastyte,   632
    The ground and mene of all oure bonechyeff;

---

601. Converted to hym . . .   612. Eke sothely *is omitted.*
618. . . . in every place.

Life of St. Anne

The houshold of clennes and honeste;
The lanterne of lyght and welle of pyte;
The consolacion of all wrechys 636
And of all trew pepyll the hope of blys;

Quene of aungellys; fountayn of mercy; *A prayer to the Virgin.*
    Mediatione of thy ineffable grace,
Whyche to all synners are euyr redy 640
    To helpe and comfort in euery space;
And to vs all worshippyng in what place
Of thys same day the gret solempnyte
She bryngeth grace of hyr benygnyte. 644

Lady of the world, make vs glad with the,
    And wit cryste Ihū oure lord, thyn owne son,
In euerlastyng ioy, for thow art verrey she,
    The blessyd modyr of redempcion. 648
    Bryng vs vnto thy sonnys hygh mansion,
To whom be parfyte honour and glory
By all the worldes now infinitely.

Now blessyd seynt Anne, of thy gret goodnes 652 *A prayer to St. Anne.*
    With my trew hert I mekely beseche the
Here my prayer and do thy besynes:
    Be mene for vs all with thy doughtres thre
To that most holy blyssyd Trynyte 656
Of hys gret mercy that we may be hys,
And when we dy to haue eternall blys. Amen. 658
    Explicat vita stē Anne matris sancte marie virginis.

642. . . worschiping and solace.   *Colophon:* Here endyth the lyff of Seynt Anne.

III

The Life of St. Anne

MS. Bodl. 10234
(Tanner 407).

[fol. 21a]

Listen to the story of St. Anne, her husbands, and her daughters.

Souereynys and serys ȝyf it be ȝour wylle
To here and to lere of thyng that is good
ffro tryflys and talys kepe ȝour tonggs stylle
and here ȝo this matere with a mylde mood   4

ffor ȝo schull here þe story þat is of seynt anne
the modyr of oure lady blyssyd mote sche bene
and of þe housbondes that sche had man aftyr manne
and of here dere dowterys and here chylderyn bedene   8

Joachim and Anne are childless twenty years.

Sent anne had a housbonde joachym was hys name
þe fyrst housbond that sche had þe soth for to telle
a ffeythfull man he was. and had a nobyll name
that meche cowde of curteseye and of good councelle   12

They weren ryght ryche folke. and therto meke and myld
and in lawe of oure lord. both þey led here lyff
but xx^{ti} yeer togedyr. cam of hem noon chyld
of thys man joachym. and anne that was hys wyff   16

I give herewith the results of a collation of the poem on the life of St. Anne contained in MS. Harley 4012 with that contained in MS. Bodl. 10234 (Tanner 407). I have not undertaken to give variant spellings; but I have endeavoured to give all the variant readings of MS. Harley 4012.

Title: Here begynnyt þe lif of Sent Anne.
1. Soueraignes & frendes . . .   3. Ffor trifelles . . .   5. Ye shall here þe storie of blessid Sent Anne.   6. . . . worship mote she bene.   7. And all hir husbondis.   10. . . . þe truþe for to tell.   11. . . . nobill fame.   12. . . . sad counsell.   13. þei were riche folke . . .   14. In þe law of *our* lorde þei led *per* lif.   15. . . . came þer ne childe.   16. Of þe man Joachym.

Life of St. Anne

A greet desyre þey had a chyld that þey myght haue
and ther of they preyd god. in al that they myght
and thys a wow þey mad. war it mayde or knave
þat it schuld servyn god be day and be nyght   20

They pray for a child and Mary is born.

So it befel as god wold withinne a schort space
þey had a chyld togedyr mari was her name
þat was weddyd aftyrward throur godds grace
to joseph a gentylman of name and of fame.   24

Mary is wedded to Joseph.

And qwow þis maryage was mad of josep and mari
30 schul here aftyrward reed in ryme.
but fyrst j wyl tell 30w a nother story.
of anne and her housbonds in þe mene tyme.   28

Joachym þe gentylman þat was oure ladyes fadyr
hym fel for to deyd as godds wylle was
and aftyr hem sent anne þat was oure ladyis modyr
toke anothyr housbond hys name was Cleophas   32

[fol. 21b]

Joachim dies and Anne marries Cleophas.

And they haddyn a dowtyr getyn of hem betwene
and she was clepyd mary. as þe boke sayes
that aftyrward was weddyd with wurchepe as j wene
to on that hythe Alpheus levyng in tho dayes   36

Their daughter is Mary, wife of Alpheus and mother of James, Joseph, Simon, and Jude.

This mary had with Alpheus þat was her housbonde
fowyr fayer chylderyn as wretyn is with penne
jamys and josep þe just man. as j vndyrstonde
symond and jude. all foure holy menne   40

Aftyr hem sent Anne. had the thredde man
his name as men seyn was salome.
and vndyr hem bothe. haddyn a woman
that was clepyd mary ful fayr and ful fre.   44

St. Anne's third husband is Salome. Their daughter is Mary, wife of Zebedee and mother of James and John.

17. And grete desire . . . 18. In þat þei praide too god þat þei myght. 19. . . . boye or knaue. 20. þat hit shulde euermore serue god boþe day and nyght. 21. So hit fell þat after in a short space. 23–24. *omitted.* 25. And how þat þe maryage . . . 30. Hym fellid for to dy . . . 31. And afterward Sent Anne . . . 33. And þei to had a doghter yofen þem betwene. 34. She was kallid mary . . . 37. This mary had by Alpheus . . . 38. iiij faire children as writen was wit penne. 40. . . . and all iij . . . 41. After þis Sent Anne had þe iij^de manne . . . 42. . . . was klepid Salomone. 43. . . . þei had a Woman.

Life of St. Anne

  And thys mary was weddyd to on ӡebede.
   that in þe lawe of god had gret loue and lyst.
   and they to haddyn to chyldryn blyssid mote þei be.
    Sent jamys þe more. and john þe wangelyst.   48

St. Anne had three husbands and three daughters named Mary.

  And thus oure ladyis moder þat hyght sent Anne.
   three housbonds she had jche after othyr.
   and with jche a mayde chyld þis is soth sertayne
    and alle three weren maryis born of on modyr.   52

  Now blyssyd be sent anne þat brouth forth þis berth
   and blyssid be these dowterys and her chylderyn infere
   and blyssed be alle tho þat make onest merth
    in þe worchepe of sent anne in thys tyme of ӡeere.   56

[fol. 22a]
St. Anne's father, mother, and sister.

  Summe wyll askyn of sent anne who was her ffadyr
   and j sey his name was kyng jsacar.
   and summe wyl aske who was her modyr
    and j sey naӡaphat and gentyll folk þey war.   60

  And sent anne had a sostyr þat hyght jsmary.
   that bar Elyӡabeth þe modyr of jon baptyst.
   and here men mowen se and knowe kyndely.
    qwow syb jon was on to ihū cryst.   64

The history of Joachim and Anne.

  Now wyl j turne aӡen and telle ӡou som what ellys.
   of joachym and Anne. of whom j spak aforen.
   and of maydyn mari as þe story tellys.
    and somwhat of her levyng & who þat sche was boren   68

  SEynt jerom þe holy man and þe holy doctour
   hath wretyn in hys boke and beryth wytnesse
   that joachym was borne wyth gret honour
    in þe Cete of naӡareth that wurchepful is.   72

---

45. þis mary was mared to one ӡebede.   48. . . John of vangeliste. 49. And þis our ladis moder . . .   50. . . eche one after oþer. 51. And wit eche one a maide chulde þis is sartayne.   53. Now *is omitted*.   56. In worship of Sent Anne in any tyme of ӡer.   58. I say his name was Sent Isakar.   59. . . will aske also . . . 60. And I say þat Masaphat . . .   61. And *is omitted*.   63. And *is omitted*.   64. How sib þat Iohn was vnto Ihū Criste.   65. What *is omitted*.   66. . . as I spake before.   68. And *is omitted* . . . wher she was borne.   69. Sent Jerom was an holi man and a doctour.   71. . . and had grete honour.

And Anne was borne in a toun besyde jerslem.
of the kynred of kynges and of kynggs blode
þe name of that Cete is clepyd bethleem
in þe whyche crist was born þat deyed on þe rode.   76

And also befel as god wold þat joachym and anne.
were weddyd togedyr ȝerys and dayes.
trewe folk and lawefull to euery manner manne.
and kept well godds lawe as the boke sayes.   80

And they haddyn werdely ryches ful gret plente
but þat ryches they partyd on three maner wyse
on parte they ȝouyn to god. with herte good and fre
to the meyntonawnse of holy chyrche and godds servyse.

Pore folk haddyn þe secunde part ȝouyn of almes.   85   [fol. 22b]
fulfyllyng þe vij dedys þat ben of mercy.
but many folk on days wyl not do þes
that han welth and weelfare ful plentewously.   88

And the thred part þei kept for her owyn fode
to hem and to here serwantys in honest degre.
and thus schuld euery man that hath mekyl goode
be þe wyl of god dapart his good in three.   92

Twenty ȝeer togedyr had þey no chyld.   *They pray for a child.*
and ofte þei mad a wow as j sayd beforne
ȝyf þei myght haue a chyld it schuld be kept vnfyld.
and put to goddys servyse aftyr it were borne.   96

So it befel on a tyme as þe lawe wold   *Joachim is reproved by the priest because he is childless.*
joachym went to cherche to make his offeryng.
on a pryncipall day as other men schuld
be þe lawe of oure lord and be hys byddyng.   100

73–76.   Anne was borne in a towne beside Jerusalem
þe name of þe cite is kallid bedlem
In whiche criste was borne þat died for vs on rode
Mankinde to redeme with his precius blode.
77. And so befelle þat Joachym and Anne.   80. And kept goddes lawes as þe boke tell saies.   81. And þei had of riches grete plente.
83. . . gaue god wit per hert fre.   84. To maintayne holy cherche.
85. þe ijde parte pore folk had in almus.   86. þat ben *is omitted*.
87. þat many folke now a day loue not to do pus.   88. þat haueth welth and welfare plenteusly.   91. So shuld euery man doo þat hath moche goode.   92. . . departe þem on iij^e.   95. If þei myght haue had one he shulde be kept unsilde.   96. And put in goddis seruice . . .

Life of St. Anne

So joachym on a day to þe offeryng he ȝede
   and his frendys infere to þe prest of þe lawe.
and whan he cam beforne þe prest and schuld do þat dede
   þe prest reprevyd hym and thys was hys sawe.   104

Thow art nouth worthy joachym offeryng to make.
   for þu hast non frute getyn of þin wombe
and þerfor þe and thyn offryng bothe j here forsake
   and joachym stode astonyid as styll as a lombe.   108

Ffor thys was þe lawe þat in that tyme was.
   that what man it were þat myght noon chyld geete.
to þe awter of gold he schuld nouth vp pas   111
   ne with hem þat haddyn chylderyn he schuld nouth be seete.

[fol. 23a]

Joachim flees to his herdsmen.

And for that joachym had noon chyld thus was he chyd.
   and for schame of hem self he would nouth be sene
but went to hys herdmen and there he hym hyd
   and meche mornyng forsothe had as j wene.   116

An angel appears to Joachim, explains why some couples are childless, and promises him a daughter, Mary.

But god of his goodnesse whan þat he saw his tyme.
   an anngel of heuene he sent to joachym.
as ȝe schall here aftyrward red in ryme.
   þe weche holy anngell on thys wyse seyd to hym.   120

I am an anngell of heuene sent to the.
   to telle þe goode tydynggs joachym be thyn name
god hath herd thyn preyowrys þat settyth in trinite
   and whow þu wer reprevyd and nouth wer to blame   124

Ffor in þat that þu hast noon with thyn wyff
   thus many dayes and ȝerys it is goddys wylle
for god wyl be lord of alle þat beryth lyff
   and namely of mankynde and that is þe skylle.   128

---

101. . . to þe cherch yode.   103. And when he kam wher þat he shuld do þe dede.   107. þerfor þe and þi offering I vtterly boþe forsake.   108. þen Ioachym stode still as a lambe.   109. Ffor þis þe law in þat tyme was.   110. þat what man þat kowde no childe get.   111. . . auter of god . . .   112. . . for to be set.   113. Ffor cauɛe he had no childe þus was he chid.   116. And made moche mornyng forsoþe as I wene.   117. . . . mercy . . .   119. . . . after in þis ryme.   120. Whiche angell þus wise saide vnto hym.   121. . . angell of god sent vnto the.   122. þe *is omitted*.   123. God hath herde þi praier sitting in trinyte.   124. . . wer not . . .   125. Ffor þat þu haste no childe wit þi wif.   127. Ffor he wil . . .   128. . . which is good skill.

Life of St. Anne

Ffor many men and women that han fleysshely lust
   they wene to han chylderyn at her owyn lykyng
but the maker of mankende that gentyl is and just
   wyl be mayster as j wene of here werkyng.   132

Ffor ȝif they haddyn chylderyn at her owyn desyre
   they wold wenyn it were of her owyn myght
but god that is her souereyn wyl be lord and syre   135
   and putte hem from her purpose as resoun wyll and ryght

And thus they may wel wete withowten ony fayle
   that they may gete noon chyld with flexly lust only
for all her lust and lykyng ful lytel schal awayle
   but god wyl help toward of hys gret mercy.   140

And many folk han no chyld for a nother skyl   [fol. 23b]
   for they wold perau(e)nter loue the chylde to meche
and mayntene it in shrewednes aȝens godds wyl
   þerfore they han no chylderyn as j trowe trewlyche.   144

And of a long tyme som folk no chyld may haue
   vnto tyme that þey come to gret age.
as Abraham and sarra þat brouth forth a knave
   ysayas þe prophete a sad man and a sage.   148

And ysayas and rebecca þat olde folk warne
   and baran and baren. be þe cours of kynde
in her elde age þey had a fayr barne
   josep þat was a lord in egypt as j fynde   152

Who was strenger in his dayes than was sampson
   who was mor holy þan was samuel.
mor strenger and more holy in that tyme was non.
   of baren women bothe wern born as oure bokys tel.   156

---

129. Ffor *is omitted* . . . which haþe . . .   131. And be maker of mankinde which is Iuge full iuste.   132. Wil be master in all þer warkinge.   133. Ffor *is omitted*.   134. . . hit wer þer awne myght.   135. Her *and* wil be *are omitted*.   136. . . as is most right.   137. And *is omitted*.   138. þat þei may haue no childrene of þer luste only.   139. . . shall preuaile.   140. But if god will help of his grete mercy.   141. Many folk haue no childerne . . .   143. . . as hit is goddis will.   145. And þerfor haue thei none þis god for þem will wirche.   146. In to þe tyme þei be of grete age.   148. . . a wise man . . .   151. ln þer wolde daies þei had a faire baron.   152. þat *is omitted*.   153. . . þen euer was samsoun.   154. And more holier þen euer Samuell.   155. So stronge and holy . . .   156. Of baren women borne boþe as I finde here tell.

And also we fyndyn wel of john þe baptyst.
þat his fader and his moder wern of gret elde
for oure lord may werke ryght as hym self lyst.
and at his owen wylle al thyng may he welde   160

Ffor thow þat þei ben weddyd in trewe wedlak
and on to long tyme no chyld mowen haue
þat schal ben a good chyld withowtyn gret lak
as many men seyn be it mayden or knaue.   164

And therfor joachym j do the to wetyn.
þat þu schal haue a chyld withinne fewe dayes.
trowe thys tale trewly thow it be not wretyn.
for god that is almyghty on to þe þis he sayes.   168

[fol. 24a] And thereto he sayes mor thy wyff is with chyld
on wetyng thy self and her self also
þer was neuer chyld þat neuer was so myld
ne neuer schal be brouth forth of to.   172

And it schal be a mayde chyld and be clepyd mary.
the worthyest woman of alle that may ben borne.
and thys may be prevyd be profecy
of ȝour owen prophetys þat wern her before   176

Ffor sche schal conceyve thurgh grace of þe holy gost
goddys sone of heuene and bere hym bodely
and a modyr and a mayden be clepyd in euery cost.
and schal be a mervely to many man suerly   180

[The angel bids Joachim return home.] And therfor joachym j bydde þe þat þu hom wynde
to þi wyff thyn frendys and þi meyne.
for thyn houswyff at home þat onest is and hende
makyth myche mornyng for love of the.   184

157. Wel *is omitted*. 158. . . boþe wer wolde. 159. . . like as hym liste. 160. At his awne will al þinge is made as hit shulde. 161. Ffor þey þat be weddid in true wedlak. 162. And so longe tyme and no childe haue. 163. Gret *is omitted*. 164. As many men be oþer childe or knaue. 167. Trust my tale true . . . 168. . . . on þis wise saes. 169. Mor *is omitted*. 170. Vnweting to hir and to þe alsoo. 171. . . þat euer was so mylde. 173. Hit shal be a maiden childe and named mary. 174. . . þat euer myght . . . 175. This may welbe proued by þe prophecy. 176. Of wolde prophitis . . . 177. . . by þe holi goste. 179. To be callid maiden and moder in euer moste. 180. And þis shalbe a maruaile to many a man truly. 181. . . loke þat home wende. 182. As I have Saide so shall hit be. 183. At home *is omitted*. 184. . ., for þe loue of þe.

Life of St. Anne 117

And j telle þe a tokene þat thow schal fynde trewe.
  þu schal mete with thyn wyff at þe goldyng gate
do as j þe rede it schal þe neuer rewe
  and joachym went his way meryly god wate   188

And aftyrward þe anngel went to sent Anne.   *The angel*
  and bad her be of good cher al schuld be wel.   *comforts*
and told her of here housbonde & wher he was sertayne   *St. Anne.*
  and al that he had told hym tol her euery del.   192

And bad her gon a good pas to þe gate of gold
  for ther sche schuld mete hym withowtyn ony fayl.
and a non sent anne walk forth sche wold
  She mad noon maner tarying in that travayl.   196

And at þe goldyn ȝate mette they togedyr   [fol. 24b]
  and eyther kyssyd other and were ful blythe   *Joachim*
and alle there goode frendys þat komyn with hem thedyr   *and Anne meet at*
  welkomyd hom joachym many fele sythe   200   *the golden gate.*

Ther was made meche merthe of lest and of most
  of alle maner pepyl as oure bokys tel
for þei were loved in euery contre and cost
  jn þat land þat þei dwellyd in. was clepyd jsrael.   204

As they went homward þey spak of þe anngel
  and what he spak to hem eyther to other gan rehers
and bothe alwayis in euery speche and spel
  they foundyn hym trewe in euery word and vers   208

And þan they thankynd god of his gret grace   *They thank*
  and of his gret goodnes and his gracyous sonde.   *God.*
and bothe knelyd doun in that same place.
  and worchepe dede to god with mowth hert and honde. 212

185. I shall tell . . .   187. Do as I þe counsaill and þu shalt hit not rue.   188. Ioachym went his way full mery . . .   189. And after þat & þe angell wento Sent Anne playne.   190. And albe of good chere for all shalbe welle.   192. And all þat he tolde hym was founde true euery dele.   193. . . go apas . . .   194. Ffor þer shulde she mete hym witouten faile.   195. . . . walkyng forþe . . .   196. She made no taryng . . .   197. And *is omitted.*   198. . . . boþe were full bliþe.   199. . . frindes kamme wit Anne þether.   200. To welcom Ioachym . . .   201. . . . and moste.   203. . . . were well loued . . .   204. þe lande where þei dwellid was callid Israell.   205. And as . . .   206. And what he tolde þem boþe ganne reherse.   207–208 *omitted.*   209. And thankid . . .   210. . . . his goodnes and gracius sonde.   212. And worship to god . . .

Life of St. Anne

Mary is born.

After þat whan tyme kome anne bar her chyld
    that was clepyd mary as j seyd beforne
a freyssh fode and a fayer with foly neuer fyld
    aftyr þe tyme that sche was of her modyr borne   216

Mary is taken to the temple and dedicated to God.

After þat this chyld was thre ȝer of age
    it was wenyd as j wene fro þe sokyng.
and aftyr comon custom and olde vsage
    þey went with þis chyld and mad her offryng.   220

On to þe grete temple of jerusalem
    þat semely is set on hey as j wene
and as men seyn þat han sen hem.
    ther be pasys vpward no lesse þan xv^{ne}.   224

[fol. 25a]

And tho be mad as men sayn al of marbyl stone
    be þe weche pylgrymys and other men pas.
and there þis chyld mary ful lythly a lone
    went vp at these pasys as ȝong as sche was.   228

And alle folk wern ameruelyd þat seyn þat selkowth syth
    þat sweche a ȝong chyld myght gon swyche a pase.
ant euery man blyssyd her. her bewte was so bryth
    fayer of feture and of face and ful of goddys grace.   232

Joachym and Anne þei left her stylle there.
    in þe forsayd temple as þei mad her a wow
þat sche schuld serue god whan þat tyme were.
    and so sche dede dewoutely j schall telle ȝou qwow.   236

She and other chylderyn þat mayden chylderyn wern
    wern take in to þe temple vnto a sertayn age.
in that place to abyden and her lawes to lern
    and so be kept in clennesse fro sythys owtrage.   240

213. . . þis childe.   216. After tyme . . . was ofter . . . 218. . . for þe sokyng.   219. After comen custome and hir wolde vsage.   220. . . þe childe and made offeringe.
221–224.   Vnto þe Tempull of Jerusalem
    þat seinly is set on his ass as I wene (*sic*)
    And as many men saith þat haþe sene þem
    þer be paises vpward moo þen xv.
226. By which . . .   227. . . full ofte alone.   228. . . all þees gresing . . .   229. All folke meruelid þat saw that sight.   232. And faire of fface and fete was of goddes grace.   233. Joachym and Anne left hir per behinde.   234. . . per avoy.   235. . . what tyme.   236. . . did she deuotely and . . .   238. Were take to . . .   239. . . to abide and per . . .   240. . . from Synne and outerage.

Life of St. Anne

And this was þe ryght rewle þat oure lady kept Mary in the temple.
  for as a wyse woman her wyl was to werk.
qwan tyme was sche wakyd qwan tyme was sche slept
  but euery day be þe morwyn sche went to þe kyrk.   244

And ther sche made her preyours tyl forforth dayes
  and aftyrward she went vnto wevyng werk
and at aftyr noone sche ȝede aȝen as þe boke sayes.
  to her preyers and her bedys tyl it was derk.   248

And euery day an anngel peryd to her.
  comfortyd her and brouth her of anngelys fode.
and ther with sche was feed sche wold take no nother
  for sche wold no werdely mete were it neuer so goode.   252

And þow euery day sche had mete and drynk   [f 1. 25b]
  of þe bysshopys of þe lawe as þe lawe wold
and her felawys also for þei schuld nouth sqwynk.
  but to godds servyse and þerto they wern bold.   256

But al þe mete þat sche toke of þe byschopis
  she departyd it ful preuyly among pore men
sche ȝaf hem her drynkyn to puttyn in her cuppys
  to drynkyn when þei woldyn & namely to women.   260

And many dyuers tymes as þe boke tellys.
  many man and woman seyn withowtyn dowte
qwat comfort sche had of holy anngellys
  and whan þey spokyn to her ful lowe gon þey lowte.   264

And qwat man it were þat had a sckenesse
  ȝif sche myghte towche hym he schuld be hool anoon.
and this was throw þe myght of her holynesse.
  now blyssyd be this lady there sche sytts in troon.   268

241. And *is omitted*.   244. Eche daie in the mornyng . . .   246. And after she went to þe . . .   247. After none agayne . . . 248. . . . and bedis till þat hit . . .   250. Hir comforting . . . angell fode.   251. þerwit was she fed she wolde haue none oþer. 252. For *is omitted*.   253. Neuerþeles . . .   255. . . for cause þei shuld . . .   256. In goddes serues and þerin wer þei bolde. 257. . . . of þe same . . .   259. . . . and put hit in þer cuppis. 266. . . . hym toche he was . . .   267. And þat was because of hir grete holines.   268. . . . þat sittithe . . .

And nowth withstondyng þat sche was þe fayrest woman
  of alle þat euer wern born. na for þat clerkys say.
ȝif a man had lokyd on her þat had be temptyd þan.
  to þe synne of lechery anoon it went a way.   272

It was gret merueyl þat mary myght do thus.
  for sche was ful of grace withowtyn ony drede
now mary and sent Anne. we pray ȝou prey ȝe for vs
  þat god ȝif vs grace wel for to spede. Amen.   276

Mary refuses to marry.

Bvt what tyme oure lady and other maydenys mo
  wer come to her ful age of fourtene ȝere
as the lawe wold þe bysshopys bad hem go.
  to be maryed to men and dwellyn no lenger there   280

[fol. 26a]

And alle these maydenys wenten as the bysshepys hem bad
  hom to her frendys save mary alone
and sche sayd sertayne a gret cause sche had.
  and therfor from the temple on no wyse wold sche gone. 284

They askyd. her þe cause and þe skyl qwy.
  that sche wold noth do as other maydenys deed.
and sche answeryd agen and seyde sekyrly
  for too causis and skyllys þat myght nouth be heed.   288

Ffor my fadyr and myn modyr maden this a wow
  þat j schuld serue god in þe terme of myn lyf
and j haue mad a wowe to kepe me chast ȝif j mow.
  serys answere to resoun and let vs nouth stryff.   292

The bysshopys wern astonyed and stoden ston stylle
  þey cowde nouth answere to her be ony resoun
for bothe þe old lawe and þe newe on this wyse wylle
  þat a good wow be kept with a good deuocion.   296

---

269. Notwithstonding she was þe ferist woman.   270. þat euer were borne ȝit as clerkes say.   271. If a man were temptid when he saw hir þan.   272. To *is omitted*.   273. Hit was no grete . . . 274. . . ane drede þen.   275. . . praie ȝe boþe for vs.   276. . . will sende vs . . . to . . .   278. . . to full age of xiij yere.   281. All þe . . . hem bade.   284. She saide for sartayne . . .   287. þen she aunswerid and saide . . .   288. Ffor þe causis and skill þat may not be hid.   289. For *is omitted*.   290. . . shall serue god the terme . . .   291. þe same wow haue I made to kepe if I mow. 294. . . bi noo reson,   295. Boþe wold law . . .   296. , , with good , ,

Life of St. Anne

Thus what for þe wow þat oure lady mad
and what for þe custom þat nedys must be kept.
þe bysshopys of þe lawe wer no thyng glad   *The bishops call a*
and therfor a councell to gedyr they kept.   300 *council.*

Of all þe wysest men þat weren in þat lond
to wete what were best in thys forsayd cas.
and alle they seyden infere it were good to fond
ȝyf good god wold helpyn hem of hys gret gras.   304

Than þese bysshopys and these men be a comyn assent
euery man preyd to god on his best wyse
þat summe trewe tokyn among hem myght be sent
er thanne þei fro ther preyers vp schuld ryse.   308

And so they loyn in her preyers þe mountennans of a myle [fol. 26b]
and anon þey herdyn a voys among hem alle   *An angel tells how*
þat bad hem bydde her bedys for within a lytel whyle   *Mary's husband*
þei schuld se with owten fayle qwat thyng schuld falle 312 *to be chosen.*

And than seyd þe anngel þat alle men myght heren
almyghty god byddyth ȝou & chargyth ȝow þerwyth
þat alle men old and ȝong in thys place aperen
that be nought weddyd and dwellyn with king dauyd   316

And that euery man schal bere in his hond a long ȝerd & a drye
in his hond opynly þat alle men mown it sene.
for that man schal be weddyd to maydyn marye.
qwose ȝerd may florych with levys that ben grene.   320

And on þe same ȝerde þe holy gost schal lyght.
in þe lyknesse of a dowe þat alle men mowe se.
and so schuln ȝo knowe be that semely syth
to qwom maydyn mary weddyd schal be   324

297. Þis was for þe wow . . .   298. Which for nedes . . .
301. . . . wisemen . . .   303. . . . saide infere it good were for to . . .
304. If god will help þem . . .   305. þat þes bisshoppis by a . . .
306. . . . praide god in his . . .   308. Or þei from per praier
shulde . . .   309. . . laye in praiere . . .   311. . . . and within
a while.   312. . . . wolde befall.   313. þen saide an angell . . .
314. . . chargiþe þerwit.   315. þat euery man . . . which . . .
þere.   316. þat þei be not . . .   317. . . . shal haue a longe
rod . . .   318. . . . may sene.   319. For *is omitted*.   320. þat
his rodd florish wit leuys grene.   321. . . . rodd . . .   324. . .
mared . . .

Life of St. Anne

The men assemble in the temple with their rods.

And þan was it comanndit be a comoun cry.
þat þo that were nouth weddyd were þei old or ȝyng.
fro þe most to þe lest saf chylderyn only
þat were dwellyng in court with dauyd þe kyng.　　　328

Joseph has no rod.

That euery man schuld haue a long ȝerd in his hond
and in þe gret temple stonde al to gedyr
and thys was don in dede as j vndirstond
but josep browt no ȝerd whan he cam thedyr.　　　332

Ffor josep was a febyl man and of gret age.
for hym to be weddyd he had non gret wylle
and therfor þat he schuld make no maryage
the ȝerd þat he schuld bere at hom he left it stylle　　　336

[fol. 27a]
No token is shown.

So whan this men wern gaderyd and togedyr stode
and euery man saf on. held vp his rod
ther was no tokene schowyd badde no goode
and the pepyl knelyd doun and preyid to good god.　　　340

That wolde schowe and telle of his mercy
qwy and wherfore they myght no tokene sene.
and they wereη answeryd agen fayr and onestly
and these wern þe werds for sothe as j wene.　　　344

Euery man hath browt a ȝerd saue only þat man
þe weche schal be weddyd to maydyn mary
and therfor loke abowte as wel as ȝe can
ȝif there be ony swych in þis company.　　　348

Joseph is sent home for his rod.

Than þey sowte and foundyn non but on
þat left his rod behyndyn hym josep be his name
and þan þe bysshopes bad hym þat hom schuld he gon
and bryng a ȝerd with hym or ellys he schuld bere blame. 352

325. And *is omitted.*　　326. All þo . . .　　327. Ffrom þe more . . .　　329. . . rod . . .　　330. . . . to stande . . .　　332. . . no rodde when þat . . .　　333. Ffor he was . . .　　334. Ffor to be weddid he had no grete wille.　　336. . . . he lefte still.　　337. So when all þe men togider þat they stode.　　339. . . . neper bad nor goode.　　340. þen . . . praid vnto god.　　341. þat he wolde shew and tell þem of his mercy.　　343. And þei wer aunswerid agayne honestly.　　345. . . . a rod sauc þat man.　　346. Which shalbe . . .　　348. . . . any suche here in þis company.　　349. þen þe sowght aboute . . .　　351. þeu þe bisshop bade hym in all haste to gone.　　352. . . . a rodde wit . . . haue blame.

Josep went forth as he bode was
    and brouth with hym a long ȝerd þat baren was & bare.
and cam agen anon into þe same plas.
    and stode with his felawis and made mechyl care.   356

And þan þe bysshopys bad hem alle þat þei schuld euery chone   *Joseph's rod flourishes.*
    holde vp here ȝerdys þat þei myght be sene.
and so þey dede in dede and after þat anone
    þe ȝerd þat josep bare sodeynly wex al grene.   360

And florysshyd ful fayre with leef & with floure.
    and the holy gost in lyknes of a dowe
he cam doun fro heuene with ful gret honoure.
    and þat al men myght it se he sat al a boue.   364

Than seyd al þe pepyl of lewyd and leryd   [fol. 27b]
    after þat þey had seyn that gloryous syth
now it is wel knowyn and sekerly schewyd
    that josep schal wedde mary of bewte so bryth   368

Bot meche folk meruelyed of þat maryage   *Why Mary was wedded to Joseph.*
    and why that god wolde ordeyne swyche a weddyng.
of so ȝong a maydyn and a man of gret age
    and what was þe cause was her carpyng.   372

And som per ben þat ȝet wyln also þe same qwestion
    why wold god hym self be born in wedlake
rather þan be syde this is here reson
    and of þis mater many men mowseng þei make.   376

But herto answeryn clerkys as j vnderstond
    and telle þe cause why. crist wold be bred
and born of a maydyn þat hath an housbond
    and nouth of a maydyn þat neuer had be weddyd   380

---

353. . . his biddyng was.   354. . . rodde þat baran and bare.
356. . . he had full mekill kare.   357. þen þe bisshop bade þat . . .
358. . . þer ȝerdes . . .   359. So þei did and after þat a nonne.
360. þe rod . . . waxid grene.   363. . . right gret . . .   364. . .
myght it se and stode euen aboue.   365. þen saide all peopill boþe
lerned and lewde.   367. Now is hit . . . openly shewde.   368. . .
mare so bright.   369. Moche peopill. . .   370. And why god
wolde . . .   371. . . and of a man of age.   372. . . cause of
ther carping.   373. And sum ther be ȝit þat will aske this question.
374. . . be borne of a maide.   375. . . is þeir resonne.   376. . .
grete musinge thei make.   377. Herto aunswerith . . .   379. .
þat neuer had husbonde.

Ffor god wold hym self þat sche schuld hym bere,
in þe lawe of wedlak þat hym self ordand
and for þat no man schuld desyre her ne dere
vnder þe same lawe he dede his moder stand. 384

Ffor ȝif sche had be maryed to no man
and had be with chyld on þe maner as sche was,
she schuld be slaunderyd with many on certayn
and haue had sorwe and schame for no trespas. 388

And therefore crist had leuer þat som folk were in dowte
on what wyse and whow he myght be borne
than sche were put to a slaunder to all folk abowte
and her name and her fame on þat wyse wer lorne 392

[fol. 28a] And for another skyl she had an housbond
iosep that was gentyl for he schuld take hede
and go with her and be with her on watyr and on lond
and be trewe wytnes of her maydenhede. 396

And oure lady bare cryst for a nother skyll
A mayden and maryed mayden and wyff
for god wyl wondrys werke at his owyn wyl
þat þe fende schal not knowe þat sterere of stryff 400

Ffor þe fende supposyd because þat sche was wedded
þat þe chyld had be getyn and brought forth of two
but he knowe nought þe mater of her maydenhed
for þat he was deseyuyd and many a jew also. 404

Ffor ȝif þe deuel had wyst þat he had be godds sone
he durst nought atempte hym withowtyn ony fayl,
but crist knowyth best. qwat is for to done
soffryd hym to tempte hym & hym to asayl. 408

383. And þat woman shuld nethir hurte ne dere. 385. . . vnto no man. 386. . . euen as . . . 387. She shulde aben slaunerd of many in sertayne. 389. þerto criste . . . 390. . . how þat he . . . 391. þen she to haue a slaunder . . . 392. Hir name and hir fame on þat wise be borne. 393. . . an husbonde. 394. . . for cause he shuld . . . 395. Euer to be with her on . . . 398. A maiden mered and also a wif. 400. . . be sterer of strif. 401. . . be cause sho . . . 402. . . brought forþe too. 405. If þe . . , he had be . . . 407. But crist þat knawith . . .

And also he soffryd hym to tempte other men
  to betraye jhū cryst throw som fals tresoun
as judas and other mo. þan vx⁽ⁿᵉ⁾ or ten
  þat put hym ful petously to his passion.   412

And other maystris of þe lawe lesse & more.
  pylat and herrowd with all her meyne
þat boffeted him and beten him ful sad & ful sore
  And alle he soffryd mekely blyssyd mote he bene.   Amen.

Nowe haue ȝe herd of þe maryage of myld mary.   417
  on qwat wyse it was don & for qwat skyl.
nowe schul ȝe here a short word of the story.
  whow crist was conceyvyd throw his owen wyl.   420

Anon as þe maryage of mary was mad   [fol. 28b]
  god sent to her his anngell gabryel   Gabriel greets Mary.
to grete her and comfort her and her to glad
  and tydynggs þat weren trewe her for to tel.   424

And thus he sayd to her with a myld steuene
  heyl mary ful of grace oure lord is with the.
þu schal conceyve and bere goddys sone of heuene
  and passyng al women blyssyd schal þu be.   428

Mary was astonyed of his tale tellyng.
  and askyd hym on qwat wyse it myght be so.
and answeryd and seyd throw þe holy gosts werkyng.
  and many good words þei had betwene hem too.   432

But at þe last oure lady on þis maner seyde   The Immaculate Conception.
  on to þe anngel þat her grette þat hyght gabryel.
thy word be wrought in me so þat god be payed
  and anon she conceyvyd crist as oure bokys tel.   436

---

409. And *is omitted*.   410. And to betray Ihū Crist with sum fals treson.   411. . . mo þen .v. or tenne.   412. *MS. blank*. 413. . . boþe lesse and more.   414. As pilate . . . þer meane. 415. þat sufferd hem and did bete þem full sore.   417. . . herd þe mariage . . .   422. God sent vnto hir . . .   423. . . comfort hir and glad.   424. *MS. blank*.   425. And þis he saide to mare wit a mylde steuen.   427. . . in heuen.   428. And *is omitted*. 430. And askid one . . . þat hit . . .   431. He aunswerid . . . 434. . . þat her grette *is omitted*.   435. . . god be presid.   436. And *is omitted*.

Life of St. Anne

  Nouth on þat maner wyse as other women done
  swych conceyvyn of men as god ordand
  and many day go þerwith be it dowter or sone
  or it waxin or qwyk as j vnderstand.   440

<small>Christ is perfect at his conception.</small>
  But in þat same tyme and in þe same oure a noon.
  Whan cryst was conceyvyd fel þis mervayl.
  cryst was a parfyte chyld of fleyssh blod & boon
  with alle his feturs fully withowtyn ony fayl.   444

  As was as wyse and as wytty on þe same day.
  þat he was conceyvyd of his modyr dere.
  as he was aftyrward as clerkys say.
  whan he had of age ful xxx^{ti} ʒere.   448

<small>[fol. 29a]</small>
<small>A prayer to Christ, Mary, and St. Anne.</small>
  Now blyssid be þis barne þat born was of a mayde
  and blyssyd be this maydyn þat brouth forth þis berth
  and blyssyd be sent anne her moder as men saye
  in þe worchep of whom we make alle oure merth.   452

  And mary and her moder maynteth this gylde
  to þe worchep of god and of his plesaunce
  and alle þat it mayntene it be it man or chylde
  god of his hey grace ʒeue hem good chaunce.   456

  Good ende and good lyff mote þei alle haue
  and crystyn folk oure fo and oure frende
  and god saue vs alle þat al thyng may saue   459
  and bryng vs to þe blys þat lestyth with owtyn ende Amen∴

---

  437. Non in þat wise as oþer women done.   438. . . haþe ordande.
439. Many daies gone be hit . . .   440. . . be waxen quycke . . .
441. In þe same tyme a hower anone.   444. Wit *is omitted*.   445.
And wise and as witty . . .   447. . . as þees clerkes say.   448. . .
had age fully xxx yere. 449. . . of mare. 450. . . þat maiden . . .
451. . . as I say.   452. Ffor of þes iij^e blessid Spronge is our myrthe.
453-54.   In þe worship of whom we be gederd all
     To be mery and glad in honest maner.
455-56. *MS. blank.*   457. And good liue and good ende þat we may
haue.   458. And all cristen folke . . .   460. . . his blis . . .

NOTES

TO THE UNIVERSITY OF MINNESOTA MANUSCRIPT

In the following notes, the lines to which the notes refer are numbered at the beginning of each note. Glosses follow the usual form. Titles and Latin quotations are italicized.

8. The reference is to the Gospel of Pseudo-Matthew. Cf. the introduction.

9, 15. **Grew** is the common M.E. spelling for Greek. Cf. *Merlin* (E.E.T.S. 36) III, 437. **Ierslem** is common also for Jerusalem. Both spellings, in these words, indicate actual pronunciations. Many such spellings and contractions are used throughout the poem. The letters supplied in expanding contractions have been italicized in the introduction, collations, notes, and text.

17. Joachim was the husband of Anne.

37-39. The account of Joachim's division of his property varies in the different versions of the story, but they all agree on the tripartite division.

47. **Meynyhe** is a Nth. form of mainē, menyē (O.F. **maisnee, mainee**), household.

52-55. Anna (Anne) is the legendary mother of the Virgin Mary. The A version of the Gospel of Pseudo-Matthew says that she was the daughter of Ysachar. The B version agrees with the text in saying that she was the daughter of Agar. She is not to be confused with Anna the Prophetess. In MS. Bodl. 10234, f. 22a, ll. 57-60, the names of Anne's parents are given as jsacar and naȝaphat.

60. This statement is contained in the B version of the Gospel of Pseudo-Matthew but not in the A version.

79. The A version of Pseudo-Matthew says that Reubin was the priest who refused Joachim's offering. The B version says it was Ysachar. See Tischendorf's *Evangelia Apocrypha*, pp. 57-58. The Gospel of the Nativity and the *Cursor Mundi* both have Issachar (Isacar).

84. Ll. 82-84 and 85-87 are transposed in the MS. This is obviously a scribal error, for both the rime and the sense require the present position.

85. **Agrysed**, afraid, in terror. Cf. Chaucer's *House of Fame*, 210. The reason for the fear is explained in the next two verses.

91. **Vised**, *ppl.* vise (O.F. **viser**), view, contemplate, regard.

107. **Whik** is a form of quik, O.E. cwic, alive. Cf. *The Death of St. Andrew* in Horstman's *Altenglische Legenden, Neue Folge*, l. 5 : And said al quik þai suld him brin.

130. In the French *Le Romanz de Saint Fanuel et de Sainte Anne et de Nostre Dame et de Nostre Segnor et de Ses Apostres* the angel appears to Joachim first. See the *Revue des langues romanes*, XXVII, 157 ff.

163. **Skyll**, cause or reason. Cf. Chaucer's *House of Fame*, l. 726.

224. "Als says þe boke." Cf. the Gospel of Pseudo-Matthew III.

128 Notes to the University of Minnesota Manuscript

229. **Swēyme**, O.E. **swēman**, to grieve; M.E. (n.) **swime**, dizziness or swoon; hence his sorrow caused him to lie in a swoon. Cf. **sweme**, also *York Plays*, XL, 40:

þat swettyng was swemyed for swetyng.

230. **Fra undron unto euensang tyme** was probably from about the middle of the forenoon until about six o'clock in the afternoon, or just before sunset, when the evening song was sung. See Skeat's discussion of **undern** in his ed. of Chaucer, VI, 275.

245. **Belefte**, to leave behind, abandon, let go. Cf. Gower's *Conf. Amantis*, II, 3458: Ther was nothing beleft.

255. Pseudo-Matthew has thirty instead of twenty days.

275. In the French poem, *op. cit. sub*. 130, there is a natural instead of a miraculous conception.

301. the **xv greces** are apparently the fifteen steps leading into the temple. See Tischendorf, *op. cit.*, p. 61. According to *Promptorium Parvolorum*, footnote, p. 209, " the term grece seems to be derived from the plural of gre, a step."

370-72. Three lines are lacking in this stanza, though there is no break in the MS. The passage is from Pseudo-Matthew VI, the context of which is as follows: *Hanc autem regulam sibi statuerat, ut a mane usque ad horam tertiam orationibus insisteret; a tertia autem usque ad nonam textrino opere se occuperet: a nona vero hora iterum ab oratione non recedebat usque dum illi angelus domini appareret, de cuius manu escam acciperet, et melius atque melius in dei laudibus proficiebat. Denique cum senioribus virginibus in dei laudibus ita docebatur, ut iam nulla ei in vigiliis prior inveniretur, in sapientia legis dei eruditior, in humilitate humilior, in carminibus Davidicis elegantior, in caritate gratiosior, in castitate purior, in omni virtute perfectior.*

409. The A version of Pseudo-Matthew says that Mary was fourteen years old, but the B version says that she was twelve. Both the Gospel of the Nativity and the *Cursor Mundi* have fourteen years.

445-56. Cf. Genesis IV. 8 and Pseudo-Matthew VII. In two articles on Chaucer's use of the expression " corones two," P.M.L.A. 26, 315 ff. and 29, 129 ff., Professor John L. Lowes has shown the relationship of the crown of roses and the crown of lilies to martyrdom and virginity. He has cited documents both prior to and contemporary with Chaucer to show that this legend was widespread and has attributed its origin to the *Legenda Aurea*. He has failed, however, to cite Ch. VII of Pseudo-Matthew, which reads as follows: *Tunc Abiathar sacerdos obtulit munera infinita pontificibus, ut acciperet eam filio suo tradendam uxorem. Prohibebat autem eos Maria dicens: Non potest fieri ut ego virum cognoscam aut me vir cognoscat. Pontifices autem et omnes eius affines dicebant ei: Deus in filiis colitur et in posteris adoratur, sicut semper fuit in Israel. Respondens autem Maria dixit illis: Deus in castitate primo omnium colitur, ut comprobatur. Nam ante Abel nullus fuit iustus inter homines, et iste pro oblatione placuit deo, et ab eo qui displicuit inclementer occisus est. Duas tamen coronas accepit, oblationis et virginitatis, quia in carne sua nunquam pollutionem admisit. Denique et Helias cum esset in carne assumptus est, quia carnem suam virginem custodivit. Haec ego didici in templo dei ab infantia mea, quod deo cara esse possit virgo. Ideo hoc statui in corde meo ut virum penitus non cognoscam.* This passage is earlier than anything cited by Professor Lowes. See *M.L.N.* XLI (1926), pp. 317-18. The late Professor O. F. Emerson has traced this flower symbolism back to St. Ambrose (P.M.L.A., XLI, 252 ff.), and Miss Roberta D. Cornelius has noted a somewhat similar symbolism in the works of St. Cyprian (P.M.L.A., XLII, 1055 ff.).

Notes to the University of Minnesota Manuscript 129

515. **Selkouð**, *adj.*, O.E. **seldcuð**, rare, strange, wonderful. Cf. the Prologue to the *Cursor Mundi*, l. 5 :

> Sanges sere of selcuth rime.

518 and 548 ff. Only here and in the B version of Pseudo-Matthew does Joseph's rod bear **nutes** (**nottes**). In all other versions of the story the rod blossoms, or bears flowers and fruit, and the dove descends from heaven and lights on the rod instead of ascending from the rod. See Tischendorf, *op. cit.*, pp. 67–68, for the various versions. The B version reads as follows : *et in cuius virga hoc signum apparebit, videlicit illa quae fronduerit et nuces protulerit, et de cuius cacumine egredietur columba et volabit ad caelos, illi tradas Mariam.*

573. **Wrake**, O.E. **wrāēc**, has the sense of revenge. Cf. the *Songs of Laurence Minot*, XI, 6.

593. Cf. Luke 1. 39 ff.

613–15. The Gospel of Pseudo-Matthew VIII, gives the names of the five maids who worked with Mary as Rebecca, Sephora, Susanna, Abigea, and Cael. *Legenda Aurea* (Graesse Ed.), p. 589, says there were seven maids ; but it gives no names.

627. **Dedeygne**, M.E. **dedaynen**, here means scorn or disdain. Cf. *York Plays*, V, 11 : And per-at dedeyned me.

653ff. According to the A version of Pseudo-Matthew, the annunciation scene is **iuxta fontem** by **angelus domini**. According to the B version it is in Mary's "habitationem."

690. **Umlap**, meaning to wrap or surround like a cover, is a contraction of **umbilappen**, which does not occur in O.E. Stratmann-Bradley's *Middle English Dictionary* gives no information concerning its origin. Cf. O.N. **um**, older **umb**, in such words as **umkringja**, to surround, and M.E. **bi-lappen**, to wrap around. Cf. the *Death of St. Andrew*, l. 243 :

> And umbilappid his bodi about. . .

Cf. also *York Plays*, XLV, 66.

709–711. In Pseudo-Matthew X, Joseph has been in **Capharnaum maritima**. See Tischendorf, *op. cit.*, p. 71.

766–68. Cf. Miss Lucy Toulmin Smith's ed. *York Plays*, XIII, 134–137.

796–98. Three lines are wanting in this stanza, but there is no break in the MS. The passage is based on Pseudo-Matthew XI, which reads as follows : *Exsurgens autem Ioseph a somno gratias egit deo suo, et locutus est Mariae et virginibus quae erant cum ea et narravit visum suum. Et consolatus est super Maria, dicens: Peccavi, quoniam suspicionem aliquam habui in te.*

801. **Bor** is probably a scribal error for **boþ**, which the context demands.

806. Here the writer seems to be following the A version of Pseudo-Matthew in calling the priest **Abyathar**. The B version has **Isachar**, as in l. 79. See Tischendorf, *op. cit.*, pp. 73–74.

820. In the MS. **ye** is crossed out after **sayd**.

865. In Pseudo-Matthew Mary prays to **dominus Adonay**.

880. *Ibid.* Mary is not led to Anna after the trial but **domuum suum**.

893. Cf. Luke ii. 1.

902. After **pay** the MS. has *t*.

906. **Syr Egryne** is probably the Cyrenius of Luke ii. 2.

907. **Lyrd** is crossed out in the MS. after **hade**.

919. The MS. has **ḱẏṁ**.

ST. ANNE. K

130   Notes to the University of Minnesota Manuscript

925. **Welke** as the reduplicated pret. indicates a conservative treatment of verbs in a text of the date of this one.

939. For **way** the MS. has **Way**.

945. For **wer** the MS. has *ð*.

963–65. Again three lines are omitted without break in the MS. The passage is based on Pseudo-Matthew XIII, par. 2: *Et cum haec dixisset, iussit angelus stare iumentum, quia tempus advenerat pariendi; et praecepit discendere de animali Mariam et ingredi in speluncam subterraneam, in qua lux non fuit unquam sed semper tenebrae, quia lumen diei penitus non habebat. Ad ingressum vero Mariae coepit tota spelunca splendorem habere, et quasi sol ibi esset ita tota fulgorem lucis ostendere; et quasi esset ibi hora diei sexta, ita speluncum lux divina illustravit; nec in die nec in nocte lux ibi divina defuit quamdiu ibi Maria fuit. Et ibi peperit masculum, quem circumdederunt angeli nascentum et natum adoraverunt dicentes: Gloria in excelsis deo et in terra pax hominibus bonae voluntatis.*

967–68. These two verses have no prototype in Pseudo-Matthew.

977. **Hatt**, reduplicated pret. See note to l. 925.

977–78. In Pseudo-Matthew the two "obstetrices" are called Zelome and Salome. The *Legenda Aurea* calls them ʒebell and Salome (p. 42).

1027. **Yhape**, O.E. **gēap**, crooked, bent, deceitful, cunning; M.E. ʒēap, eager, bold, prompt. Cf. yaprely and ʒappele (O.E. **gēaplīce**) in *York Plays*, XXX, 331, and XLIV, 127.

1066. **Hōgely**, O.F. **ahuge** + O.E. -lice, hugely. Wyclif, Gen. XVII. 2, has **hugeli**. The *Wars of Alexander*, l. 269 of E.E.T.S. ed., Sec. Series 47, has: ʒe behold me sa hogely quare-on is ʒour mynd ?

1107. This verse does not rime with the following verses. It probably should read "gette."

1126–52. This part of the story does not appear in Pseudo-Matthew. There are, however, similar accounts in *Legenda Aurea*, p. 41, and in Peter Comester's *Historia Scholastica* (Migne's *Patrologia*, Tom. 198, Col. 1539).

1157. Pseudo-Matthew XV has the sixth instead of the seventh day. Other accounts have the eighth day. Cf. Luke ii. 21.

1171. The purification takes place thirty-two days after the circumcision, or thirty-nine days after the nativity. Pseudo-Matthew XV says that it was according to the law of Moses, which would place the purification on the fortieth day after the Nativity. See Leviticus xii. The Arabic Gospel of the Infancy and *Legenda Aurea*, p. 159, both say that the purification took place on the fortieth day after the nativity.

1189–92. Pseudo-Matthew XV gives the age of **Simon** (Simeon) as 112 years. Cf. Luke ii. 25 ff.

1210–12. These lines are omitted without break in the MS. The passage is following Pseudo-Matthew XV, par. 3, which reads as follows: *Erat autem in templo domini Anna prophetissa, filia Phanuel, de tribu Asser, quae vixerat cum viro suo annis septem a virginitate sua; et haec vidua erat iam per annos octoginta quatuor; quae nunquam discessit a templo domini, ieiuniis et orationibus vacans. Haec accedens adorabat infantem dicens quoniam in isto est redemptio seculi.* Cf. Luke ii. 36–38. The writer of the French *Le Romanz de Saint Fanuel, op. cit.*, erroneously conceived Phanuel, the father of Anna the Prophetess, as the father of Anna, the mother of the Virgin Mary.

1225 ff. The A version of Pseudo-Matthew does not give the names of the three kings. The B version gives the names as Guaspar, Melchior, and Balthasar. See

Tischendorf, op. cit., pp. 83-84. The *Historia Scholastica*, op. cit., Tom. 198, Col. 1542, follows the B version. *Legenda Aurea*, p. 88, and *Cursor Mundi*, ll. 11492 ff., have the same names as the poem in ll. 1330-39.

1294-96. Three lines are omitted, but there is no break in the MS. The gap is bridged in Pseudo-Matthew XVI, end of par. 1, as follows: *Tunc Herodes rex vocavit magos ad se et diligenter inquisivit ab eis quando eis apparuit stella. Et misit eos in Bethleem dicens: Ite et interrogate diligenter de puero; et cum inveneritis eum, renuntiate mihi, ut et ego veniens adorem eum.*

1367. He is written over þai in the MS.

1424. **Spayned**, Nth. and Scot., weaned; cf. O.E. **spanan**, to allure, entice, persuade, seduce, Ger. Dutch **spänen**, **spenen**. Cf. also *Cursor Mundi*, 3018: Quen he was spaned fra þe pap.

1427. Pseudo-Matthew does not give the number of innocents slain by Herod. *Cursor Mundi*, l. 11579, has the same number as the poem, 144,000.

1436. Herod does not slay himself in Pseudo-Matthew. In *Cursor Mundi*, ll. 11797 ff., he is slain by traitors at the instigation of his son, the Archylaus of l. 1438.

1448 ff. Pseudo-Matthew XVIII and XIX has two accounts of the homage paid to Jesus by the wild beasts of the desert, whereas this poem has only one. The poem adds Joseph's thanks to Jesus for saving the party from the wild beasts.

1476. **Whaht**, O.E. hwæt, augury, fortune, fate. **Wahat** is written on the next line in the MS.

1489. In the MS. a has been added by another hand before **aurneye**.

1498 ff. The **was** of l. 1498 is repeated in the MS. The date tree under which Mary rested is called a palm tree in Pseudo-Matthew.

1503. The MS. has menȝe on the next line.

1534. After **well**, w^t wat^o is crossed out in the MS.

1540 ff. Cf. Revelations xxii.

1552. **To mary** is crossed out after **Ihesus** in the MS.

1564. The MS. is defective and the reading uncertain in the middle of this line.

1573 ff. In the A version of Pseudo-Matthew XXII, **sotinen** is the name of the city in which Joseph took refuge. Here he lodges in the temple. In the B version the name of the city is **Sotrina**. Here Joseph and his family lodge in the house of a widow. The poem, as usual, follows the B version, which differs greatly from the A version beyond this chapter.

1596. The MS. has **yklone**.

1614. **Farly** is crossed out after **was** in the MS.

1635. After the last word in the line, -ght is added below.

1675 ff. For variant versions of this incident, see Tischendorf, op. cit., p. 91.

1705 ff. Cf. Exodus xiv.

1727 ff. At this point the A version of Pseudo-Matthew records the return from Egypt. The B version records a miracle of grain and dead fish. Neither incident is in the poem. From this point to l. 2076 there is considerable variation from all versions of Pseudo-Matthew. Cf. variants in Tischendorf, op. cit., pp. 92 ff. Events not recorded in Pseudo-Matthew include an account of the return from Egypt, the miracle of Jesus and the outlaw, the fall of the false gods in Judea, the account of Mary Magdalene, and the anointing scene at the house of Simon the Leper. These differences, with some other incidents, might lead one at first glance to suspect that the poem is a redaction of the French *Le Romanz de Saint Fanuel*. A close comparison of the two texts has convinced me, however, that this is not the case. The differences between this poem and the French one are much more numerous and significant than those between this poem and the B version of Pseudo-Matthew. It seems reasonable to suppose that if the writer had been following a poem already complete, he would have followed his source more closely than this poem follows *Le Romanz de Saint Fanuel*. The additions to and variations from the B version of Pseudo-Matthew seem to be drawn from the author's knowledge of the gospels and of popular legends rather than from another poem.

1765. The small letter *b* is written in the margin of the MS.

1774. The word **at** is written in the margin of the MS.

1793. **Tytter,** Nth. Dial., comp. *of* **tite,** adv., more readily, more willingly, sooner, rather. N.E.D. Cf. *Cursor Mundi*, 28120 (Cott.):

> And titter wald i lesyng make
> þat man my worde vn-trew to take.

2014. **Salbour** is apparently drawn from M.E. **slaberen,** to slobber. Here it seems to mean the perspiration taken from Jesus' face.

2022. The MS. has **Solowed** instead of folowed.

2032. After **and, hyse** is crossed out in the MS.

2039. **Pop** is probably a derivative of the O.F. **popiner,** though the origin is uncertain. It means to paint, to adorn with a cosmetic. N.E.D.

2076. The rime is imperfect. Perhaps "ʒette" was intended, or perhaps the poet replaced rime by assonance.

2077-2232. In the A version of Pseudo-Matthew XXX, XXXI, and XXXVIII Zachyas is both the advisor of Joseph and Mary and the teacher of Jesus, who puts him to shame by the display of superior wisdom. The B version combines this account into a single series of incidents regarding the attempt to educate Jesus. The poem follows the B version.

2079. This line does not rime with the remainder of the stanza. It rimes with the preceding couplet instead.

2119. "Manstate at draw," *i.e.* he began to draw to man's estate.

2207. **For** is written in the margin of the MS. before this line.

2233-2256. Pseudo-Matthew gives no account of this incident.

2257-80. In the A version of Pseudo-Matthew Jesus, not the maid, is sent to the well. The B version is similar to the poem.

2281-2304. The A version of Pseudo-Matthew XXXIV gives the miracle of the wheat Cf. ll. 2614 ff. The B version gives this and the James Alpheus incident. Following this, the A version, XXXV and XXXVI, gives a miracle of Jesus and a lioness and one of the partition of the waters of the Jordan. These are in neither the B version nor the poem. The James Alpheus incident is given in ch. xli of the A version, but there the victim is James, son of Joseph.

2305-2367. The A version of Pseudo-Matthew says that Jesus lengthened the beam for Joseph. It does not give the incident of leaping onto the sunbeams. The B version gives both incidents but says that Jesus lengthened the beam for "quidam architector lignifaber." The poem follows B. Chapters XXXVIII and XXXIX of the A version give a second series of incidents attending the attempt to educate Jesus according to the accepted method. The B version includes these incidents in Chapters XXX and XXXI. Cf. ll. 2077-2232 of the poem.

2317. **Sayd** is repeated in the MS.

2377-2940. These lines have no counterpart in Pseudo-Matthew, nor have I been able to find sources for them except in the few cases noted below.

Notes to the University of Minnesota Manuscript

2455-81. This incident is related in the poem printed in Horstmann's *Altenglische Legenden*, Paderborn, 1875, pp. 24 ff.

2474. At the point where I have read i*hesus* the MS. has been changed and is illegible.

2592. For a discussion of the **somer play** see Chambers' *Mediaeval Stage*, 1, 114, 126, 173, and 183. Note that all the children were singing and that each one carried a green branch in his hand. The passage shows a power and exactness of portrayal indicating personal knowledge. Doubtless the author had witnessed many of these popular summer feasts and plays.

2665-2772. Cf. Horstmann, *op. cit.*, pp. 39 ff. The Arabic Gospel of the Infancy XXXVII has a variant account of this incident.

2726. After **may** in the MS. **W** is written.

2769. **Blan** is pret. of **blinnen**, *to cease*.

2793. A **shout** is a flat-bottomed boat used on canals and shallow rivers. It is still used in England, according to the *Century Dictionary*.

2845-2940. Cf. *Cursor Mundi*, ll. 12577 ff., and Luke iii. 41-52, for slightly different versions of this part of the story. I find no account exactly similar to that in the poem.

2941-2988. The A version of Pseudo-Matthew XLII gives an account of a banquet of Joseph and his sons. The B version notes Joseph's death and gives an account of Anne's three husbands and her children by each husband. Variants are to be found in the Latin Gospel of Thomas XV and in *Cursor Mundi*, ll. 12485 ff. Cf. also the corresponding account in the poem from MS. Bodl. 10234 printed herewith. The Gospel of Pseudo-Matthew ends at this point in the story.

2989-3042. Cf. Matthew ix. 27-32, which has two men.

3043-3126. See notes on ll. 2941-88. The same account is to be found in *Legenda Aurea*, p. 586 (Graesse ed.). *Cursor Mundi*, ll. 12517 ff., omits the death of Joseph.

3127-92. Cf. Matthew viii. 2-14.

3130-32. This stanza lacks three verses, but there is no break in the MS. See Matthew, *ibid.*, for the context.

3160. **Bonetyuouse** is a peculiar spelling of **bountevous**. For the latter form see Chaucer's *Troilus*, I, 883.

3174-76. Three lines missing without break in the MS. Cf. Matthew viii. 5-14.

3193-3240. Cf. Matthew ix. 9, and Luke v. 1-12.

3241-3324. Cf. John ii. 1-12, and Horstmann, *op. cit.*, p. 58.

3267. According to rime, this line belongs with the preceding stanza; but the stanzaic structure demands the present position. **All** is probably a scribal insertion.

3337-72. Matthew **xx**. 30-34 has two men.

3373-3408. Cf. Matthew xix. 27-30.

3409-57. This same source is given in the B version of Pseudo-Matthew XLII. Cf. Tischendorf, *op. cit.*, pp. 111-12.

NOTES

TO MS. TRINITY COLLEGE, CAMBRIDGE, 601
(English Poets R. 3. 21)

1. After the **incipit** the name of Lydgate is added in a different hand from that in which the MS. is written. It has already been suggested that this is probably an addition by Stow.

32. **Parage**, birth, perhaps generalized to status, rank, nature. Cf. Chaucer's *Canterbury Tales*, D 250. The line probably means "which are devoid of reason by their very nature."

99. Lydgate's name is added after the prologue as in 1.

106. **This day** is Saint Anne's Day (July 26).

129. **Cardyd**, purified as wool is when carded.

169. See the apocryphal Gospel of the Nativity of Mary, I, 1-3.

215. **Of oure fadyr Iacob, lowsyng the bond** refers to God's covenant with Jacob and the promise of a Redeemer. Cf. Numbers xxiv. 17-19, and 1 Chronicles xvi. 17.

218. Cf. Genesis xxxv. 22.

223. Cf. Ezek. xxiv. 24 and Matthew i. 8-9.

229. **Lemes**, O.E. lēoma, flames. Cf. Chaucer's *Canterbury Tales*, B 4120.

232. This Iudas is not Judas Iscariot but Judas, brother of Jesus. Cf. Matthew xiii. 55. Levi is the son of Alpheus. Cf. Mark ii. 14.

236. Cf. Eph. ii. 20, where Christ is called the **chief corner stone of the building**.

247. Cf. note to l. 106.

295. Professor Carleton Brown suggested to me that **boose** might be a spelling of **busch**, which the context requires. That his suggestion was correct is evidenced by the following passage from E.E.T.S., Extra Series 19, p. 296 : "By this busshe ys vnderstonde our lady *that* was fyred & brente not. for she was moder with*out* losse of maydenhod." And William of Shoreham, vi. 19, "þou art þe bosche of synay."

297. **Gloose**, deceit. Cf. *Cursor Mundi*, 26774 :

> þai come to scrift a glos to make.

302 ff. This allegory of the thorns seems to be an application of Matthew xiii. 18-23 to the Jews.

312 ff. This stanza is largely a repetition of ll. 169-175. The author has wandered away from his theme and now picks it up at the beginning.

319 ff. This tripartite division of wealth, as has been noted, is common to all the accounts of Joachim and Anna.

397. The reference here is to the feeding of Mary by the angels during her sojourn in the temple. This legend is common to all the apocryphal narratives.

414 ff. The references to Matthew are doubtless to the apocryphal Gospel of Pseudo-Matthew, which was popular in both France and England.

417. **A rew** is equivalent to on row, in a row, in order. Cf. Chaucer's *House of Fame*, 1692, and *Canterbury Tales*, D 506.

421. **Omely**, or homily, is, of course, the common name for a sermon or utterance of truth. Apparently it is here used in the abstract sense and not with reference to any particular homily.

432 ff. Cf. Genesis xv. 18 and Matthew i. 1.

440. Cf. Matthew i. 1–18.

468. **Syndony**, a thin fabric of cotton, linen, or silk. *Cent. Dic.* Cf. *Joseph of Arimathia* (E.E.T.S. ed.), p. 37:

> So Joseph layde Ihesu to rest in his sepulture,
> And wrapped his body in a cloth called sendony.

509. **Rother**, rudder.

532. **Fynaunce** is here used in the sense of ransom. Cf. *Rom. of Partenay* (E.E.T.S. 22), l. 1853.

576. **Prefynyte**, *L.* **praefinitus**, *p.p.*, predetermined.

597. The same hand that wrote the remainder of the MS. has written in the left margin *Deus pars hereditate mee*.

598 ff. Cf. Psalm xvi. 5.

618. **Conspect**, F., a general view, in the sight of.

630. Anne is Hannah, mother of Samuel. Cf. 1 Samuel ii. 21.

633. **Bonechyeff**, O.F. **bon chief**, good fortune, happiness.

659. Lydgate's name is again written at the end of the poem by the same hand that wrote it in the other places.

NOTES

TO MS. BODLEY 10234
(Tanner 407)

Throughout this poem there are certain stops or periods. It is impossible to tell whether these are the result of carelessness on the part of the scribe in allowing his pen to rest after a given word or are an attempt at an elementary sort of punctuation. In any event, the text is both more interesting and more exactly reproduced by allowing it to stand without additional punctuation. It is therefore reproduced with these marks as they appear in the MS.

36 ff. Note that Mary, daughter of Anne and Cleophas and wife of Alpheus, is the mother of four children. In the Minnesota MS. version, ll. 3063 ff., she is the mother of James and Joseph only.

56. **Thys tyme of ʒeere** is the time of the Feast of St. Anne (July 26).

61. The sister of Anne is called Emeryne in the Minnesota MS. version, l. 3053.

64. **Syb**, related to, akin to. Cf. Chaucer's *Romaunt of the Rose*, 1199, and *Canterbury Tales*, B 2565.

69. The book of St. Jerome might be either the Gospel of the Nativity or the Gospel of Pseudo-Matthew, for both were attributed to him. Apparently the former is meant here, for the author follows it more closely than the latter.

103. The priest, according to the Gospel of the Nativity, was Issachar.

141. **Skyl**, cause, reason. Cf. note to Minnesota MS. version, l. 169.

149. Cf. Genesis xxx. 24 and the Gospel of the Nativity, ch. iii. Joseph was not the son of Isaac and Rebekah but of Jacob and Rachel. For the preceding ll., cf. Genesis xvii. 16–19 and xxi. 1–5.

153. Cf. Judges xiii. 24 and the Gospel of the Nativity iii.

157. Cf. Luke i. 5–20. John the Baptist is not mentioned in the Gospel of the Nativity.

224. The Minnesota MS. version, l. 301, has **xv greces**. The Gospel of the Nativity has *quindecim graduum psalmos quindecim ascensionis gradus*. Cf. note on l. 301 of the Minnesota MS. version. It is possible that the scribe had before him a version containing **grecys** and that he misread it as **pasys**.

265 ff. The miraculous powers of the Virgin Mary are not given in the Gospel of the Nativity. They are given in Pseudo-Matthew. Cf. the Minnesota MS. version, ll. 379 ff.

274. The Minnesota MS. version, following the B version of Pseudo-Matthew, has twelve instead of fourteen years as the age of Mary at this time. The Gospel of the Nativity has twelve years; so has the Protovangelion of James.

309. **Mountenans**, the length of. Cf. Chaucer's *Troilus*, ii. 1707.

316. The author freely but inaccurately renders *familia David* as **dwelling wit kyng dauyd**.

Notes to MS. Bodley 10234

373 ff. The reasons for the virgin birth are not given in the Gospel of the Nativity.

376. **Mowseng,** musing, meditation.

411. Cf. Matthew xxvi. 47 and Luke xxii. 47. These do not give any idea of the number accompanying Judas. They simply say **a great multitude.**

443. I find no other account of the completeness and perfection of Christ at the time of his conception. This is probably an original adornment on the part of the author.

453. **This gylde** is important because it indicates that the poem was made especially for a guild celebration. The guild for which it was made was possibly the St. Anne's Guild in the "Parish of St. Peter at the Skinmarket," Lincoln, which was founded in 1344. See A. F. Westlake's *The Parish Gilds of Mediaeval England,* p. 168, and the discussion in that part of the introduction devoted to sources and authorship.

BIBLIOGRAPHY

Baring-Gould, S., *Lives of the Saints*, London and New York, 1898.
Bibliorum Sacrorum Iuxta Vulgatam Clementinam, Nova Editio, Mediolani, 1922.
Björkman, Erik, "Scandinavian Loan-Words in Middle English" in *Studien zur Englischen Philologie*, VII and XI.
Block, K. S., *Ludus Coventriae or The Plaie Called Corpus Christi* (E.E.T.S., Extra Series, cxx), London, 1922.
Bonnard, Jean, *Les Traductions de la Bible en Vers Francais au Moyen Age*, Paris, 1884.
British Historical MSS. Commission, the, *14 Report of, Appendix B*.
Brown, Carleton, *A Register of Middle English Religious and Didactic Verse*, 2 Vols., Oxford, 1916 and 1920.
Budge, Sir E. A. Wallis, *Legends of Our Lady Mary the Perpetual Virgin and Her Mother Hanna*, London, 1922.
Bülbring, Carl D., *Altenglisches Elementarbuch*, Heidelburg, 1902.
Chambers, E. K., *The Mediaeval Stage*, 2 Vols., Oxford, 1903.
Craig, Hardin, *Two Coventry Corpus Christi Plays*, E.E.T.S., Extra Series, 87.
Cursor Mundi, E.E.T.S., 57, 62, 66, 68, 99, and 101.
Emerson, O. F., *A Middle English Reader*, New York, 1912.
England, G., and Pollard, A. W., *Towneley Plays*, E.E.T.S., Extra Series, 71.
Englische Studien, XII.
Furnivall, F. J., *An Old English Miscellany Presented to*, Oxford, 1901.
Furnivall, F. J., Ed., *Digby Plays*, E.E.T.S., Extra Series, 70.
Gerould, G. H., *Saints' Legends*, Boston, 1916.
Gerould, G. H., *The North English Homily Collection*, Oxford, 1902.
Gower, John, *Complete Works of*, Macaulay Ed., Oxford, 1899–1902.
Graesse, Thomas, Ed., *Legenda Aurea*, 3rd Ed., Lipsiae, 1890.
Greg, W. W., *Bibliographical and Textual Problems of the English Miracle Cycles*, London, 1914.
Greg, W. W., *The Assumption of the Virgin. A Miracle Play from the N-Town Cycle*, Oxford, 1915.
Halliwell, J. O., Ed., *Ludus Coventriae* (Shak. Soc.), London, 1841.
Hone, William, *Ancient Mysteries Described*, London, 1823.
Horstmann, C., *Altenglische Legenden*, Paderborn, 1875.
Horstmann, C., *Altenglische Legenden, Neue Folge*, Heilbronn, 1881.
Horstmann, C., *Osbern Bokenams Legenden*, Heilbronn, 1883.
Jespersen, Otto, *Growth and Structure of the English Language*, 4th Ed., New York, 1923.
Jespersen, Otto, *Modern English Grammar*, Vol. 1, Heidelberg, 1909.
Joseph of Aramathia, E.E.T.S., 44.

Bibliography

Kaluza, Max, *Historische Grammatik der englischen Sprache*, 2 Vols., Berlin, 1907.
Kramer, M., *Sprache und Heimat des sogen. L.C.*, Halle, 1892.
Lyndesey, Sir David, *Works*, E.E.T.S. Ed., 11, 19, 36, 37, and 47.
Merlin, E.E.T.S., 36.
Migne, J. P., *Patrologia Latina*, 1884–1902.
Minot, Laurence, *The Poems of*, Hall Ed., Oxford, 3rd Ed., 1915.
Modern Language Notes, XXXVII and XLI.
Modern Language Review, IX.
Moore, Samuel, *Historical Outlines of English Phonology and Middle English Grammar*, Ann Arbor, 1919.
Morsbach, Lorenz, *Mittlenglische Grammatik*, Halle, 1898.
Noreen, Adolf, *Altislandische Grammatik*, Halle, 1923.
Pollard, A. W., *English Miracle Plays, Moralities, and Interludes*, Oxford, 1909.
Promptorium Parvulorum, Mayhew Ed., E.E.T.S., Extra Series, 102.
Publications of the Modern Language Association of America, 26, 29, 41, and 42.
Publications of the Surtees Society, VII.
Revue des langues romanes, XXVII.
Romania, XV, XVI, and XXV.
Romauns of Parthenay, E.E.T.S., 22.
Skeat, W. W., *The Complete Works of Geoffrey Chaucer*, 7 Vols., Oxford, 1894–97.
Skeat, W. W., *Principles of English Etymology*, First Series, Oxford, 1892.
Smith, Lucy T., Ed., *York Plays*, Oxford, 1885.
Sweet, Henry, *A History of English Sounds*, Oxford, 1888.
ten Brink, B., *History of English Literature to Wyclif*, Kennedy Translation, New York, 1889.
Tischendorf, C., *Evangelia Apocrypha*, Leipzig, 1876.
University of Minnesota Studies in Language and Literature, I.
Unwin, George, *The Guilds and Companies of London*, London and New York, 1909.
Wells, J. E., *A Manual of the Writings in Middle English*, London and New Haven, 1916.
Westlake, H. F., *The Parish Gilds of Mediaeval England*, London, 1909.
Wright, Joseph and E. Mary, *Old English Grammar*, 2nd Ed., London and New York, 1914.
Wright, Joseph and E. Mary, *An Elementary Middle English Grammar*, London and New York, 1923.
Wright, Thomas, Ed., *Chester Plays* (Shak. Soc.), London, 1843–47.

Printed and bound by CPI Group (UK) Ltd, Croydon, CR0 4YY